Better Homes and Gardens®

1983 RECIPE YEARBOOK

Better Homes and Gardens.

Editor GORDON G. GREER
Managing Editor KATE KEATING   Art Director GERALD PREATOR

Food and Nutrition Editor DORIS EBY
Senior Food Editor NANCY BYAL   *Senior Food Editor–Books* SHARYL HEIKEN
Senior Food Editor–Special Interest Publications SALLY PEDERSON
Recipe Development Editor MARION VIALL
Associate Editors ELIZABETH WOOLEVER   ROSEMARY HUTCHINSON
SANDRA GRANSETH   MARLENE BROWN   PAT TEBERG   JOY TAYLOR
MARCIA STANLEY   DIANA McMILLEN   JULIA MALLOY   DIANE YANNEY
JILL BURMEISTER   NANCY WALL   JANET FIGG   ALETHEA SPARKS
LINDA HENRY   JULIE HENDERSON   CATHERINE COOK   LINDA FOLEY

Copy Chiefs MARY ANN ROBERTSON   ELIZABETH HAHN BROOKS
Makeup Editor KATIE NORRIS
Associate Makeup Editor DOROTHY GRANT
Assistant Makeup Editor JUDY HUNSICKER

Associate Art Director (Creative) BRYAN E. McCAY
Associate Art Directors (Managing) DON NICKELL   KRISTIN FRANTZ
Senior Graphic Designer CHRIS GRECO   *Graphic Designer (Covers)* SUSAN MAHER
Graphic Designers JUDY H. NEIGHBOR   SUSAN KOCH
KEVIN S. LUDGATE   KENT W. MAUCK
Art Production Director JOHN BERG
Art Production Associates JOE HEUER   KATHRYN DAVIDSON

New York–Shopping Editor ANN LIVELY

Group Editorial Services Director DUANE L. GREGG
Executive Art Director WILLIAM J. YATES
Director of Editorial Planning RICHARD W. ROYER

Books: *Editor* GERALD KNOX *Managing Editor* DAVID A. KIRCHNER
Art Director ERNEST SHELTON   *Associate Art Director (Managing)* RANDALL YONTZ
Associate Art Directors (Creative) NEOMA ALT WEST   LINDA FORD
Assistant Art Directors HARIJS PRIEKULIS   TOM WEGNER
Graphic Designers ALISANN DIXON   LYNDA HAUPERT   LYNE NEYMEYER
BILL SHAW   D. GREG THOMPSON   MIKE EAGLETON   MIKE BURNS
DEB MINER   TRISH CHURCH-PODLASEK   STAN SAMS   DARLA WHIPPLE
Copy and Production Editors DAVID A. WALSH
NANCY NOWISZEWSKI   MARY HELEN SCHILTZ

Director, Editorial Research C. RAY DEATON   *Associate* CAROLYN A. HAMILTON
Administrative Editor ROSE ANDERSON   *Art Business Office Manager* CECILEE LEWIS
Test Kitchen Director SHARON STILWELL   *Photo Studio Manager* DON WIPPERMAN

PUBLISHING GROUP PRESIDENT **JACK D. REHM**
Publishing Group Vice-Presidents: JAMES A. AUTRY General Manager, Magazines
NEIL KUEHNL Editor-in-Chief   **ROBERT E. GERHARDT** Administration
FRED STINES General Manager, Books and Newspapers

Director of Book Publishing ROBERT B. NELSON
Director of Book Retail Marketing JAMIE MARTIN
Director of Book Direct Marketing ARTHUR HEYDENDAEL

Publisher J. WESLEY SILK
Publishing Services Director AL NEY
Advertising Sales Director LENNOX E. H. STUART

CORPORATE OFFICERS: **Chairman of the Board E. T. MEREDITH III**
President ROBERT A. BURNETT
Group Presidents JACK D. REHM, Publishing   **WALTER A. VOSS**, Printing
JAMES CONLEY, Broadcasting
Vice-Presidents DONALD L. ARNOLD, Corporate Relations
THOMAS G. FISHER, General Counsel and Assistant Secretary
HERB SCHULTE, Corporate Planning   **WILLIAM H. STRAW**, Finance
GERALD D. THORNTON, Administrative Services
Secretary BETTY CAMPBELL MADDEN   Treasurer MICHAEL A. SELL

Our seal assures you that every recipe in
the *1983 Recipe Yearbook* is endorsed by the
Better Homes and Gardens Test Kitchen. Each
recipe is tested for family appeal, practicality,
and deliciousness.

CONTENTS

JANUARY
Home-Cooked Meals in Short-Order Time —— 6

FEBRUARY
Classic Cooking Techniques to Make Simple Fare Sensational —— 20

MARCH
Treasured Family Recipes for Spring Celebrations —— 34

APRIL
Kids Cooking —— 46
Wonderful One-Pot Meals —— 56

MAY
Affordable Fish and Seafood —— 64
Show-Off Cake Decorating Made Easy —— 74

JUNE
Outdoor Living: Bring on the Guests —— 80

JULY
New Pizzazz for Old Favorites —— 96

AUGUST
Fresh-from-the-Farm Fruit and Vegetable Recipes —— 108

SEPTEMBER
How to Make Meals More Nutritious —— 124

OCTOBER
Look-Ahead Meal Planning —— 136

NOVEMBER
Bedazzling Recipes for Special Occasions —— 148

DECEMBER
Sharing the Spirit of Christmas —— 160

INDEX —— 188

In a year's time *Better Homes and Gardens*® magazine publishes hundreds of delicious recipes covering a wide variety of cooking trends. In this book you'll find a rich assortment of the recipes published in 1982. No longer will you have to remember to clip and save your favorite recipes. With this easy-to-use volume you'll have a year's worth of good eating all in one place—right at your fingertips.

JANUARY

January 1982 • $1.25

Better Homes
and Gardens.

Food: Timesaving recipes with great old-fashioned flavor
Quick and easy decorating ideas • Affordable open-plan house
Education: New options for adults who want to learn
Just-for-fun houseplant ideas • Create a classy home office
Health: Medical breakthroughs that could lengthen your life

AMISH-STYLE
Quilt

Stitch it up in 5 hours for under $50
Instructions inside

SUPER-SIMPLE CRAFT PROJECTS
YOU CAN MAKE IN A JIFFY

BH&G Home Improvement Contest: Win big cash prizes!

HOME-COOKED MEALS
IN SHORT-ORDER TIME

Chances are you don't need to be sold on the wholesomeness and goodness of homemade meals. Where you probably need help is finding the time to prepare them. If that's the case, you've come to the right place. The following pages are filled with beat-the-clock techniques, dinner ideas, and recipes. On page 14 is a collection of hints to cut your kitchen time even more.

By Rosemary Hutchinson

FIX A TWO-FOR-ONE DINNER

Double-batch cooking is nothing new, but the timesaving principle behind it is still valid. You make two batches of a recipe in nearly the same time it takes to make one. Cheese rarebit fans will rave about *Shrimp in Cheddar Sauce (left)*. Freeze half of the shrimp-and-vegetable sauce; serve the rest tonight in crispy patty shells. Ground pork, ham, and a bouquet of herbs star in *Cranberry-Pork Loaf (right)*. Freeze one loaf and half of the spunky cranberry-chili sauce for a no-fuss dinner later.

PLAN A HEAD-START ENTRÉE

Believe it or not, you can turn leftovers into mouth-watering meals
and save time all at once. Plan to cook an extra amount when you prepare the first meal so
you can use the surplus food as the basis for a second meal.
To test out the idea, try our peanutty *Zucchini-Bulgur Stir-Fry (left)*. It includes
extra bulgur and vegetables so you can stir up a completely different
main dish—*Sausage-Bulgur Soup (right)*—tomorrow or the next night in under 30 minutes.

BUILD ON A FROZEN BASE

One smart way to cut down on dinnertime hassle is to capitalize on your freezer. During your less hectic hours, mix up *Frozen Meat Base,* featuring round steak, onion, green pepper, carrot, and green beans. Stash this versatile concoction in your freezer (the base keeps up to several months). Then whenever you're faced with a time bind, the base can give you a head start on meal-makers like these.

Blend applesauce and poultry seasoning into the *Frozen Meat Base* for *Applesauce-Beef Pie (left).* Or add taco sauce, corn, ripe olives, coriander, and taco chips to the *Frozen Meat Base* to produce *Tortilla-Beef Casserole (right).*

It has all the flavor of a long-simmering Mexican stew but goes together in less than an hour. For another delicious spin-off meal, see page 16.

START WITH A HOMEMADE MIX

On those days when "What's-for-dinner?" needs an answer lickety-split,
turn to a do-it-yourself convenience mix. Our version, *Onion-Mushroom Rice Mix,* is as easy as
stirring together uncooked rice, dry soup mix, parsley, and basil.
When you embellish the rice mix with broccoli and add a Muenster cheese topping, you have
Easy Broccoli Eggs (left), an elegant meatless entrée. Prepare the mix pilaf-style to create
Pecan-Pork Chop Casserole (right). You can pop this one-step casserole right
into the oven without browning the chops. For another rice-mix-based main dish, see page 17.

CHILL A MAKE-AHEAD MEAL

With a little culinary sleight of hand, you can design meals to chill and forget until you need them. At mealtime, just arrange the foods, garnish, and serve. A perfect example is *Curried Rice Dinner Platter (front).* You marinate rice, apple, green pepper, green onion, and raisins overnight in the refrigerator with a curry-garlic dressing. Before serving, arrange the rice mixture on a lettuce-lined platter with summer sausage, cheese, egg wedges, and almonds. Round out the menu with pita bread or breadsticks and squares of your favorite cake.

BAKE AN OVEN MENU

Can you see yourself with your feet up as dinner time approaches? It's possible when your oven contains the whole meal—everything from the main dish to the dessert. Besides eliminating last-minute cooking, oven meals save energy because several dishes bake at once. And if you plan a one-dish meal, you'll save time on pot and pan washing, too. The headliner of this oven meal, *Beef and Potato Bake (right),* is a mushroom-ground beef loaf placed on a bed of vegetables and drizzled with a mustard sauce. Serve the entrée right from the baking dish with your favorite warm rolls. For dessert, bake *Coconut-Pear Crisp (front left),* a coconut cream and pear pudding topped with a crunchy pecan and cinnamon topper.

FIX A MEAL FROM CUPBOARD FINDS

A well-stocked cupboard can be a busy cook's best friend. Here's how to
produce a three-course dinner from ingredients you have on hand. It's as easy as one-two-three.
Step I: Cook the pasta for *Ham-Mushroom Rotini (center).* Just before serving,
toss the pasta with ham, tomatoes, mushrooms, a creamy sauce, and mozzarella cheese.
Step 2: Mix fruit and walnuts in rich orange-rum sauce for
Rum-Raisin-Peach Sundaes (front right). Keep the sauce warm during dinner.
Step 3: Assemble the spinach, beets, and onion for *Beet-Spinach Salad*
(front left) and toss them with bottled Italian dressing and crumbled blue cheese.

PREPARE A SHOP-AND-SERVE SUPPER

Forget to thaw some meat for dinner? Don't panic—help is as near
as the neighborhood delicatessen or the convenience section of your supermarket.
Begin by purchasing sliced meat and hard rolls for *Horseradish-Beef
Sandwiches (front).* At home, just heat the meat and pile it on the rolls along with sandwich
condiments. Place a relish tray or deli bean salad alongside. To wind up the
meal, serve *Fruit Salad Dessert (center right),* a layered ambrosia of purchased fruit salad,
walnuts, and spice cookies.

TIMESAVING, WORK-SAVING COOKING TIPS

With more and more demands on your time, it's important to get the most out of every minute you spend in the kitchen. Here are some work-saving hints that will help you maximize your KP time.

GET ORGANIZED

• Plan several days' or a week's worth of meals at a time so you can compile one master grocery list. This will reduce the number of trips to the grocery store and eliminate last-minute confusion over what to serve.

• Keep meals simple. Limit them to two or three courses and use a pre-prepared food for one of the courses (such as frozen yogurt for dessert or canned fruits or vegetables with cottage cheese for a salad).

• To simplify assembling your grocery list, keep a note pad handy to jot down ingredients just before they run out.

• Be sure to keep a good supply of staple foods for last-minute meals.

• Arrange your kitchen for maximum efficiency. Position often-used utensils in convenient drawers and cupboards. Keep frequently used ingredients in easy-to-open containers at the front of your shelves.

• Read your recipes carefully before you begin; then gather the ingredients and utensils you'll need.

• Interweave as many of the steps in a meal or recipe as possible. In our Meal from Cupboard Finds, for example, you can cook the pasta for the main dish while you're fixing the salad and dessert.

CALL ON TIMESAVING APPLIANCES

Store your most often used appliances in easy-to-reach locations. Then be alert to new ways to use them.

• Rely on your blender for more than just drinks. It's also great for making bread crumbs, crushing cookies, chopping nuts, pureeing or chopping vegetables and fruits, and grating cheese. A blender also is handy for preparing frozen fruit juice concentrates and for dissolving gelatin.

• Use your food processor when you need to shred cheese, snip parsley, chop hard-cooked eggs, make nut butters or salad dressings, slice or chop large amounts of fruits and vegetables, and chop or grind meats. Processing dry foods before wet ones saves time because you needn't wash the work bowl repeatedly.

• Even when you're preparing a conventional recipe, enlist your microwave oven. The oven can do a speedy job of melting butter, margarine, and chocolate; softening cheese; toasting nuts and coconut; cooking bacon and vegetables; and thawing frozen foods.

• Use your pressure cooker to prepare normally slow-cooking vegetables, stews, ribs, and roasts in a third of the regular time.

USE TIMESAVING INGREDIENTS

• A number of convenience foods can save you time and work at little or no added cost. Some examples are dried onion, parsley, and garlic; frozen juice concentrates; canned and dried soups; canned meat, fish, and poultry; quick-cooking rice and potatoes; and sliced or grated cheese.

• Make your own convenience foods. Chop large batches of onion, green pepper, or nuts and freeze them in small units. Shred cheese for a week's worth of meals, then chill or freeze it in recipe-size portions. Shape ground meat into patties so you can thaw a few at a time for hamburgers. Freeze homemade casseroles, soups, stews, and chilies in serving-size portions for faster thawing and reheating.

SHORT-CUT PREPARATIONS

• To cut up canned tomatoes quickly, use kitchen shears and snip the tomatoes right in the can.

• To simplify snipping fresh parsley and herbs, place uncut sprigs in a measuring cup and snip finely with shears.

• To separate frozen fruits and vegetables easily, put them in a colander and rinse them under hot tap water.

• Grease and flour baking pans in one step. Thoroughly mix ½ cup *shortening* and ¼ cup all-purpose *flour,* then use a pastry brush to apply the coating to the pans. Store any remaining coating, covered, at room temperature.

• Use as few utensils as possible to cut dishwashing time. For example, mix a casserole in its baking dish. Or use a saucepan as a mixing bowl, then use the same pan for the cooking.

• Except for cakes and breads, omit the step of preheating the oven.

• To shape meatballs speedily, use a small ice cream scoop or shape the meat mixture into a log and cut off slices to roll into balls.

• To reduce thawing time, place wrapped one-pound packages of fish under cold running water. Or, better still, cook the fish without thawing. Simply let the block stand at room temperature 20 to 30 minutes. Then slice the block into one-inch, ½-inch, or ¼-inch slices or into one-inch cubes. Use the still-icy cubes in soups or stews. Bake the slices in a 450° oven 15 minutes for 1-inch slices, 8 minutes for ½-inch slices, and 5 minutes for ¼-inch slices.

• Chill foods quickly by placing them in the freezer for 20 to 30 minutes.

• Make gelatin salads in 20 to 25 minutes by placing them in individual molds or custard cups and chilling them in the freezer. To quick-set gelatin for folding into other ingredients, chill the mixture over ice cubes.

January

CRANBERRY-PORK LOAF

2 beaten eggs
½ cup milk
1½ cups crushed whole wheat
    crackers (30 crackers)
2 medium onions, chopped
3 tablespoons dried parsley
    flakes
1 teaspoon dried marjoram,
    crushed
1 teaspoon dry mustard
½ teaspoon dried sage, crushed
3 pounds ground pork
1 pound ground ham
1 8-ounce can (1 cup) whole
    cranberry sauce
1 cup chili sauce
½ cup water

Combine eggs, milk, cracker crumbs, onion, parsley flakes, marjoram, mustard, sage, ¼ teaspoon *salt,* and ¼ teaspoon *pepper.* Add pork and ham; mix well. Divide mixture in half. Pat *one half* of the mixture into an 8½x4½x2-inch loaf pan. Unmold. Wrap in moisture-vaporproof material. Seal, label, and freeze. Pat remaining meat mixture into the same loaf pan. Bake in loaf pan or unmold into a shallow baking pan. Bake, uncovered, in 350° oven for 1½ hours. Drain. Meanwhile, combine cranberry sauce, chili sauce, and water. Divide mixture in half; freeze half. Heat remaining. Serve with loaf. Makes 8 servings per loaf.

To bake frozen loaf: Unwrap and place frozen loaf in shallow baking pan. Bake, uncovered, in 350° oven for about 2 hours. Drain fat. Meanwhile, heat frozen sauce and serve as above.

Microwave directions: Assemble loaves as above except shape meat into two rings in 8-inch round baking dishes. Micro-cook unfrozen loaf, covered with clear plastic wrap, at MEDIUM-HIGH for 18 to 20 minutes or till done, giving dish a half-turn once. Drain off excess fat. Let loaf stand 5 minutes. (Internal temperature of loaf should be 180°.) Meanwhile, heat sauce in small bowl at HIGH for 1 minute.

For frozen loaf: Micro-cook, covered with clear plastic wrap, on MEDIUM for 15 minutes, giving dish a half turn once. Let stand 10 minutes. Cook at MEDIUM-HIGH for 18 to 20 minutes or till done, giving dish a half-turn once. Let stand 5 minutes. Meanwhile, heat sauce in small bowl at HIGH for 4 to 5 minutes or till hot.

SHRIMP IN CHEDDAR SAUCE

1 16-ounce package frozen peas
    and carrots
1¼ pounds frozen peeled and
    deveined shrimp
½ cup butter *or* margarine
⅔ cup all-purpose flour
½ teaspoon paprika
¼ teaspoon pepper
3 cups milk
½ cup chopped green onion
¾ cup dry white wine
2 cups shredded sharp cheddar
    cheese (8 ounces)
    Frozen patty shells, baked

Rinse frozen peas and carrots with hot water; set aside. Cook shrimp according to package directions; drain and set aside. Meanwhile, in 3-quart saucepan melt butter or margarine; blend in flour, paprika, and pepper. Stir in milk and green onion. Cook and stir till mixture is thickened and bubbly. Cook and stir 1 minute more. Stir in wine. Add shrimp, peas and carrots, and cheese; stir till cheese is melted. Pour *half* the mixture into a 5- or 6-cup freezer container. Cool quickly by setting container in a bowl of ice water. Seal, label, and freeze. Spoon remaining half into six prepared patty shells. Serve immediately. Makes 2 (6-serving) portions.

To heat frozen mixture: Heat in covered saucepan over low heat for 45 minutes or till hot, stirring frequently. Serve as above. Serves 6.

ZUCCHINI-BULGUR STIR-FRY

Save a third of this mixture to make Sausage-Bulgur Soup—

4 cups water
2 tablespoons instant beef
    bouillon granules
2 cups bulgur wheat
2 tablespoons cold water
2 teaspoons cornstarch
2 tablespoons soy sauce
1 tablespoon cooking oil
3 cups thinly sliced carrots
1 clove garlic, minced
1½ teaspoons grated gingerroot
2 small zucchini, sliced
¼ cup sliced green onion
1 cup peanuts
½ teaspoon grated lemon peel

In a saucepan combine the 4 cups water and bouillon granules. Bring to boiling. Pour over bulgur. Let stand 1 hour; drain. Set bulgur aside. Combine the 2 tablespoons cold water and the cornstarch. Stir in soy sauce. Set aside.

Preheat a wok or large skillet over high heat; add cooking oil. Stir-fry carrots, garlic, and ginger for 8 minutes. Add zucchini and green onion. Cook 2 minutes more or till crisp-tender. Stir soy mixture. Add to vegetables; cook and stir till thickened and bubbly. Cook and stir 1 to 2 minutes more. Remove a third of the vegetable mixture and a third of the bulgur. Cover and chill separately for Sausage-Bulgur Soup. Stir remaining bulgur, peanuts, and lemon peel into wok. Toss gently till heated through. Remove a few slices of zucchini and carrot for garnish, if desired. Makes 4 servings.

SAUSAGE-BULGUR SOUP

Serve this main-dish soup with crisp salad and dark bread—

12 ounces Polish sausage, cut into
    ½-inch chunks
½ cup chopped onion
3½ cups water
1 16-ounce can tomatoes, cut up
    Reserved vegetable and bulgur
    mixtures from Zucchini-
    Bulgur Stir-fry
2 teaspoons instant beef bouillon
    granules
1 teaspoon Worcestershire sauce

In 3-quart saucepan cook sausage and onion till meat is browned and onion is tender. Drain off fat. Add water, *undrained* tomatoes, reserved vegetable mixture, bouillon granules, and Worcestershire sauce. Bring mixture to boiling. Reduce heat and simmer, covered, 10 minutes. Add reserved bulgur mixture; heat through. Serves 6.

FROZEN MEAT BASE

- **4 pounds beef round steak, cut in ¾-inch cubes**
- **2 tablespoons cooking oil**
- **1 cup water**
- **1 cup chopped onion**
- **½ cup chopped green pepper**
- **2 tablespoons instant beef bouillon granules**
- **1 20-ounce package frozen sliced carrots**
- **1 16-ounce package frozen cut green beans**

In a 12-inch skillet brown meat, about ⅓ at a time, in hot oil. Add water, onion, green pepper, and bouillon granules. Bring to boiling. Cover; simmer about 1 hour or till meat is tender, stirring occasionally. Chill. Stir in carrots and beans. Spoon mixture into 4 moisture-vaporproof containers. Seal, label, and freeze. Makes 4 (3½-cup) portions.

BEEF PAPRIKASH

- **1 3½-cup container Frozen Meat Base**
- **¼ cup water**
- **¾ cup dry red or white wine**
- **1 tablespoon paprika**
- **1 bay leaf**
- **½ teaspoon dried savory, crushed**
- **¼ teaspoon salt**
- **½ cup dairy sour cream**
- **1 tablespoon all-purpose flour**
- **Hot cooked spaetzle or noodles**

Thaw Frozen Meat Base by placing mixture in a 3-quart saucepan with the ¼ cup water; cover and cook over medium-low heat for 15 to 20 minutes, breaking up mixture with a fork. Cook 5 minutes more. Add wine, paprika, bay leaf, savory, and salt. Cover and simmer 15 minutes. Combine sour cream and flour; add to meat mixture. Cook and stir till thickened and bubbly; cook and stir 1 minute longer. Remove bay leaf. Serve over hot cooked spaetzle or noodles. Makes 6 servings.

APPLESAUCE-BEEF PIE

For a slightly sweet pie, use regular applesauce—

- **1 3½-cup container Frozen Meat Base**
- **¼ cup water**
- **1 8-ounce can unsweetened applesauce**
- **¼ cup hot-style catsup**
- **3 tablespoons all purpose flour**
- **1½ teapoons poultry seasoning**
- **¼ teaspoon salt**
- **Pastry for a 2-crust 9-inch pie**
- **1 slightly beaten egg**

Thaw Frozen Meat Base by placing mixture in a large saucepan with the ¼ cup water. Cover and simmer over medium-low heat for 15 to 20 minutes; break up mixture with a fork. Cook 5 minutes more. Stir together applesauce, hot-style catsup, flour, poultry seasoning, and salt. Add to meat mixture. Cook and stir till thickened and bubbly; cook and stir 1 minute more.

Roll *half* of the pastry to a 12-inch circle. Line a 9-inch pie plate with pastry; spoon meat mixture into crust. Roll remaining pastry to a 10-inch circle. Cut into 6 triangles. Place atop filling, points toward center; fold outside edges under bottom crust. Flute edges. Brush pastry with egg. Bake in a 375° oven for 30 to 35 minutes. Let stand 10 minutes before serving. Makes 6 servings.

Microwave method: Thaw Frozen Meat Base by placing mixture in a 1½-quart nonmetal casserole with the ¼ cup water. Cover and micro-cook on HIGH 7 minutes, stirring once or twice with fork to break up mixture. Combine applesauce, catsup, flour, poultry seasoning, and salt; add to casserole. Cook 8 minutes more or till thickened and bubbly, stirring every 2 minutes. Cook 1 to 2 minutes more. Roll out pastry, assemble pie, and bake conventionally as above.

TORTILLA-BEEF CASSEROLE

To save time, thaw the Frozen Meat Base in the refrigerator overnight. Then heat the mixture five minutes and proceed with the recipe—

- **1 3½-cup container Frozen Meat Base**
- **¼ cup water**
- **1 8-ounce can tomato sauce**
- **1½ cups shredded sharp cheddar cheese (6 ounces)**
- **1½ cups tortilla chips or broken corn tortillas**
- **1 8¾-ounce can whole kernel corn, drained**
- **¼ cup taco sauce**
- **½ cup sliced pitted ripe olives**
- **2 teaspoons snipped fresh coriander or ½ teaspoon ground coriander (optional)**
- **1 teaspoon sugar**
- **1 teaspoon chili powder**
- **½ teaspoon ground cumin**

Thaw Frozen Meat Base by placing mixture in a large saucepan with the ¼ cup water. Cover and cook over low heat for 15 to 20 minutes; break up mixture with a fork. Cook 5 minutes more. Stir in tomato sauce, *1 cup* of the cheese, *1 cup* of the chips, corn, taco sauce, olives, coriander if desired, sugar, chili powder, and cumin. Spoon meat mixture into a 2-quart casserole. Bake, covered, in a 350° oven for 30 to 35 minutes or till hot. Sprinkle with remaining tortilla chips and cheese. Bake, uncovered, 5 minutes more or till cheese melts. Makes 6 servings.

Microwave method: Thaw Frozen Meat Base mixture by placing in a 2-quart nonmetal casserole with the ¼ cup water. Cover and micro-cook on HIGH 7 minutes; break up mixture with fork. Cook 2 minutes more. Assemble as above. Cook, uncovered, 10 minutes or till hot and vegetables are tender, stirring once. Sprinkle with remaining tortilla chips and remaining cheese. Return to microwave and cook 1 minute more or till cheese melts. Makes 6 servings.

EASY BROCCOLI EGGS

Serve this attractive main dish for a brunch or Sunday supper—

- 1 10-ounce package frozen cut broccoli
- ⅔ cup dry Onion-Mushroom Rice Mix
- 1⅓ cups water
- 1 2-ounce jar pimiento, drained and chopped
- ½ teaspoon salt
- 4 eggs
- ½ cup shredded Muenster or cheddar cheese

Rinse broccoli under hot running water to separate; drain well. In an 8-inch round baking dish combine broccoli, rice mix, water, pimiento, and salt. Bake, covered, in 350° oven for 40 minutes or till rice is almost tender. Make 4 depressions in rice mixture with back of spoon. Carefully break 1 egg into each depression. Bake in 350° oven, covered, for 10 minutes. Uncover; sprinkle with cheese. Bake 2 to 3 minutes more. Makes 4 servings.

PECAN-PORK CHOP CASSEROLE

If you like, remove chops and fluff rice with a fork just before serving—

- 6 pork loin chops, cut ½ inch thick
- 1 cup sliced celery
- 1 tablespoon cooking oil
- 1 cup dry Onion-Mushroom Rice Mix
- 2 cups water
- ½ cup broken pecans
- 2 tablespoons soy sauce
  Paprika

Trim excess fat from chops; set chops aside. In saucepan cook celery in oil till tender. Stir in rice mix and water. Bring to boiling. Remove from heat; stir in nuts. Turn mixture into a 13x9x2-inch baking dish. Arrange chops atop rice. Brush chops with soy sauce; sprinkle with paprika. Bake, covered, in 350° oven for 25 minutes. Uncover and bake 10 minutes more or till chops and rice are tender. Makes 6 servings.

ONION-MUSHROOM RICE MIX

- 3 cups long grain rice
- 1 envelope regular onion-mushroom soup mix
- ¼ cup dried parsley flakes
- 2 teaspoons dried basil, crushed

Combine all ingredients. Store in an airtight container for up to several months. Stir before measuring.

To prepare mix: In a saucepan combine 1 cup mix and ¼ teaspoon *salt* with 2 cups *water.* Bring to boiling; reduce heat. Cover and simmer 20 minutes or till rice is tender. Makes 3 cups.

SEAFOOD-RICE CHOWDER

You can make this soup with cod, croaker, flounder, haddock, halibut, red snapper, sole, or whiting—

- 12 ounces fresh *or* frozen fish fillets
- 1 clove garlic, minced
- 1 tablespoon cooking oil
- ⅓ cup dry Onion-Mushroom Rice Mix
- 2 cups water
- 1 10-ounce package frozen chopped spinach
- 1 7½-ounce can tomatoes, cut up
- ½ cup dry white wine
- 2 teaspoons instant chicken bouillon granules
  Several dashes bottled hot pepper sauce
- 1 7½-ounce can minced clams

Let frozen fish stand at room temperature 15 to 20 minutes. Remove skin from fillets and cut into 1-inch cubes. Set aside. Meanwhile, in a 3-quart saucepan cook garlic in hot oil for 30 seconds. Add rice mix, water, spinach, *undrained* tomatoes, wine, bouillon granules, and bottled hot pepper sauce. Bring to boiling; reduce heat. Cover; simmer 15 minutes or till rice is almost tender. Add fish cubes and *undrained* clams. Bring just to boiling. Reduce heat; cover and simmer 5 to 7 minutes or till fish is done. Makes 6 servings.

CURRIED RICE DINNER PLATTER

- 2 cups cooked rice
- 1 medium apple, cored and chopped
- 1 small green pepper, chopped
- 2 tablespoons sliced green onion
- 2 tablespoons raisins
- 2 tablespoons olive oil
- 2 tablespoons white wine vinegar
- 2 teaspoons sugar
- 1 teaspoon curry powder
- ¼ teaspoon garlic salt
  Toasted sliced almonds
- 8 ounces summmer sausage, cut into ½-inch cubes
- 6 ounces cheddar cheese, cut into ½-inch cubes
- 2 hard-cooked eggs (optional)

Combine first 5 ingredients. Mix the olive oil, vinegar, sugar, curry powder, garlic salt, ¼ cup *water,* and ⅛ teaspoon *pepper.* Stir into rice mixture. Cover; chill overnight. Spoon rice mixture down center of lettuce-lined platter, if desired. Sprinkle with nuts. Combine summer sausage and cheese cubes; spoon on each side of the rice. Garnish with egg wedges, if desired. Serves 8.

COCONUT-PEAR CRISP

- 3 medium fresh pears, peeled, cored, and sliced
- 1¼ cups milk
- 1 4-serving-size package *instant* coconut cream pudding mix
- ¾ cup all-purpose flour
- ¼ cup chopped walnuts
- 2 tablespoons sugar
- ½ teaspoon ground cinnamon
- ¼ cup butter *or* margarine
- 1 beaten egg
- ½ teaspoon vanilla

Arrange pears in an 8-inch round baking dish. Mix milk and *half* the pudding mix. Pour over pears. Combine remaining pudding mix, flour, walnuts, sugar, and cinnamon. Cut in butter till the size of coarse crumbs. Mix egg and vanilla. Stir into dry mixture till well combined. Crumble mixture over top of pears. Bake, uncovered, in a 350° oven 40 minutes. Serves 4 to 6.

BEEF AND POTATO BAKE

1 cup thinly sliced carrots
2 medium potatoes, peeled,
    halved, and thinly sliced
    (2 cups)
1 medium onion, thinly sliced
2 tablespoons chopped green
    chili peppers (optional)
¾ teaspoon salt
⅛ teaspoon pepper
1 10¾-ounce can condensed
    cream of mushroom soup
¼ cup quick-cooking rolled oats
¼ teaspoon salt
⅛ teaspoon pepper
1 pound lean ground beef
1 teaspoon prepared mustard
    Snipped parsley

Combine carrots, potatoes, onion, chili peppers, the ¾ teaspoon salt, and the first ⅛ teaspoon pepper. Add about *one-third* of the canned soup; mix well. Spoon into a 10x6x2-inch baking dish. Combine a second third of the soup, the oats, and the remaining salt and pepper. Add meat; mix well. Form into a loaf and place atop vegetables. Bake, uncovered, in a 350° oven for 1¼ hours. Meanwhile, combine the remaining soup with the mustard. Spread atop meat; return to oven and bake, uncovered, for 15 minutes more. Sprinkle with snipped parsley. Serves 4.

RUM-RAISIN-PEACH SUNDAES

2 tablespoons raisins
2 tablespoons brown sugar
2 tablespoons orange juice
2 tablespoons butter *or*
    margarine
1 8-ounce can peach slices,
    drained
2 tablespoons rum
2 tablespoons chopped walnuts
    Vanilla ice cream

In small saucepan stir together raisins, brown sugar, orange juice, and butter or margarine. Cook and stir 5 minutes or till hot. Stir in peach slices and rum. Heat through. Add walnuts. Serve over ice cream. Serves 4.

HAM-MUSHROOM ROTINI

7 ounces rotini corkscrew
    macaroni *or* elbow macaroni
2 tablespoons butter *or*
    margarine
8 ounces fully cooked ham,
    cubed
1 7½-ounce can tomatoes, cut up
1 4-ounce can sliced mushrooms
1 5⅓-ounce can evaporated milk
3 egg yolks
¼ cup snipped parsley
¼ teaspoon ground nutmeg
⅛ teaspoon pepper
¼ cup shredded mozzarella
    cheese
2 tablespoons grated Parmesan
    cheese

Cook rotini or macaroni according to package directions; drain and keep warm. Meanwhile, in a skillet melt butter or margarine. Stir in ham, *undrained* tomatoes, and *undrained* mushrooms. Beat together evaporated milk, egg yolks, parsley, nutmeg, and pepper. Add to skillet; cook and stir till slightly thickened. Add mozzarella cheese. Cook and stir till cheese is melted. Toss with pasta. Sprinkle Parmesan cheese atop. Makes 4 servings.

BEET-SPINACH SALAD

If you have time, chill the beets ahead—

8 ounces torn spinach (6 cups)
1 8-ounce can sliced beets,
    drained
1 small onion, sliced and
    separated into rings
⅓ cup Italian salad dressing
¼ cup crumbled blue cheese *or*
    shredded cheddar cheese

In a large salad bowl combine spinach, beets, and onion. Sprinkle with salt and pepper. Toss dressing with greens. Top with cheese. Serves 4.

HORSERADISH-BEEF SANDWICHES

12 ounces thinly sliced cooked
    roast beef, ham, *or* turkey
½ cup mayonnaise *or* salad
    dressing
1 tablespoon prepared
    horseradish
1 tablespoon prepared mustard
¼ teaspoon salt
    Several dashes ground red
    pepper
2 medium green peppers, sliced
    into rings
2 tablespoons butter *or*
    margarine
4 hard rolls, halved horizontally
    Leaf lettuce

Wrap meat in foil; heat in a 350° oven for 20 minutes or till warm. Meanwhile, combine mayonnaise or salad dressing, horseradish, mustard, salt, and red pepper. Cook green pepper in butter or margarine till almost tender.

To assemble sandwiches, line bottom halves of rolls with lettuce. Top with meat, horseradish mixture, and green pepper. Add roll tops. Makes 4 servings.

To heat meat in microwave oven: wrap in clear plastic wrap; micro-cook on HIGH 3 to 4 minutes.

FRUIT SALAD DESSERT

For company, layer in parfait glasses—

1 pint (2 cups) creamy fruit salad
    (from the deli)
¼ cup broken walnuts *or* pecans
¼ teaspoon almond extract
1 cup coarsely crumbled spice,
    molasses, chocolate chip, *or*
    sugar cookies

In a bowl combine salad, nuts, and almond extract. Fold in *half* of the crumbled cookies. Spoon mixture into a 3- or 4-cup bowl. Top with remaining cookies. Chill in freezer 20 minutes or till serving time. Makes 4 servings.

FEBRUARY

COOKING TECHNIQUES
To Make Simple Fare Sensational

By Joy Taylor

Flambé! Deglaze! Glacé! Caramelize! Sound mysterious? And difficult? Don't believe it! These cooking methods, and other classic techniques, are actually simple tricks used by cooking pros to liven up the flavor of familiar foods.

On the following pages, we demystify seven classic cooking techniques so that you can incorporate them into your everyday meals. Flambe gets you off to a flashy start. Then you'll learn the tricks of the trade for bouquet garni, caramelizing, reducing, deglazing, pureeing, and glaceing. Expand your cooking expertise even more with our food term guide on page 28.

FLAMBÉ
Ignite Spirits for Glowing Finales

Flambé (French for "flamed") is more than a striking way to serve food. It also adds the flavor of liquor, minus any harshness from the alcohol, to a variety of foods. Choose a spirit that's compatible with your recipe and at least 70 proof. In a ladle or saucepan, warm ¼ to ½ cup of the libation. Ignite the warm liquid with a long match and pour the glowing spirit over the food. Allow the flames to subside, then stir the food to distribute the flavor.

Photograph: Hedrich/Blessing; Mike Dieter. Food stylist: Fran Paulson

Southern Comfort and hot pepper sauce make **Frisky Shrimp** *(left)* live up to its name. Colorful shrimp with tails, bias-sliced celery, green onions, and toasted slivered almonds are accented by the zesty tomato sauce.

What makes **Meringue and Fruit Flambé** *(right)* especially inviting is the brandied fruit sauce that's spooned over the chocolate meringue shells and vanilla ice cream.

Orange liqueur adds zip to **Dessert Omelet Flambé** *(middle)*, filled with fresh kiwi slices and strawberry preserves. Powdered sugar, singed with a hot metal rod, adds a decorative finish to the top of this elegant omelet.

Richly brewed **Flaming Tea Punch** *(upper right)* is spiked with a blend of cognac and Amaretto. Orange pinwheel slices accent the citrus base of this warm drink.

CARAMELIZE
Melt Sugar for Sweet Creations

Put the heat to granulated sugar and it **caramelizes** into a liquid with a brand-new amber color and rich flavor. This melted mixture can give breads, desserts, sauces, and vegetables a distinctive caramel taste and tint. Let the sugar brown slightly over low heat in a heavy skillet. Caution: Don't stir till the melting begins or the sugar

will get lumpy. After the sugar starts to melt, stir it constantly over low heat for eight to ten minutes or till golden brown. The longer it's cooked, the more pronounced the flavor. When the melted sugar is removed from the heat, it will harden quickly. To remelt it, a liquid or melted butter is often stirred into the mixture.

Pineapple chunks and apple wedges team up in a caramelized syrup and bake under a rich pastry in **Pineapple Tarte Tatin** *(back right).* The frozen puff pastry dough makes short work of

this elegant dessert that will impress your family and friends.

Caramelized sugar replaces the traditional corn syrup in the glaze for **Whole Wheat Caramel Rolls** *(left);* they're

filled with wheat germ, chopped nuts, and raisins. In **Caramelized Onions in Squash** *(front),* the sugar syrup is accented with orange peel that complements the vegetable combo.

BOUQUET GARNI
Bag Up Herbs for Savory Seasoning

Wrap several parsley sprigs, garlic cloves, fresh or dried thyme, and a whole bay leaf in cheesecloth and you have one **Bouquet Garni.** Just drop one, two, or even three of these simple seasoning bags into a simmering soup, stew, sauce, or braising liquid to give the food a robust taste and aroma. The cooking liquid remains speckle-free and you can easily fish out all of the herbs at the end of the cooking time.

Tie up a batch of these wonder-bags to keep close at hand for fast flavoring. For this purpose, be sure to use the dried thyme in the mix since the fresh thyme loses its potency when stored. for any length of time.

Versatile is the word for bouquet garni, as these three recipes demonstrate. **Bouquet Garni Jelly** *(left)* is especially good when spooned over biscuits, but try it on a peanut butter sandwich, also. Two bouquet garni bags give **Herbed Béchamel Sauce** *(right)* its sophisticated flavor. Serve this sauce over cooked vegetables, eggs, or fish. **Herbed Lentil Vegetable Soup** *(back)* makes a hearty meal that is enriched not only by the bouquet garni, but also by the tomato-juice-based broth.

PUREE
Sieve Foods for Extra Body

You can add an intriguing new look, taste, and texture to commonplace foods by **pureeing** some of the recipe ingredients. When you substitute purees for other liquids in a recipe, you stir in body and richness, and often subtract calories since thickeners may be omitted. You can add fullness to a cream sauce by stirring in pureed

vegetables. Or, blend extra fruitiness into a molded salad with processed berries.

Start with almost any food—fruit, vegetable, or meat—and mash it with a sieve, food mill, blender, or food processor. No matter how you do it, or how many foods you mix, the outcome is the same: a rich puree ready to impart its flavor to many dishes.

Peaches, mandarin orange sections, and ricotta cheese are pureed together to form stately **Peach Mousse with Raspberry Sauce** *(back)*. The elegant, but easy sauce is made from sieved frozen berries and orange liqueur.

Potatoes, celery, onion, plus your choice of any winter squash, are the beginnings of **Cream of Winter Vegetable Soup** *(front)*. A portion of the cooked vegetables is pureed to provide the thick, creamy base of this robust soup. To add satisfying crunch, salted sunflower nuts are sprinkled on top of each serving.

24

DEGLAZE
Capture Drippings to Add Richness

Don't discard the tasty pan drippings when you roast or pan-fry food. Instead, **deglaze** the pan. When the cooking vessel is deglazed, those crispy brown morsels are loosened and become the basis for a full-bodied gravy or sauce.

To get started, remove the cooked food from the skillet and keep it warm.

Add your choice of liquid to the hot pan —milk, fruit juice, wine, coffee, bouillon, or any other liquid you happen to have on hand in the kitchen. Scrape up the crusty bits with a metal spatula while the liquid boils, stirring in additional liquid and seasonings as needed. The result: A rich-tasting sauce that turns plain food into extra-special fare.

Ham with Onion Sauce *(back)* capitalizes on the drippings left in the skillet after boneless ham slices have been fried. A hint of coffee in the deglazing liquid makes the sauce similar to the Southern favorite, red-eye gravy.

Add apple juice to the flavorful bits in the pan bottom for **Curried Lamb Chop Platter** *(front)* and stir up extra flavor. Then, blend curry powder, green pepper, onion, and dried fruits into the juice mixture and you have a colorful sauce to spoon over the meat.

REDUCE
Boil Down Liquids to Boost Flavor

Does your sauce have a thin consistency, a thin taste, or both? **Reduce** it! Just simmer a big-batch sauce for hours, or vigorously boil a small-scale sauce for minutes, to evaporate the liquid and concentrate the flavors. Almost any sauce or condiment can be enriched via reducing (catsup and apple butter are two old

standbys). Just remember to first reduce the liquid, then add ingredients such as meat or vegetables and simmer just till they're done.

And if you're trying to reduce (your weight, that is), you'll discover that reducing (your sauce) can help because it may allow you to omit thickening ingredients, thus calories.

Rosemary Chicken *(back)* features chicken-sausage bundles simmered in a mixture of bouillon, wine, and herbs. For the cream sauce, the braising liquid is reduced before cream is added. The sauce is boiled down again to a velvety consistency, and then it's spooned over the poultry roll-ups.

For **Pasta with Fish Sauce** *(front)* a tomato-clam sauce slowly simmers till it is thick enough to coat linguine. Just a few minutes before serving, cubes of whitefish and sliced pimiento-stuffed olives are added to and cooked with the spunky Italian-style sauce.

GLACÉ
Spoon on a Glossy Finish

If you've ever enjoyed glazed strawberry pie or main dishes sealed in delicate aspics, you already know the virtues of **glacéing.** It forms a glistening topper that enhances both the looks and the flavor of foods, including vegetables, meats, and candies. Of course, you'll want to choose a sweet or savory glaze that complements the food. In addition, remember that the jelly, thickened sauce, or gelatin-based mixture should set up on the food. When glazing individual portions, place the unglazed food on a wire rack so that any excess glaze can run off. Gently spoon on the glossy finish, then refrigerate the food. In a short time, your creation will be all set.

Jellied chicken broth and soy sauce make up the see-through topping for **Oriental Vegetable Tart** *(back).* Purchased refrigerated dough is used for the bread shell of this colorful vegetable side dish. The shell is topped with a cheese layer, then pea pods, tomatoes, mushrooms, and water chestnuts.

Glacéed Sandwiches *(front)* get their richness from the whipping cream that is stirred into a thickened salad dressing. Spoon this sauce over layers of rye bread, ham, sour cream, cheese, and nuts, and garnish with decoratively cut foods to suit your fancy.

Cook's Guide to Food Terms

If you're stumped by the terminology used in recipes and restaurant menus, this list of food terms will provide the help you need. You'll discover that many of those baffling terms are simply fancy (or foreign) phrases for cooking techniques you're already using.

Cooking Terms

- **aged**—Foods and beverages such as cheese, beef, spirits, and wine that have been stored under controlled conditions for days, months, or years. Besides maturing the flavor, aging often improves the color and/or texture of the food.
- **al dente (al-DEN-tay)**—A phrase describing pasta that has been cooked just to the point that it is slightly chewy. (Italian)
- **beurre manié (boor-mun-YAY)**—A mixture of softened butter and flour that's shaped into small balls, then used to thicken sauces. (French)
- **candied**—A term describing fruits or nuts that have been coated with a sugar syrup to enhance the flavor and also to preserve the food.
- **clarify**—To clear a liquid (such as beef stock or melted butter) by removing the solid particles.
- **crystallize**—To allow crystals of sugar to form on foods such as candy. The size and number of crystals determine the quality of the finished food.
- **degrease**—To remove excess fat from soups, stocks, pan juices, or sauces by skimming the surface of the hot liquid with a spoon or chilling the liquid and removing the hardened fat.
- **duxelles (dewk-SELL)**—A combination of mushrooms, shallots, and herbs that is cooked till it's reduced to a paste. Then the mixture is used as a garnish or as an ingredient in sauces, stuffings, or meats. (French)
- **gratiné (grah-tee-NAY)**—Meats and vegetables that have been sprinkled with buttered bread crumbs or cheese and then broiled to brown the foods or give them a crust. (French)
- **macerate**—To soak food, especially fruit, in a flavored liquid so that the food can absorb the flavor.
- **roux (ROO)**—A blend of flour and fat that is cooked and used to thicken sauces and gravies. How long the roux is cooked affects the color and flavor of the sauce.
- **sauté (saw-TAY)**—To cook foods, often vegetables, quickly over high heat in a small amount of fat. (French)
- **score**—To place shallow slits partway through the outer surface of food, usually meat or bread, for functional or decorative purposes. Scoring meat allows fat to drain and tenderizes tough connective tissue.

Menu Terms

- **a la Grecque (ah-la-GREK)**—A phrase meaning "in the Greek style." Vegetables prepared in this manner are seasoned with oil, vinegar, and spices and are served chilled. (French)
- **avgolemono sauce (AHV-go-LEM-uh-no)**—An egg-lemon sauce that is served over meats, fish, poultry, or vegetables or is used to thicken soup. (Greek)
- **blanquette (blan-KET)**—A chicken, veal, or lamb stew made with a creamy white sauce and thickened with egg yolk. Onions and mushrooms often are added to the stew. (French)
- **blintze**—A main-dish or dessert pancake rolled round a meat, cheese, or fruit filling and served with sour cream, applesauce, or jam. (Yiddish)
- **Bourguignonne (boor-gween-YON)**—Meats, fish, and poultry that have been cooked in a red wine sauce with onions and mushrooms. The cooking style originated in the Burgundy region of France. (French)
- **braciola (bra-chee-O-la)**—A flattened piece of meat rolled around a stuffing and cooked in a wine sauce. (Italian)
- **brûlé (brew-LAY)**—Any food made or served with a caramelized sugar topping or sauce. (French)
- **cacciatore (catch-a-TOR-ee)**—The Italian word for "hunter." The term is applied to meat or poultry that's been prepared with onions, garlic, herbs, wine, and tomatoes. (Italian)
- **Chantilly**—A term describing a dessert prepared or served with whipping cream. (French)
- **en daube (ahn-DOB)**—A meat, poultry, or fish stew made with wine, vegetables, and herbs. (French)
- **en papillote (ahn-POP-e-lowt)**—A method of baking and serving food, such as fish, in parchment or brown paper. (French)
- **Florentine**—An adjective that is used to describe a food prepared with spinach. (Italian)
- **maison (may-ZOHN)**—The French word for "house." It's applied to a food prepared according to the chef's own recipe. (French)
- **Niçoise (nee-SWAZ)**—Foods prepared with tomatoes and garlic, a style that originated in Nice, France. (French)
- **Paella (pie-AY-yah)**—An elaborate rice, seafood, and poultry casserole seasoned with saffron. (Spanish)
- **paprikash (PAP-ra-kesh)**—The term referring to foods that are seasoned with paprika. (Hungarian)
- **paysanne (pay-ZAHN)**—The French word for "peasant," used for meat or poultry that is braised with vegetables.
- **Provencale (pro-vin-SAHL)**—Foods cooked in the style of Provence (a region in southern France). A liberal amount of garlic, plus tomatoes and oil, is used. (French)
- **ratatouille (ra-too-TWEE)**—A well-seasoned vegetable stew that includes eggplant, squash, green pepper, tomatoes, garlic, and olive oil. (French)
- **roulade (roo-LAHD)**—A word meaning "roll" which refers to a thin slice of meat that has been wrapped around a stuffing, then cooked. (French)
- **Saint Germain (san-zher-MAYN)**—A French city's name, applied to foods made with green peas. (French)
- **Véronique (ver-ro-NEEK)**—A meat or fish dish that contains seedless white grapes. (French)

FRISKY SHRIMP

¼ **small lemon**
2 **stalks celery, bias sliced into 1-inch pieces**
3 **green onions, sliced into 1-inch lengths**
1 **clove garlic, minced**
3 **tablespoons butter**
¾ **pound large shelled shrimp with tails**
1 **7½-ounce can tomatoes, cut up**
¼ **teaspoon dried basil, crushed**
    Dash bottled hot pepper sauce
¼ **cup slivered almonds, toasted**
¼ **cup Southern Comfort**
2 **cups hot cooked rice**

With zester or sharp knife, cut lemon peel into thin strips. Set aside. In skillet cook celery, green onion, and garlic in the butter till onion is tender but not brown. Add shrimp. Cook 2 to 3 minutes or till shrimp are pink. Stir in *undrained* tomatoes, basil, hot pepper sauce, ¼ teaspoon *salt,* and dash *pepper.* Stir over low heat for 2 minutes or till heated through. Stir in the toasted almonds.

In separate saucepan heat Southern Comfort and lemon peel just till warm. On serving platter, arrange shrimp mixture atop rice. Using a long match, ignite the liquor. Pour over shrimp mixture. Allow flames to subside. To serve, toss together the shrimp mixture and rice. Serves 4.

FLAMING TEA PUNCH

6 **cups strong almond-flavored tea *or* regular brewed tea**
1 **cup orange juice**
1½ **cups Amaretto/cognac blend**
¼ **cup sugar**
    Orange slices (optional)

In a blazer pan or chafing dish combine the brewed tea, orange juice, *1 cup* of the liquor blend, and sugar. Heat through. Add orange slices, if desired, to punch. Heat the remaining liquor just till warm. Using a long match, ignite the liquor. Pour flaming liquor into tea mixture; stir. After flames subside transfer to heatproof punch bowl, if desired. Makes 16 (4 ounce) servings.

MERINGUE AND FRUIT FLAMBÉ

The individual meringue shells can be made a day ahead and stored in an airtight container—

3 **egg whites**
1 **teaspoon vanilla**
½ **teaspoon cream of tartar**
¾ **cup sugar**
¼ **cup unsweetened cocoa powder**
2 **medium oranges**
    Orange juice
1 **tablespoon cornstarch**
¼ **teaspoon ground allspice**
1 **tablespoon lemon juice**
2 **small fresh peaches, sliced, *or* one 8-ounce can peach slices, drained**
1 **small banana, sliced**
¼ **cup raisins**
8 **scoops vanilla ice cream**
¼ **cup brandy**

Let egg whites come to room temperature. For meringue shells, cover baking sheet with brown paper or foil. Draw eight 3-inch circles. Set aside. Add vanilla, cream of tartar, and dash *salt* to egg whites. Beat to soft peaks (tips curl over); gradually add ½ cup of the sugar. Continue beating to stiff peaks (tips stand straight). Combine the remaining ¼ cup sugar and the cocoa powder; gradually beat into egg whites being careful not to overbeat. Pipe meringue mixture through a pastry tube or spoon and spread the mixture to cover each of the eight circles, forming high edges. Bake in a 275° oven for 1 hour. Turn off oven. Let stand 2 hours in oven. Cool. Peel off paper.

For sauce: Section oranges over bowl to catch juices. Drain orange sections, reserving juice. Add additional orange juice to make ¾ cup liquid. In saucepan combine cornstarch and allspice. Stir in the ¾ cup orange juice and the lemon juice. Cook and stir over medium heat till thickened and bubbly. Remove from heat; stir in orange sections, peaches, banana, and raisins; heat through, stirring gently.

To serve, place a scoop of ice cream in each meringue shell. In small saucepan heat brandy just till hot. Using a long match, ignite the brandy. Pour into fruit sauce; stir. Ladle sauce over ice cream. Serve immediately. Makes 8 servings.

DESSERT OMELET FLAMBÉ

If desired, make a decorative criss-cross design on the omelet by singeing the surface with a hot metal skewer before adding the flaming liqueur—

3 **egg whites**
¼ **teaspoon vanilla**
    Dash salt
3 **tablespoons granulated sugar**
3 **egg yolks**
1 **tablespoon butter *or* margarine**
2 **kiwis, peeled and sliced**
2 **tablespoons strawberry preserves**
    Sifted powdered sugar
3 **tablespoons orange liqueur**

In large mixer bowl beat egg whites, vanilla, and salt at medium speed of mixer to soft peaks (tips curl over). Gradually add granulated sugar, beating at high speed till stiff peaks form (tips are straight). In a mixer bowl beat the egg yolks at high speed about 5 minutes or till they are thick and lemon-colored. Fold egg yolks into beaten egg whites.

In a 10-inch skillet with an ovenproof handle, heat the butter *or* margarine till a drop of water sizzles. Pour in egg mixture, mounding it slightly higher at the sides. Cook over low heat, uncovered, for 8 to 10 minutes or till eggs are puffed and set and bottom is golden brown. Place skillet in a 325° oven. Bake 10 minutes or till a knife inserted near center comes out clean. Loosen sides of omelet with a metal spatula. Make a shallow cut across the omelet, cutting slightly off center. Combine kiwis and preserves; spoon over larger portion of omelet. Fold the smaller portion of omelet over. Slide omelet onto platter. Sprinkle powdered sugar over omelet. Heat the 3 tablespoons liqueur just till warm. Using a long match, ignite the liqueur; pour over omelet. Serve immediately. Makes 2 or 3 servings.

February

WHOLE WHEAT CARAMEL ROLLS

1 to 1½ cups all-purpose flour
1 package active dry yeast
½ cup raisins
1 cup boiling water
3 tablespoons cooking oil
3 tablespoons honey
½ teaspoon salt
1 egg
1½ cups whole wheat flour
1 cup sugar
⅓ cup water
¼ cup butter *or* margarine
¼ cup chopped nuts
2 tablespoons wheat germ
1 teaspoon ground cinnamon

In a large mixer bowl combine *1 cup* of the all-purpose flour and the yeast. Soak raisins in the 1 cup boiling water for 5 minutes. Drain, reserving ⅔ cup liquid. Set raisins aside. Stir the oil, honey, and salt into reserved liquid; cool to 115° to 120°. Add honey mixture to flour mixture; add egg. Beat at low speed of electric mixer for ½ minute, scraping constantly. Beat 3 minutes at high speed. Stir in the whole wheat flour and raisins. Stir in as much of the remaining all-purpose flour as you can mix in with a spoon. On floured surface, knead in enough of the remaining all-purpose flour to make a moderately stiff dough that is smooth and elastic (6 to 8 minutes total). Shape into a ball and place in a lightly greased bowl; turn once to grease top. Cover; let rise in warm place till double (about 1 hour).

Meanwhile, in 10-inch skillet heat the sugar over medium-low heat till it begins to melt. Heat and stir for 5 to 10 minutes or till golden brown. Remove from heat. Stir in the ⅓ cup water and *2 tablespoons* of the butter; return to heat. Cook and stir to remelt sugar. Immediately pour mixture into a 13x9x2-inch baking pan; swirl to coat pan bottom. Set aside.

Punch dough down. Cover; let rest 10 minutes. On a lightly floured surface roll dough out to a 15x10-inch rectangle. Melt the remaining 2 tablespoons butter; brush over dough. Mix nuts, wheat germ, and cinnamon; sprinkle over dough. Roll up dough jelly-roll style, starting at long end. Pinch edges and ends together to seal. Cut into 15 slices.

Arrange dough slices atop caramelized sugar in prepared pan. Cover pan; let rise in warm place till double (about 45 minutes). Bake, uncovered, in a 375° oven for 20 to 25 minutes or till golden brown. Immediately turn rolls out onto wire rack with waxed paper underneath. Serve warm with butter or margarine, if desired. Makes 15 rolls.

PINEAPPLE TARTE TATIN

¾ cup sugar
¼ cup butter *or* margarine
¼ teaspoon ground cloves
5 medium cooking apples, peeled, cored, and cut into 8 wedges each
1 16-ounce can pineapple chunks, drained
1 10-ounce package frozen patty shells, thawed

In 10-inch skillet heat the sugar over low heat without stirring till it begins to melt. Heat and stir for 3 to 5 minutes or till light brown. Stir in butter or margarine and ground cloves. Add apple wedges; cook over medium-low heat, stirring occasionally, about 7 minutes or till apples are nearly tender. Remove apples using a slotted spoon. Gently boil mixture in skillet till the consistency of corn syrup, stirring occasionally. Pour into a 9- or 10-inch flan pan. Decoratively arrange apples and pineapple chunks in pan. Bake in a 425° oven for 10 minutes.

Meanwhile, on lightly floured surface press patty shells together and roll into a 9- or 10-inch circle to fit flan pan. Trim and flute edge. Place atop hot fruit. Bake 15 to 18 minutes more or till pastry is golden brown. Cool in pan on a wire rack for 30 minutes. Invert onto platter. Serve warm. Makes 6 to 8 servings.

CARAMELIZED ONIONS IN SQUASH

2 small acorn squash
⅓ cup sugar
2 large onions, sliced and separated into rings, or chopped
2 tablespoons butter
½ teaspoon finely shredded orange peel

Cut squash in half lengthwise. Remove seeds and strings. Place squash, cut side down, in shallow baking pan. Bake in 350° oven 30 minutes. Turn cut side up; bake 15 to 20 minutes more.

Meanwhile, in heavy skillet heat sugar over medium heat without stirring till it just begins to melt. Heat and stir about 3 minutes or till golden brown. Add onions, butter and orange peel. Cook and stir for 7 to 8 minutes or till onions are tender and glazed, and liquid is consistency of corn syrup. To serve, spoon onions and syrup into each squash half. Serves 4.

BOUQUET GARNI

2 cloves garlic, halved
1 bay leaf
4 sprigs parsley
2 teaspoons snipped fresh thyme *or* ¾ teaspoon dried thyme

Cut a 2-inch square from several thicknesses of cheesecloth; place all ingredients in center of cheesecloth. Bring corners of cheesecloth together to form a bag. Tie with string. Makes 1 bouquet garni.

BOUQUET GARNI JELLY

6½ cups sugar
2 cups water
1 cup red wine vinegar
3 Bouquet Garni
1 6-ounce package liquid fruit pectin (2 foil pouches)

Combine sugar, water, vinegar, and Bouquet Garni. Bring to boiling. Stir in pectin. Bring to full rolling boil; boil hard 1 minute. Discard Bouquet Garni. Pour hot liquid into clean, hot jelly jars, leaving ¼ inch headspace. Seal jars, using metal lids or paraffin. Makes 7 half-pints.

HERBED BÉCHAMEL SAUCE

- ½ cup water
- 2 Bouquet Garni
- 1 teaspoon instant chicken bouillon granules
- 1¼ cups milk
- 1 tablespoon all-purpose flour
- 3 slightly beaten egg yolks

In small saucepan combine water, Bouquet Garni, and bouillon granules. Bring to boiling. Reduce heat. Simmer, covered, for 10 minutes. Stir milk into flour; add to the bouillon mixture. Cook and stir till thickened and bubbly. Cook and stir 1 minute more. Discard Bouquet Garni. Stir *half* of the hot mixture into egg yolks. Return all to saucepan. Cook and stir constantly over low heat for 2 to 3 minutes or till thickened. Serve immediately over cooked vegetables, eggs, or fish. Makes 1½ cups.

HERBED LENTIL-VEGETABLE SOUP

- 1 cup dry lentils
- 3 cups water
- 1 18-ounce can tomato juice
- 1 large onion, cut into wedges
- 1 tablespoon Worcestershire sauce
- 2 teaspoons instant beef bouillon granules
- ½ teaspoon salt
- ¼ teaspoon pepper
- 1 Bouquet Garni
- 2 potatoes, peeled and cubed
- 1 10-ounce package frozen cut green beans
- 1 cup shredded cheddar cheese

Rinse lentils. In a large saucepan combine lentils, water, tomato juice, onion, Worcestershire sauce, bouillon granules, salt, and pepper. Bring to boiling. Reduce heat. Add the Bouquet Garni. Cover and simmer for 25 minutes. Add potatoes. Cover and simmer 20 minutes more or till vegetables are nearly tender. Add green beans; cover and simmer 5 to 10 minutes more or till all vegetables are tender. Discard Bouquet Garni. Sprinkle cheese atop each serving. Makes 6 servings.

CREAM OF WINTER VEGETABLE SOUP

- 2 cups chopped peeled potatoes
- 1½ cups chopped peeled winter squash
- ½ cup chopped celery
- 1 small onion, chopped
- 1 clove garlic, minced
- 2 tablespoons snipped parsley
- 1 teaspoon dry mustard
- 1 teaspoon finely shredded lemon peel
- 1 10¾-ounce can condensed chicken broth
- 1¼ cups milk *or* light cream
  Sunflower nuts

In saucepan combine potatoes, squash, celery, onion, garlic, parsley, mustard, lemon peel, and ⅛ teaspoon *pepper.* Stir in chicken broth. Bring to boiling. Reduce heat; cover and simmer 20 minutes. Transfer about 2 cups of the vegetable-broth mixture to blender container or food processor bowl. Cover; process till smooth. Return pureed mixture to saucepan. Stir in milk. Heat through. Season to taste. Sprinkle nuts atop each serving. Serves 6 to 8.

HAM WITH ONION SAUCE

- 6 slices fully cooked boneless ham cut ¼ inch thick
- 2 tablespoon cooking oil
- ½ teaspoon instant coffee crystals
- ½ cup sliced green onion
- 1 teaspoon Worcestershire sauce
- 1 tablespoon all-purpose flour

In large skillet cook the ham slices in hot oil about 5 minutes per side or till heated through. Remove ham slices to platter; keep warm. Add coffee crystals and 1 cup *water* to skillet drippings. Bring to boiling, scraping up any browned bits in skillet. Add green onion and Worcestershire. Blend flour into 2 tablespoons cold *water;* add to skillet juices. Cook and stir till thickened and bubbly. Cook and stir 1 minute more. Spoon gravy over ham. Garnish with green onion fans, if desired. Makes 4 to 6 servings.

PEACH MOUSSE WITH RASPBERRY SAUCE

- 1 29-ounce can peach slices (syrup pack)
- 1 11-ounce can mandarin orange sections, drained
- 1 15-ounce carton ricotta cheese
- 2 teaspoons lemon juice
- ⅓ cup sugar
- 2 envelopes unflavored gelatin
  Dash salt
- 1 egg yolk
- 1 egg white
- 2 tablespoons sugar
- ½ cup whipping cream
- 1 recipe Raspberry Sauce
  Peach slices and mandarin orange sections (optional)

Drain peaches, reserving ¾ cup syrup. In blender container or food processor bowl combine the peach slices, mandarin orange sections, ricotta cheese, lemon juice, and ¼ cup of the reserved peach syrup. Cover and process till smooth. (Or, press peaches and oranges through a fine-mesh wire sieve; set aside. Press cheese through sieve. In bowl combine sieved fruits, cheese, lemon juice, and ¼ of the cup peach syrup.)

In small saucepan combine the ⅓ cup sugar, the gelatin, and salt. Stir in the remaining ½ cup reserved peach syrup and egg yolk. Cook and stir till mixture just comes to a boil and gelatin is dissolved. Pour into a large bowl; cool to room temperature.

Stir the ricotta cheese mixture into the gelatin mixture. Beat egg white to soft peaks (tips curl over). Gradually add the 2 tablespoons sugar; continue beating to stiff peaks (tips stand straight). Fold beaten egg white into gelatin mixture. Beat the cream to soft peaks; fold into gelatin mixture. Spoon mixture into a 6½-cup mold. Chill till firm. To serve, unmold onto plate. Drizzle Raspberry Sauce over mousse; pass remaining sauce. Garnish with peach slices and orange sections, if desired. Makes 8 to 10 servings.

Raspberry Sauce: Combine one 10-ounce package frozen *red raspberries,* thawed, with 1 teaspoon *cornstarch.* Cook and stir till bubbly. Cook and stir 2 minutes more. Sieve; discard seeds. Add 1 tablespoon *orange liqueur.* Chill.

CURRIED LAMB CHOP PLATTER

2 slices bacon
6 lamb leg sirloin chops, cut ¾ inch thick
½ cup apple cider *or* apple juice
2 teaspoons curry powder
1 cup chicken broth
½ cup apple cider *or* apple juice
1 large onion, chopped (¾ cup)
½ cup chopped mixed dried fruits
1 green pepper, cut into strips
    Hot cooked couscous *or* rice
4 teaspoons cornstarch
    Peanuts

Cook bacon till crisp. Remove bacon, reserving drippings. Crumble bacon; set aside. Brown chops on both sides in hot bacon drippings. Sprinkle with salt, if desired. Remove chops from skillet. Remove skillet from heat; add ½ cup apple cider and curry powder. Return skillet to heat. Cook over medium heat 5 minutes; scrape up any browned bits on bottom of skillet.

Return chops to skillet. Add chicken broth, the remaining ½ cup apple cider, and onion. Cover; simmer for 20 minutes. Add dried fruits and green pepper. Cover; simmer 10 minutes more. Remove chops; arrange atop couscous on serving platter; keep warm. Blend cornstarch into 2 tablespoons *cold water;* stir into liquid in skillet. Cook and stir till thickened and bubbly. Cook and stir 1 to 2 minutes more. Spoon sauce over chops; sprinkle with crumbled bacon. Pass peanuts. Makes 6 servings.

GLACÉED SANDWICHES

12 slices rye bread
½ cup dairy sour cream
¼ cup bottled creamy Italian salad dressing
½ cup chopped nuts
½ teaspoon dry mustard
1½ cups shredded cheddar cheese
12 ounces fully cooked sliced ham
2 teaspoons unflavored gelatin
2 cups mayonnaise
⅓ cup whipping cream
    Sandwich toppers*

Cut each bread slice into a 3- or 4-inch circle or square, removing crusts. Combine sour cream, salad dressing, chopped nuts, and dry mustard. Stir in cheddar cheese. Spread cheese mixture on one side of each piece of bread. Cut 2 or 3 ham slices to fit each bread piece; place atop cheese mixture to form an open-face sandwich. Cover; chill.

In small saucepan combine gelatin and 3 tablespoons *cold water.* Let stand 5 minutes. Stir over low heat till gelatin is dissolved. Remove from heat; cool slightly. Combine mayonnaise and whipping cream; stir in dissolved gelatin. Place sandwiches on wire rack. Spoon mayonnaise mixture over each sandwich, allowing mixture to drip down sides of bread to coat evenly. Decorate with sandwich toppers.* Cover; chill about 1 hour or till set. Makes 12.

*Use walnuts, sliced ripe olives, pimiento, green pepper, parsley, green grapes, ham pieces, asparagus tips, and avocado slices as desired.

ORIENTAL VEGETABLES TART

1 3-ounce package cream cheese
1 package (4) refrigerated crescent rolls
¼ cup mayonnaise
1 teaspoon soy sauce
1 6-ounce package frozen pea pods, thawed
1 cup sliced fresh mushrooms
½ cup sliced water chestnuts
5 cherry tomatoes, halved
1½ teaspoons instant chicken bouillon granules
1½ teaspoons soy sauce
1 tablespoon cornstarch

Soften cream cheese; set aside. Separate crescent roll dough. Press dough on bottom and 1 inch up sides of a 10x6x2-inch baking dish. Bake in a 375° oven for 10 to 12 minutes. Cool. Remove crust; place on serving tray. Mix cream cheese, mayonnaise, and the 1 teaspoon soy sauce. Spread cheese mixture over bottom of crust. Drain vegetables well. Arrange pea pods, mushrooms, water chestnuts, and tomatoes atop cheese layer. Combine bouillon granules, remaining 1½ teaspoons soy sauce and ¾ cup *water.* Blend in the cornstarch. Cook and stir till thickened and bubbly. Cook and stir 2 minutes more. Spoon hot glaze evenly over vegetables. Cover; chill. To serve, carefully cut into squares. Makes 6 to 8 servings.

PASTA WITH FISH SAUCE

1 large onion, chopped (¾ cup)
1 clove garlic, minced
2 tablespoons butter
1 28-ounce can tomatoes, cut up
1 5½-ounce can clam-tomato juice cocktail (⅔ cup)
½ teaspoon dried oregano, crushed
¼ teaspoon dried basil, crushed
1 7½-ounce can minced clams
1 16-ounce package frozen fish fillets
¼ cup sliced pimiento-stuffed olives
    Hot cooked linguine

Cook onion and garlic in butter till onion is tender. Stir in next 4 ingredients and ⅛ teaspoon *pepper.* Drain clams; reserve liquid. Set clams aside. Add clam liquid to tomato mixture. Bring to boiling; reduce heat. Simmer, uncovered, for 45 to 50 minutes or till very thick; stir occasionally. Meanwhile, let fish stand at room temperature 20 minutes; cut into 1-inch cubes. Add fish, olives, and clams to sauce. Bring to boiling. Reduce heat. Cover; simmer for 5 to 7 minutes. Serve over pasta. Serves 6.

ROSEMARY CHICKEN

Skin 2 whole medium *chicken breasts;* halve lengthwise and bone. Place each half between two pieces of clear plastic wrap; pound to ¼-inch thickness. Using 4 *smoked sausage links,* wrap *each* half around a link. Secure with wooden picks. In skillet brown chicken rolls in 2 tablespoons *butter.* Add ¼ cup *dry white wine;* ¼ cup *water;* ¼ cup chopped *onion;* 1 stalk *celery,* chopped; 1 teaspoon *instant chicken bouillon granules;* and ¼ teaspoon *dried rosemary,* crushed. Bring to boiling; reduce heat. Simmer, covered, 20 minutes. Remove rolls to platter. Remove picks; keep chicken warm. Skim fat from pan juices. Bring juices and vegetables to boiling. Boil hard for 3 minutes or till juices and vegetables are reduced to ½ cup. Add ⅓ cup *whipping cream.* Boil gently, uncovered, for 3 to 4 minutes or till slightly thickened; stir occasionally. Spoon sauce over chicken. Serves 4.

MARCH

Treasured Family Recipes
For Spring Celebrations
By Nancy Byal

**Never let it be said that great holiday feasting comes but once a year!
Look around and you'll discover family celebrations cropping up right along
with the first blossoms of spring. For openers, meet the Richmans, the
Havens, and the Ferraras, who uniquely preserve the heritage of Passover,
Easter, and St. Joseph's Day respectively by cooking up delicious and
festive foods. Now let's visit these families. You're sure to find ideas
to enrich your own celebrations (and enliven everyday meals, too).**

*L*ike many Jewish parents, Sheila and Hal Richman look forward to Passover as a time to share Jewish history and food customs with their children. "Passover is our most important holiday," says Sheila. "It commemorates the liberation of the children of Israel from slavery in Egypt some 3,000 years ago. Hal and I believe that the home is the most important place to express the Jewish heritage. So we've made it our responsibility to pass on the traditions to our children, just as my husband's parents and mine passed them on to us," explains Sheila.

The first and most elaborate dinner of the Richmans' week-long celebration is the Seder (meaning "order of service"). This is a family meal interwoven with solemn religious ceremony and playful customs that appeal to and inspire the children. "An elegant table setting, the children's happy voices, the family's singing, and the reading of the Haggadah (the story of Passover) all enrich the occasion," Sheila says.

One intriguing aspect of Passover food is that no leavened bread or regular flours of any kind are used throughout the week's celebration. Instead, the unleavened bread, matzo, is used to symbolize the unleavened bread the children of Israel ate during their Exodus—unleavened because there wasn't time to wait for the bread to rise before the Exodus.

Through the years, resourceful Jewish cooks have devised infinite ways to use whole matzo crackers as well as coarsely ground matzo known as farfel and finely ground matzo called cake meal. "Matzo products are available all year long," explains Sheila, "so you needn't limit their use to the Passover season." The

Passover
A Dinner of Reaffirmation

Top: The Seder dinner ceremony is centered around the Seder plate. Each food on the plate is symbolic of the Exodus: *(clockwise from top left)* a roasted egg, a roasted lamb shank, salt water, **Haroseth** (a blend of apples, nuts, and wine), sweet herbs, and bitter herbs. **Bottom:** Sheila, Hal, and their children, Ann and Adam, enjoy the dinner with Sheila's and Hal's parents. **Right:** Dishes enjoyed during Passover are: *(clockwise from front)* **Chicken Soup With Matzo Balls, Farfel Pudding, Spinach Matzo Pie, Orange-Glazed Chicken With Matzo-Nut Stuffing, Passover Carrot-Nut Cake, Fruit Tzimmes.**

crunchy texture and mild flavor of matzo enhance a variety of foods, from entrées to desserts. Here are some of the Richmans' favorites:

Orange-Glazed Chicken With Matzo-Nut Stuffing—Farfel is combined with vegetables and nuts in the citrus-flavored stuffing.

Chicken Soup With Matzo Balls—Sheila, like her mother before her, sets great store on homemade chicken soup. This elegant version is a clear broth dotted with sliced carrots, parsnips, celery, and parsley. Sheila says that the matzo balls have a light and delicate texture because carbonated water is mixed with the matzo meal.

Spinach Matzo Pie—This spinach and egg side dish is capped with whole matzo crackers. An egg "wash" gives the crackers their shiny, golden appearance.

Farfel Pudding—Sheila's version of this bread-pudding-like dessert is lavished with sour cream, cottage cheese, raisins, and nuts. According to Jewish dietary restrictions, meat and dairy products cannot be eaten at the same meal, so this dessert would be served in a fish or meatless menu.

Passover Carrot-Nut Cake—The light, fine texture of this moist cake comes from well-beaten egg yolks, beaten egg whites, and the flourlike matzo called cake meal.

Fruit Tzimmes—"Although the word *tzimmes* means fuss or excitement, making tzimmes is actually easy," says Sheila. "My mother's recipe features mixed dried fruits, but you can use almost any combination of meat, vegetables, or fruits in tzimmes. Usually the dish is served in place of a vegetable side dish."

Photographs: Bradley Olman; Mike Dieter

Easter
An Ecumenical Brunch

For the past several years Sharon and Clayton Haven have enlarged their annual Easter breakfast from a small family affair to a celebration brunch for the neighborhood. According to Sharon, "It was important that our children, Matt and Amy, understand and appreciate Easter as something more than the arrival of the Easter bunny. Since we have no relatives living nearby, we decided to share traditions with our immediate neighbors." Because their neighboring families represent many different backgrounds, the Havens put together an ecumenical sampling of traditional Easter foods.

Sharon and Clayton believe it's important to convey to their children the significance of different recipes and serving traditions. Consequently, the brunch menu changes slightly from year to year as Sharon discovers foods that are new to her family. "We are not purists about the dishes that we serve," Sharon says. "Some of the dishes are no longer strictly associated with Easter. They've become so popular over the centuries that they're served at other times of the year, too. And we may include a dish that isn't really an Easter food but that *might* be served at Easter, or a food that's a family Easter tradition among the people we know."

While they are preparing the foods, the Havens like to explain to Matt and Amy the religious or cultural background of each recipe. Here are some of the delicious foods and interesting facts:

Aebleskivers—Sharon says, "My family always had these Danish doughnuts on Easter morning served with homemade preserves and Danish sausages, but we also ate them on other occasions throughout the year. I make the Aebleskivers in a special pan that my grandmother

brought from Denmark." For our version, you can opt to use a skillet or griddle.

Strawberry Bavarian Dressing—Sharon has turned the popular German Easter dessert, Bavarian Cream, into a salad dressing that's centered on a platter with an assortment of fresh fruits and greens. "Flavor the dressing with fresh strawberries for a springlike taste," she suggests.

Ham and Asparagus Bundles—These open-faced sandwiches served with Hollandaise-based sauce are favorite Easter recipes that Sharon obtained from some Dutch friends. Two traditional Easter foods—eggs and ham—are featured in this brunch entrée.

Kulich—This festive fruit bread is part of the elaborate Russian Orthodox Easter feast that breaks the Lenten fast. Sharon also displays intricately decorated Ukrainian eggs called *pysanki* to announce the arrival of Easter. Since these hollow eggs are time-consuming to decorate, the Havens make just one or two each year to add to their collection of Easter decorations.

Fromajadas—Cheese-filled pastries, scored with signs of the cross, are part of some Easter-caroling processions in Spain. Carolers go from house to house singing a hymn of praise and receive these savory tarts from the appreciative homeowners. As a result, the hymn itself has taken on the name "Fromajadas" or "Cheesecake Song."

Greek Eggs—The Haven table always includes these hard-cooked eggs colored with a special red dye to symbolize Christ's blood. According to Greek tradition, the eggs are cracked against each other as one family member says "Christ is risen," and the other replies, "Truly, He is risen."

Top: The association of eggs with Easter stems from pre-Christian times when eggs symbolized the seeds of creation and renewal. These **Leaf Eggs** are made with natural ingredients according to an old Swiss dyeing technique.

Bottom: The Havens and guests toast the holiday with **Easter Punch,** a mixture of champagne, orange juice, and rose water.

Right: To simplify serving, the brunch foods are displayed buffet style: *(clockwise from front left)* **Strawberry Bavarian Dressing, Fromajadas, Aebleskivers, Kulich,** and **Ham and Asparagus Bundles.**

Photographs: Brian Leatart

St. Joseph's Day

A Feast of Thanks

Joe Ferrara and his sisters, Mary Puccio and Vicky Strano, have an incredible recipe for a spring celebration held every March 19: Recruit a dozen close relatives and friends, cook up tablefuls of food (using some 60 pounds of pasta, 25 gallons of tomato sauce, 100 pounds of ricotta cheese, and 100 pounds of flour!), and invite 500 to 1,000 guests for a St. Joseph's Day Feast. "Ask most Americans what this day represents," says Mary, "and they won't know what you're talking about. This is an old Sicilian holiday that our relatives always celebrated."

Although other ethnic cultures observe St. Joseph's Day, the Sicilian version is the most elaborate. Joe explains the holiday: "Throughout the Catholic Church, St. Joseph has always been regarded as the family protector. Several centuries ago, a severe famine in Sicily caused considerable suffering and starvation. The peasant farmers turned in prayer to St. Joseph for help. The famine soon ended, and in gratitude, the farmers honored St. Joseph by filling an altar with their most prized possession—food." St. Joseph's altars have evolved into immense family open houses, intended as thanks for special prayers that have been answered. The guests include family and friends as well as anyone in need.

Because of the time and work involved in putting on a St. Joseph's Day Feast, the Ferrara event is one of the few that's still family-organized. When asked what prompts them to keep the tradition going, Joe answered without hesitation, "We do it because it brings back memories of our childhood. But more important, it takes people—young and old—out of their own four walls to give thanks together."

Top: Besides the large loaves of **St. Joseph's Bread** that are served, a small piece or loaf of bread is given to each guest along with a lucky fava bean.

Bottom: Children are an important part of this celebration. It's customary to have three children, blessed by the priest, represent the Holy Family at a special dining table.

Right: Here's a tasting of Feast Day foods: *(clockwise from front)* **Pasta con Sarde, Fried Cod With Tomato-Olive Sauce, Sesame Cookies, Fig-Filled Cookies, Pignolatti, Cannoli, Sfinghi, and Stuffed Artichokes.**

In keeping with tradition, there is always a great quantity of food, and the dishes are meatless because the celebration falls during Lent. At least one month in advance, Joe recruits his "crew" to cook and freeze the foods. He suggests serving one or two Feast Day foods for a Sunday or special-occasion dinner.

St. Joseph's Bread—"The most essential food is this crusty Italian yeast bread," Joe says. The bread is often made in different sizes and shapes, including the braid shown, wreaths, crosses, and staffs.

Pasta con Sarde—This tomato-based dish is another St. Joseph's Day classic. The slightly sweet flavor of fennel predominates in the sauce.

Fried Cod With Tomato-Olive Sauce—"I serve this as a first course on St. Joseph's Day, and as a dinner entrée on other occasions," Joe says.

Stuffed Artichokes—For this popular appetizer, each artichoke leaf is seasoned with bread crumbs, Parmesan cheese, basil, and wine.

Cannoli—Pastry cylinders house a rich ricotta-chocolate filling. Joe says cannoli are popular at Christmas, too.

Sfinghi—Ricotta cheese is the basis for these light yet moist fritters.

Fig-Filled Cookies—Every one of these pastrylike cookies contains an extraordinary dried fruit and nut filling.

Sesame Cookies—Grains, nuts, and seeds are popular St. Joseph's Day ingredients, in keeping with the holiday's rural origin. These rich butter cookies, for example, are lavished with sesame seed.

Pignolatti—This mound resembling a pinecone cluster is made up of many fried pastry pieces, all of them glazed with honey brittle.

Photographs: Hedrich-Blessing

MATZO BALLS

    1 cup matzo meal
    1 teaspoon salt
      Dash pepper
    4 slightly beaten eggs
    ¼ cup chicken fat
    ¼ cup carbonated water

In mixing bowl combine matzo meal, salt, and pepper. Beat in eggs and chicken fat till well blended. Stir in carbonated water. Cover and chill at least 2 hours. With wet hands, shape dough into 1-inch balls. Carefully drop dough into gently boiling salted water. Cover; simmer 30 minutes or till matzo balls test done (they should be light and cooked all the way through). *Leave cover on pot until end of cooking.* Remove carefully with slotted spoon. Serve in hot Chicken Soup. Makes about 30 balls.

SPINACH MATZO PIE

    6 10-ounce packages frozen
      chopped spinach
    1 medium onion, chopped
    ½ cup margarine
    2 teaspoons salt
    2 teaspoons sugar
    2 teaspoons ground nutmeg
    1 teaspoon pepper
   12 eggs
    2 eggs
    2 matzo crackers

In large saucepan cook spinach *without water,* covered, over medium-low heat for 30 to 35 minutes or till thawed. Drain spinach, pressing out excess liquid. Return spinach to saucepan. Stir in onion, margarine, and seasonings. Cook 4 to 5 minutes more or till onion is tender. Remove from heat; cool slightly. Turn into large mixer bowl. Beat the 12 eggs, one at a time, into spinach mixture with electric mixer. Turn into 12x7½x2-inch baking dish. Beat the remaining 2 eggs. Dip whole matzo crackers, one at a time, in the beaten egg. Overlap matzos in center of spinach mixture. Bake in a 350° oven for 50 minutes or till filling is set. Serves 15.

HAROSETH

Haroseth means "sweet like freedom." It symbolizes the building mortar used by Jewish slaves—

    2 tart unpeeled apples, finely
      chopped
    ½ cup ground walnuts
    3 tablespoons Passover wine
    3 tablespoons honey
    ¼ teaspoon ground cinnamon

Combine all ingredients; let stand 1 hour. Makes 2 cups.

CHICKEN SOUP WITH MATZO BALLS

For a main-dish soup, remove the meat from the bones, cube the meat, and return it to the broth with the vegetables in Dutch oven—

    1 4- to 5-pound stewing chicken
   2½ quarts water
    2 onions, cut up
    1 leek, sliced
    3 stalks celery, sliced
    1 tablespoon salt
    ¼ teaspoon pepper
    2 carrots, sliced
    2 parsnips, sliced
    4 or 5 parsley sprigs
    4 fresh dill heads *or* ¼ teaspoon
      dried dillweed (optional)
    1 recipe Matzo Balls

Place chicken in 8- to 10-quart Dutch oven; add water, onions, leek, celery, salt, and pepper. Bring to boiling. Reduce heat; simmer, covered, 1½ hours or till chicken is almost tender. Add carrots and parsnips; simmer, covered, 30 minutes more or till chicken and vegetables are tender. Remove chicken; refrigerate meat for another use. Lift vegetables from broth with slotted spoon. Strain broth. Return vegetables to broth. Add parsley and dill, if desired. Heat through. Serve with Matzo Balls. Serves 15.

FARFEL PUDDING

    3 eggs
    ¼ cup sugar
    2 cups farfel *or* 4 matzo crackers,
      coarsely crushed
    2 cups cream-style cottage
      cheese
    1 cup dairy sour cream
    ⅓ cup margarine, melted
    ½ cup raisins
    ½ cup apricot preserves
    ½ cup finely chopped walnuts
    2 tablespoons sugar
    1 teaspoon ground cinnamon

In mixing bowl beat eggs till light; gradually beat in ¼ cup sugar till fluffy. Soak farfel in cold water till moistened; squeeze out excess water. Add farfel, cottage cheese, sour cream, margarine, raisins, and preserves to egg mixture; blend well. Turn into a 12x7½x2-inch baking dish. Mix nuts, sugar, and cinnamon. Sprinkle atop farfel mixture. Bake in 350° oven for 40 to 45 minutes. Serve warm or cool. Makes 10 to 12 servings.

PASSOVER CARROT-NUT CAKE

    6 egg yolks
    1 cup sugar
    1 cup ground walnuts
    1 cup ground carrots
    1 teaspoon vanilla
    ¾ cup matzo cake meal
    6 egg whites
      Powdered sugar

In small mixer bowl beat egg yolks till light (about 5 minutes); gradually add 1 cup sugar, beating till thick and lemon-colored (about 5 minutes longer). Blend in walnuts, carrots, and vanilla; stir in matzo meal. Wash beaters thoroughly. In large mixer bowl beat egg whites to stiff peaks (tips stand straight). Fold some of the egg whites into matzo mixture to lighten; then fold matzo mixture into egg whites. Turn batter into *ungreased* 8- to 8½-inch springform pan. Bake in 350° oven for 40 to 50 minutes or till cake tests done. Invert cake in pan on rack to cool completely. When cake is cool, remove it from pan. Sprinkle top with powdered sugar. Makes 10 to 12 servings.

ORANGE-GLAZED CHICKEN WITH MATZO-NUT STUFFING

Use a roasting chicken or a capon for this festive entrée—

- ⅓ cup finely chopped onion
- ⅓ cup finely chopped celery
- ⅓ cup chopped almonds
- ⅓ cup chicken fat
- 5 matzo crackers, coarsely crushed *or* 2½ cups farfel
- 1 10¾-ounce can condensed chicken broth
- 1 egg
- 1 tablespoon finely shredded orange peel
- ½ teaspoon salt
- ⅛ teaspoon pepper
- 1 5- to 6-pound capon *or* roasting chicken
- 1 teaspoon finely shredded orange peel
- ½ cup orange juice
- 2 tablespoons honey
- 2 tablespoons chicken fat (schmaltz), melted, *or* vegetable oil
- Red grapes (optional)
- Parsley sprigs (optional)

Cook onion, celery, and almonds in the ⅓ cup chicken fat till vegetables are tender but not brown. Add coarsely crushed matzos or farfel; brown lightly. In large bowl combine the chicken broth, egg, the 1 tablespoon orange peel, the salt, and pepper. Add matzo mixture and blend well. Let stand 15 minutes to absorb broth.

Rinse bird; pat dry with paper toweling. Spoon some of the stuffing loosely into neck cavity of bird; pull neck skin to back of bird and fasten securely with a small skewer. Lightly spoon remaining stuffing into body cavity. If opening has a band of skin across tail, tuck drumsticks under band (or tie legs securely to tail). Twist the wing tips under back of capon or chicken. Place bird, breast up, on rack in shallow roasting pan. Combine the remaining orange peel, orange juice, honey, and 2 tablespoons chicken fat. Roast bird, uncovered, in a 375° oven for 2¼ to 2½ hours, basting with glaze the last ½ hour of roasting. Garnish with red grapes and parsley sprigs, if desired. Makes 8 servings.

FRUIT TZIMMES

This dish also makes a delicious dessert compote; make it ahead and chill till serving time—

- 2 11-ounce packages mixed dried fruits
- 2 cups water
- ½ cup dry white Passover wine
- 3 inches stick cinnamon
- 1 tablespoon orange peel cut in thin strips
- 1 cup orange juice
- ⅓ cup honey
- ¼ cup lemon juice
- ¼ teaspoon ground allspice
- ¼ teaspoon ground ginger
- ¼ teaspoon ground cinnamon

In 3-quart saucepan combine mixed dried fruits, water, wine, and stick cinnamon. Bring to boiling; reduce heat. Simmer, covered, 15 to 20 minutes or till fruit is tender. With slotted spoon transfer fruit to bowl. Discard cinnamon stick. Add orange peel to liquid in saucepan; simmer 2 to 3 minutes. Stir in orange juice, honey, lemon juice, allspice, ginger, and ground cinnamon. Return fruit to saucepan; heat to boiling. Remove from heat; cool to room temperature. Serve at room temperature or chilled. If desired, drain fruit before serving. Serves 10.

EASTER PUNCH

Rose water is available at drugstores and pharmacies. It adds a springtime fragrance to this easy punch—

- 1 12-ounce can frozen orange juice concentrate, thawed
- 4½ cups water
- 2 750-milliliter bottles champagne, chilled
- 3 to 4 teaspoons rose water
- Ice

Combine orange juice concentrate and water; pour into punch bowl. Slowly pour champagne down side of bowl; add rose water. Stir gently with an up-and-down motion. Add ice. Makes about 12 cups punch.

STRAWBERRY BAVARIAN DRESSING

- 1½ cups fresh *or* frozen unsweetened strawberries
- ¼ cup cream sherry
- 1 teaspoon unflavored gelatin
- 3 tablespoons sugar
- 1 egg
- 1 teaspoon vanilla
- ½ cup whipping cream
- Fresh fruit

Thaw strawberries, if frozen. Crush ½ cup of the berries. In small saucepan soften gelatin in crushed berries and sherry. Cook and stir over low heat till gelatin is dissolved. Cool slightly. Place gelatin mixture in blender container or food processor bowl; cover and blend on high speed for 30 to 45 seconds. Add sugar, egg, and vanilla; cover and blend 5 seconds. Add remaining berries; blend 5 seconds more. With blender or food processor running, add whipping cream; continue blending 20 to 30 seconds more. Chill several hours or overnight. Serve with fresh fruit. Makes about 2 cups.

FROMAJADAS

- 2 slightly beaten eggs
- ½ teaspoon ground cinnamon
- ¼ teaspoon ground nutmeg
- ⅛ teaspoon ground red pepper
- 1½ cups grated sharp cheddar cheese (6 ounces)
- Pastry for 2-crust 9-inch pie

In mixing bowl blend together eggs, cinnamon, nutmeg, and red pepper; stir in cheddar cheese. Divide pastry dough in half. On floured surface roll half the dough to ⅛-inch thickness. Cut into seven 4-inch circles. For each pastry round, cut a small cross pattern on one half of round. Spoon about 1 tablespoon filling on uncut half of round. Fold slashed half of dough over filling. Moisten edges with water and press together gently to seal.

Repeat with remaining dough and filling. Place pastries on an ungreased baking sheet. Bake in a 350° oven for about 25 minutes or till pastries are golden brown (filling will puff through the cross). Cool pastries slightly; serve warm. Makes 14 pastries.

KULICH

Kulich is usually baked so it's tall and rounded at the top to represent the dome of a Russian church—

½ cup light raisins
2 tablespoons rum
¼ teaspoon ground saffron
1 package active dry yeast
¼ cup warm water (110° to 115°)
½ cup milk
⅓ cup butter *or* margarine
¼ cup sugar
½ teaspoon salt
3½ cups all-purpose flour
2 eggs
½ cup mixed candied fruits and peels
¼ cup chopped almonds
¼ teaspoon almond extract
1 beaten egg yolk
1 recipe Powdered Sugar Icing
Candied cherries (optional)

Combine raisins, rum, and saffron. Soften yeast in warm water. In saucepan combine milk, butter or margarine, sugar, and salt. Heat and stir till warm (115° to 120°) or till butter almost melts. Combine milk mixture and *2 cups* of the flour; beat well. Add yeast and eggs; beat well. Stir in raisin mixture, candied fruits and peels, almonds, extract, and enough remaining flour to make a soft dough. Knead on floured surface 8 to 10 minutes. Shape in ball. Place in greased bowl; turn once to grease surface. Cover; let rise till double (about 1½ hours). Punch down; turn onto floured surface. Divide in half (or thirds). Cover; let rest 10 minutes.

Grease bottom and sides of two 29-ounce cans (or three 16-ounce cans); place upright on baking sheet. Shape dough into balls; place one ball of dough in each can. Cover; let rise 45 minutes. Brush dough with beaten egg yolk. Bake in 350° oven about 40 minutes for small cans or about 50 minutes for large cans. Remove from cans; cool. Drizzle with Powdered Sugar Icing. Garnish top of each loaf with a candied cherry, if desired.

To make Powdered Sugar Icing: Mix 1 cup sifted *powdered sugar*, ¼ teaspoon *vanilla*, and enough *milk* (about 1½ tablespoons) to make the mixture spreadable.

AEBLESKIVERS

2 cups all-purpose flour
1 teaspoon baking soda
½ teaspoon baking powder
2 well-beaten egg yolks
1½ cups buttermilk
2 tablespoons butter or margarine, melted
2 egg whites
Cooking oil
Powdered sugar
Assorted jams and jellies

Stir together flour, soda, baking powder, and ½ teaspoon *salt*. In mixing bowl beat egg yolks well with rotary beater; blend in buttermilk and butter. Add to flour mixture, beating till smooth. Wash beaters thoroughly. Beat egg whites to stiff peaks (tips stand straight); fold into batter.

To cook: heat aebleskiver pan over medium-low heat; oil each cup lightly. Spoon about 2 tablespoons batter into each cup. Cook till bubbles form and edges appear dry, about 3 minutes. Gently turn with 2 wooden picks. Cook till second side is golden brown, about 2 minutes. Remove from pans; keep warm. Repeat with remaining batter. Dust with powdered sugar. Serve warm with assorted jams and jellies. Makes about 30.

Note: batter may also be cooked on lightly greased griddle, using about 2 tablespoons batter per pancake. Cook about 3 minutes on first side, 2 minutes on second side.

HAM AND VEGETABLE BUNDLES

2 pounds fresh asparagus spears
16 slices boiled ham
8 hard-cooked eggs, sliced
8 English muffins, halved and toasted, *or* Dutch rusks
1 recipe Maltaise Sauce

Clean and trim asparagus. Cook asparagus, covered, in a small amount of boiling salted water about 10 minutes. Drain; cool. Roll a few asparagus spears in each ham slice. Place one roll and a few hard-cooked egg slices atop each muffin half. Prepare Maltaise Sauce; pass to spoon over each serving. Garnish with fresh watercress, if desired. Serves 16.

To prepare Maltaise Sauce: Place 6 *egg yolks* in blender container or food processor bowl. Cover and blend about 5 seconds or till mixed. In saucepan heat 1 cup *butter* or *margarine*, 1 teaspoon finely shredded *orange peel*, ¼ cup *orange juice*, 1 tablespoon *lemon juice*, and ⅛ teaspoon *ground red pepper* till butter is melted. With lid ajar and blender or food processor running at high speed, slowly pour in butter mixture. Blend about 30 seconds or till thick and fluffy. Keep warm over hot, but not boiling, water.

ST. JOSEPH'S BREAD

1½ cups warm water (110° to 115°)
2 packages active dry yeast
2 tablespoons shortening
1 tablespoon sugar
1 tablespoon olive oil
4 to 4½ cups all-purpose flour
1 beaten egg
¼ cup sesame seed

Combine the warm water, the yeast, shortening, sugar, oil, and 2 teaspoons *salt*. Let stand 5 minutes. Place 2½ cups of the flour in large mixer bowl; add liquid mixture. Beat on low speed of electric mixer or stir by hand till all ingredients are thoroughly blended. Stir in as much of the remaining flour as you can mix in with a spoon. Turn out onto lightly floured surface. Knead in enough of the remaining flour to make a moderately stiff dough that is smooth and elastic (6 to 8 minutes total). Shape into a ball. Place in lightly greased bowl; turn once to grease surface. Cover; let rise in warm place till double (45 to 60 minutes). Punch down; divide dough into six equal pieces. Cover; let rest 10 minutes. Roll each piece into a 12-inch-long rope. Using three ropes for each loaf, braid dough; secure ends. Place on greased baking sheets. Cover; let rise till nearly double (30 to 45 minutes). Brush sides and top of loaves with beaten egg. Sprinkle with sesame seed. Bake in 400° oven 25 minutes or till bread tests done and is golden brown. Remove bread from baking sheet; cool on wire rack. Makes 2 braids.

FRIED COD WITH TOMATO-OLIVE SAUCE

2 pounds salt cod
1 medium onion, chopped
1 tablespoon snipped parsley
½ lemon, sliced
2 eggs
⅓ cup all-purpose flour
2 teaspoons olive oil
  Cooking oil for deep-fat frying
1 recipe Tomato-Olive Sauce

Soak cod in enough cold water to cover for 24 to 48 hours, changing water several times. Drain well. Skin and bone cod; cut into 2- to 3-inch squares. Place cod in large saucepan and cover with water (about 6 cups). Add onion, parsley, and lemon slices. Bring to boiling; cover and boil 1 minute. Remove from heat. Let stand, covered, for 15 minutes. Drain cod; pat dry with paper toweling. In mixing bowl beat eggs and ¼ cup *water* with rotary beater; beat in flour till smooth. Stir in olive oil. Let stand 30 minutes.

In a deep saucepan or deep-fat fryer heat cooking oil to 375°. Dip cod squares, one at a time, in batter. Fry a few squares at a time in hot oil for 1 to 2 minutes or till golden, turning once. Remove from fat with a slotted spoon; drain on paper toweling.

Keep cooked cod warm in oven while frying remaining pieces. Place cod in shallow serving dish. Spoon Tomato-Olive Sauce atop. Garnish with a fresh basil or parsley sprig, if desired. Makes 8 to 10 servings.

TOMATO-OLIVE SAUCE

In saucepan cook ½ cup chopped *onion* in 2 tablespoons hot *olive oil* till tender but not brown. Add one 14-ounce can peeled *Italian-style tomatoes,* cut up and 1 cup *dry white wine.* Bring to boiling. Reduce heat and simmer, uncovered, 20 minutes or till sauce is reduced to about 2 cups. Stir in ½ cup *pitted green olives,* sliced; ¼ cup *pitted black Greek olives,* sliced; 1 tablespoon snipped *parsley;* 4 teaspoons *capers;* and a dash *garlic powder.* Simmer, uncovered, 10 minutes more. Makes 2⅔ cups sauce.

SESAME COOKIES

½ cup butter
½ cup margarine
¾ cup sugar
3 egg yolks
½ teaspoon vanilla
2½ cups all-purpose flour
1 teaspoon baking powder
3 egg whites
¾ cup sesame seed

In mixer bowl beat butter, margarine, and sugar on medium speed of electric mixer till fluffy. Blend in egg yolks and vanilla; beat well. Mix flour and baking powder. Gradually add to creamed mixture; beat till well blended. With fork beat egg whites slightly. Pinch off a piece of dough the size of a walnut; shape in a ball. Dip in beaten egg whites; roll in sesame seed. Repeat with remaining dough, egg whites, and sesame seed. Place on greased cookie sheet. Bake in 375° oven 12 to 15 minutes. Cool. Makes about 42.

PASTA CON SARDE

4 medium onions, chopped (2 cups)
¼ cup olive *or* cooking oil
1 29-ounce can tomato puree
1 tomato can (29 ounces) water
2 tablespoons sugar
1 15-ounce can (2 cups) condimento per pasta con sarde*
¼ cup pine nuts
2 cups dry bread crumbs
2 tablespoons olive *or* cooking oil
  Hot cooked spaghetti

In large, heavy saucepan or Dutch oven cook onion in the ¼ cup hot oil till tender but not brown. Add tomato puree, water, and sugar. Simmer, uncovered, 10 to 15 minutes. Break up fish in condimento per pasta con sarde; add condimento to tomato mixture in pan along with pine nuts. Simmer, uncovered, 2 hours, stirring frequently. Stir every 5 to 10 minutes the last 30 minutes to prevent sticking. In heavy skillet toast bread crumbs with the 2 tablespoons oil and several dashes *pepper.* Serve sauce over hot spaghetti; sprinkle with bread crumbs. Makes 10 to 12 side-dish servings.

If you cannot locate canned condimento per pasta con sarde, you can make a substitute as follows: Cook 4 cups coarsely shredded *romaine,* covered, in ½ cup *water* for 5 minutes or till limp. Puree one 3¾-ounce can *undrained sardines.* Add sardine puree; one 3¾-ounce can whole *undrained sardines;* ¼ cup *raisins;* 1 tablespoon *lemon juice;* 1 tablespoon *dried fennel seed,* crushed; 1 tablespoon *pine nuts;* 1 teaspoon *salt;* and ¼ teaspoon *pepper* to the romaine. Bring to boiling; reduce heat. Cover; simmer 5 minutes. Uncover; simmer 5 minutes longer or till mixture is of thick-puree consistency. Makes 2 cups.

PIGNOLATTI

2 cups all-purpose flour
3 eggs
½ teaspoon vanilla
  Cooking oil for deep-fat frying
1 cup sugar
½ cup honey
2 tablespoons butter
  Multicolored decorative candies

In a large bowl combine flour and ¼ teaspoon *salt.* Make a well in center. Combine eggs and vanilla; add to flour mixture. Mix well to make a stiff dough. On lightly floured surface knead dough 10 to 12 times. Roll dough to a 12x7-inch rectangle, ¼ inch thick. With pastry wheel or knife cut dough into ¼-inch-wide strips. Cut strips into ½-inch-long pieces. Heat oil in deep saucepan or deep-fat fryer to 365°. Drop as many pieces of dough as will float, uncrowded, in one layer in the hot oil. Fry dough for 2 to 3 minutes or till lightly browned, turning once. Drain on paper toweling.

Repeat with remaining dough. In small saucepan with buttered sides combine the sugar and honey. Cook and stir over medium-low heat till sugar is dissolved and mixture boils. Cook, stirring occasionally, to 270°, about 3 minutes. Remove from heat. Stir in butter. Pour over deep-fried pastries in large bowl. Stir constantly to coat well. With buttered hands form the honey-coated pieces into a cone-shaped mound on serving platter. Sprinkle with decorative candies. Let cool to harden. To serve, break off individual pieces. Serves 10 to 12.

CANNOLI

The cannoli tubes used for shaping and frying the pastries are metal cylinders about 4 inches long and 1 inch in diameter; they're sold at Italian import shops and some gourmet cookware shops—

2¼ cups all-purpose flour
¼ cup granulated sugar
½ teaspoon ground cinnamon
¼ teaspoon ground cloves
⅓ cup shortening
2 well-beaten eggs
⅓ cup dry white wine
  Cooking oil for deep-fat frying
2 pounds ricotta cheese, well drained
1½ cups sifted powdered sugar
1 teaspoon vanilla
3 drops oil of cinnamon (optional)
½ cup German sweet cooking chocolate, coarsely chopped
¼ cup chopped candied citron
  Pistachio nuts (optional)
  Powdered sugar (optional)

In mixing bowl stir together flour, granulated sugar, cinnamon, and cloves. Cut in shortening till mixture resembles small peas. Combine eggs and wine; add to flour mixture. Stir till dough forms a ball. On a lightly floured surface knead dough 10 to 12 strokes. Divide dough in fourths. Roll each fourth to slightly less than ¹⁄₁₆-inch thickness. Using a knife and a paper pattern, cut dough into ovals 5 inches long and 4 inches wide. *Do not reroll trimmings.* Beginning with long side, roll dough loosely onto cannoli tubes. Moisten overlapping dough with water; press gently to seal. Fry, a few at a time, in deep hot oil (375°) for 1 to 1½ minutes. Drain on paper toweling. When shells are cool enough to handle, remove them from tubes and cool. Cool tubes before reusing.

For filling: Beat cheese with electric mixer till fluffy. Add powdered sugar, vanilla, and oil of cinnamon; beat about 3 minutes. Blend in chocolate and citron; mix well. Cover; chill. No more than 1 hour before serving, fill shells, using a pastry tube to force cheese mixture into shells. If desired, garnish with pistachio nuts; sift powdered sugar atop. Makes 24 cannoli.

SFINGHI

To reheat, place the cold Sfinghi in a baking pan, cover with foil, and heat in a 350° oven for 10 minutes—

2 eggs
¼ cup granulated sugar
½ cup ricotta cheese (4 ounces)
1½ cups all-purpose flour
2 teaspoons baking powder
¼ teaspoon ground cinnamon
½ cup milk
  Cooking oil for deep-fat frying
  Powdered sugar

In mixer bowl beat eggs and sugar with electric mixer till light. Add ricotta cheese; beat well. Thoroughly stir together flour, baking powder, cinnamon, and ⅛ teaspoon *salt.* Add flour to egg mixture alternately with milk; blend well.

Drop dough by tablespoonfuls into deep hot oil (375°); fry 2 to 3 minutes or till golden, turning once. Drain well. Sift powdered sugar over. Serve warm. Makes 30.

STUFFED ARTICHOKES

4 artichokes
  Lemon juice
1¼ cups fine dry French bread crumbs (5 slices bread)
1 small clove garlic, minced
¼ cup snipped parsley
¼ cup grated Parmesan cheese
¼ teaspoon dried basil, crushed
⅛ teaspoon crushed dried red pepper
2 tablespoons olive oil
2 tablespoons dry white wine

Wash, trim stems, and remove loose outer leaves from artichokes. Cut off 1 inch from tops; snip off sharp leaf tips with kitchen shears. Brush cut edges with lemon juice. Invert; drain well.

Combine the bread crumbs, garlic, parsley, Parmesan cheese, basil, and pepper; stir in oil and wine. Starting from bottom and working up, put a small amount of crumb mixture on each artichoke leaf. Steam stuffed artichokes over boiling water 25 to 30 minutes. Makes 4 servings.

FIG-FILLED COOKIES

6 ounces dried figs (about 1 cup)
4 ounces pitted dates (about ⅔ cup)
4 ounces raisins (about ¾ cup)
2 tablespoons candied citron
4 ounces almonds, chopped and toasted (about 1 cup)
¼ cup marmalade
¼ cup pineapple preserves
¼ cup orange liqueur
½ teaspoon ground cinnamon
¼ teaspoon ground cloves
2½ cups all-purpose flour
⅓ cup sugar
1¼ teaspoons baking powder
⅛ teaspoon salt
½ cup lard *or* shortening
1 tablespoon butter *or* margarine
2 eggs
2 tablespoons milk
½ teaspoon vanilla
1 recipe Lemon Glaze
  Candied citron (optional)

Steam figs over boiling water 2 to 3 minutes to soften. Grind through food chopper along with dates, raisins, and 2 tablespoons citron. Blend in almonds, marmalade, preserves, liqueur, cinnamon, and cloves.

In large mixing bowl thoroughly stir together flour, sugar, baking powder, and salt. Cut in lard and butter or margarine till mixture resembles fine crumbs. Combine eggs, milk, and vanilla; add to flour mixture till well blended. Divide dough in half. On lightly floured surface roll each half to a 12x8-inch rectangle.

Place one of the 12x8-inch sheets on a lightly greased baking sheet. Spread with the fig filling. Top with the second pastry sheet. Score top in 2x1-inch diamonds. Bake in 350° oven for 15 to 18 minutes. Remove to wire rack to cool. When cookies are cool, cut into diamonds.

Glaze cookies with *Lemon Glaze:* Blend 4 cups sifted *powdered sugar,* 1 teaspoon *vanilla,* ½ teaspoon *lemon extract,* and enough *milk* (¼ to ⅓ cup) to give the mixture a glaze consistency. Garnish diamonds with additional candied citron, if desired. Makes 4 dozen cookies.

APRIL

New treatments for depression–our number one mental health problem

Family Travel: Appalachian Vacations en route to World's Fair '82

Better Homes and Gardens.

April 1982 • $1.25

GARDENING
Vegetable crop
season-stretchers

REMODELING
How to light up your
house with the sun

DESIGNER BATHS
Four roomfuls of great ideas
you can adapt

**WONDERFUL
ONE-POT MEALS**
Recipes for range top, oven,
microwave, crockery pot

MONEY
How to figure your own
Consumer Price Index

KIDS COOKING
A small-fry's guide to
fun-to-fix food

DECORATING
Big style for
small rooms

See recipe page 187.

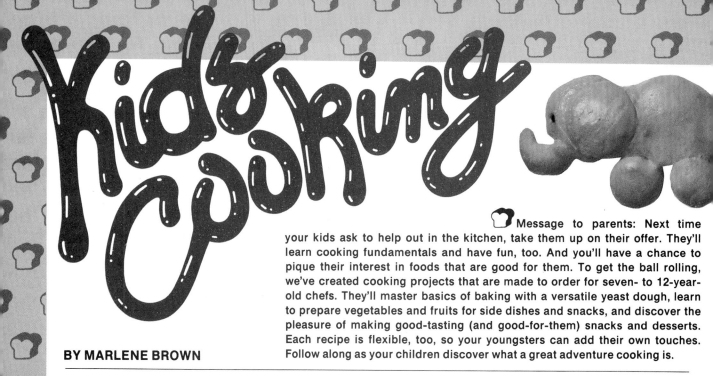

Kids Cooking

Message to parents: Next time your kids ask to help out in the kitchen, take them up on their offer. They'll learn cooking fundamentals and have fun, too. And you'll have a chance to pique their interest in foods that are good for them. To get the ball rolling, we've created cooking projects that are made to order for seven- to 12-year-old chefs. They'll master basics of baking with a versatile yeast dough, learn to prepare vegetables and fruits for side dishes and snacks, and discover the pleasure of making good-tasting (and good-for-them) snacks and desserts. Each recipe is flexible, too, so your youngsters can add their own touches. Follow along as your children discover what a great adventure cooking is.

BY MARLENE BROWN

HOW TO MAKE BREAD DOUGH

With just a few simple ingredients—flour, sugar, salt, shortening, water, and yeast—you can open up your own home-sized bread bakery. It's the yeast that makes the dough puff up and gives the bread a light, spongy texture. After the dough stands (rises) in a warm place for an hour or so, you punch it down and knead it. Kneading means that you turn and fold the dough over and over

Photographs: Mike Dieter

again with your hands until it's smooth and no longer sticky. This gets out bubbles and makes the bread tenderer and softer inside. Now you're ready to shape the dough any way you like.

To get off to an easy start, use a hot roll mix, which contains all the basic dry ingredients. We'll show you how to make animal-shaped breads and bagels (rolls that look like doughnuts). Then you can advance to adding fillings—such as chili and cheese for a hot snack, or dried fruit for a sweet treat.

HOW TO MAKE SHAPES

Shaping dough is just like working with clay—except you get to eat the results! First, sprinkle some flour on the counter or tabletop—a small handful should be enough. (Or, put a kitchen towel on the counter, and sprinkle some flour on that.) To make your **Animal Breads,** first shape a teddy bear as Susan is *(above):* pull off a medium-sized piece of dough and make a smooth

ball for a head; then make smaller balls for ears, hands, and feet. Use a bigger piece for the body, and stretch it with your fingers till it's the right shape. Then decorate each of your animals with flavorful tidbits. **Mini Bagels** like Abby's *(left)* are simple shapes to make. Just divide all the dough into 36 pieces, roll each piece into a ball, and poke your finger right through the middle. Then shape into a doughnut by pulling the dough around the hole to make a smooth ring.

HOW TO ADD A SWEET FILLING

You can add a special filling to the dough to make extra-delicious breads, like these **Thumbprint Sweet Rolls** *(above)*. To make the tasty filling, you can use mixed dried fruit or just one kind, like dried apricots, prunes, apples, or raisins. Start by dividing the bread dough into 16 equal pieces. Lightly flour your hands. Shape each piece into a ball, then flatten each ball with the palms of your hands to make a flat circle. Make a dent in each ball with your thumb, then spoon the fruit filling into each hole. After you bake the rolls, you can drizzle on icing and serve them to your friends. Try other fillings such as nuts, granola, jam, or jelly, too.

TRY AN UNSWEET FILLING

Steve *(right)* filled his bread dough with chili for a hot snack *(above)*. Here's how you do it: First, use a rolling pin to roll the dough into a big flat sheet. (If your dough snaps back when you roll it, just cover the dough and let it rest for ten minutes.

Then try rolling it again.) For the next step, spread canned chili over the dough and sprinkle peanuts and parsley on top. Roll up the dough with the filling inside. Pinch all the ends together so no filling leaks out during baking. Then sprinkle cheese on top and let it melt. Abracadabra —**Cheesy Chili Roll**!

continued

Kids Cooking

Besides having all those vitamins and minerals your parents talk about, vegetables and fruits are fun ingredients. First of all, they come in a rainbow of colors and textures—from bright red apples, strawberries, and tomatoes to vibrant green broccoli, lettuce, and grapes, and to sunny yellow beans, corn, and bananas. Some vegetables and fruits are crunchy, and others are soft and juicy. But one thing they all have in common is—they taste wonderful!

CREATE A VEGETABLE/DIP SNACK

You can assemble a beautiful basket of ready-to-eat vegetables that are perfect for snacking with a creamy dip *(below)*. To make your basket look good enough to eat, pick several different colors, shapes, and textures (some vegetables that crunch and others that don't). Darrin *(right center)* used broccoli, tomatoes (the cherry tomatoes are the perfect bite size), celery, carrots, and cauliflower. You might also use sliced zucchini, mushrooms, or green pepper cut into strips.

To begin, rinse the vegetables thoroughly in cold water; but don't let them soak or they'll lose some of the precious vitamins. Drain the vegetables on paper toweling. Use a small sharp knife called a *paring knife* to *carefully* cut the vegetables (use a wooden board for a cutting surface). Then whip up a batch of **Very Cheesy Dip** to serve with your vegetables.

Watch how fast they disappear!

MAKE A SUPER SALAD

Susan says that the best part about making a salad is tossing it *(above, right)*. Start by washing the lettuce—rinse the leaves gently and dry them between paper towels. Tear up the lettuce into a bowl. Then add your favorite cut-up vegetables.

You can turn the salad into a main dish by adding chopped meat or tuna, hard-cooked eggs, or cheese strips. Susan added cooked pasta for her **Spaghetti Salad.** To make the dressing, shake together salad oil, vinegar, and seasonings in a covered jar, then pour the dressing over the salad. Now you're ready to toss—and enjoy!

FRUITS FOR SPECIAL TREATS

Fresh fruits are a breeze to fix anytime you want a snack or dessert. If you're using fruits like apples, pears, peaches, grapes, or berries, there's no need to peel them. Cut up other fruits, just before you eat them, because that way they'll taste the best (and be the best for you). Fruits make perfect snacks and desserts all by themselves. But you also can use your favorite fruits to make fancy parfaits, fruit ice cream sundaes, and fruit faces to decorate cookie tarts.

the fruit pieces for a short time so they don't overcook. You can use canned peaches or pineapple, or sliced banana to make **Spicy Fruit Sundaes** *(bottom center)* in about five minutes!

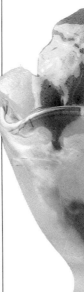

FRUIT PARFAITS

One great way to enjoy fruit is in a **Fruit 'n Granola Parfait** *(bottom left)*. You choose the fruit, then layer it in a tall glass with granola and ice cream, pudding, or fruit-flavored yogurt. Sliced strawberries and grapes with homemade granola make a crunchy delight. Or try this concoction: lemon- and orange-flavored yogurt layered with mandarin oranges and granola. You also can use the granola for a breakfast parfait—just top the granola with cut-up fruit and pour on the milk!

HOT FRUIT SUNDAES

It's a snap to cook up fruit if you follow a few simple tips: be sure to use a low temperature and cook

FRUIT 'N COOKIE TARTS

You can choose any designs for your **Fruit 'n Cookie Tarts** *(top and right)*. Start with refrigerated cookie dough to make the giant cookies for the base. (Either sugar, peanut butter, or oatmeal cookies work well.) Bake the cookies and let them cool on wire racks. Then spread on some vanilla or butterscotch pudding with the back of your spoon. Now decorate the tarts with some pieces of cut-up fruit and some nuts and coconut. Caryn *(above)* spread vanilla pudding on an oatmeal cookie; then she used red and green grapes and a slice of orange to give the cookie a funny face. (Shredded toasted coconut is great for the hair.)

The Snack Shop

Sunflower Cheese Balls

▲ If you like cheese, you already know it's a great-tasting snack food. You can spread the word by serving a tray of these cheesy balls to your friends. Roll 'em (the cheese balls, not your friends!) in sunflower seeds and wheat germ for extra crunch.

Fresh Fruit Snow

▼ Use a blender to mix up fresh fruit chunks with water and honey; then freeze the snow, beat and freeze it again. Don't eat this snow too fast though, or it will tickle your tongue!

HOW TO MAKE NUTRITIOUS SNACKS

If you get hungry after school or play, these kids have some terrific ideas for tasty nibbles you can make. You'll find some more ideas for jiffy refreshments below.

Chunky Peanut Butter Spread

▼ This nifty spread combines peanut butter, cream cheese, honey, plus your choice of raisins or apricots, and it won't even stick to the roof of your mouth! Try the spread on apple slices or crackers for a neat treat, or on bread for an open-face sandwich.

Lollipop Cookies

▲ If you want to make a great cookie better, put it on a stick! Use a cookie mix to make your favorite cookies, then insert wooden sticks in them, decorate with small candies, raisins, nuts, or cut-up gumdrops, and bake.

Snack-in-a-Glass

▼ Drinks can be delicious snacks, too. This one tastes like fruit-flavored eggnog that's made with yogurt. You can whip the drink up fast in the blender. Save a few pieces of the fruit to decorate each frothy serving.

MORE IDEAS FOR MUNCHIES

• Spread nut bread slices, or English muffin or bagel halves, with softened cream cheese. Top with your favorite fruit-flavored jam and a sprinkling of nuts.
• Spread peanut butter on a bread slice. Cut bread in half. Top with peanuts, raisins, or sliced banana. Give half to a friend.
• Thread chunks of fruit, cheese, and lunch meat alternately on skewers.

• Make pickle dogs: wrap a big sweet or dill pickle with a piece of ham or lunch meat, then dip the dogs in catsup or mustard.
• Fill ready-made mini tart shells with pudding, ice cream, or frozen yogurt; top with a drizzle of honey or jam and nuts.
• Make ice cream sandwiches: Slice a block of ice cream into ½-inch-thick slices; cut in quarters. Place each quar-

ter between two big oatmeal cookies. Eat the sandwiches immediately or wrap and freeze them.
• Make vegetable mini-pizzas: Cut thick slices of zucchini, cucumber, or tomato; place them on a baking sheet. Top each slice with a small piece of cheese or a spoonful of cheese spread. Sprinkle pizzas with sliced olives or mushrooms. Bake at 350° for 1 to 2 minutes till cheese melts.

Photographs: Mike Dieter

April

Note to kids: before you begin a recipe, read through it carefully to be sure you have all of the ingredients you'll need. If you don't understand some of the cooking terms, look them up in a general cook book.

SPICY FRUIT SUNDAES

Top your favorite ice cream flavor with this yummy, warm sauce—

Ingredients You Will Need:
  1 15- *or* 16-ounce can sliced
    peaches *or* pineapple chunks
    (juice pack); *or* 3 medium
    bananas
  2 tablespoons butter *or*
    margarine
  ¼ cup packed brown sugar
  ½ teaspoon ground cinnamon
  ⅓ cup reserved fruit juice *or*
    orange juice
  2 teaspoons cornstarch
    Ice cream, sherbet, *or* frozen
    yogurt

Steps for Making Sundaes:
1. Collect all ingredients.
2. If using canned fruit, drain fruit in a strainer, but save the juice. If using bananas, peel and slice them.
3. In a medium saucepan melt the butter or margarine over medium-low heat; stir in the sugar and cinnamon.
4. Add desired fruit. Cook and stir for 2 minutes.
5. If you used the canned fruit, measure ⅓ cup of the reserved drained juice. Stir cornstarch into the juice. *Or,* if you use bananas, stir cornstarch into ⅓ cup orange juice.
6. Stir juice mixture into saucepan. Cook and stir till sauce gets thick and bubbly. When bubbles appear, cook and stir the sauce 2 minutes longer.
7. Scoop ice cream, sherbet, *or* frozen yogurt into sundae dishes. Spoon the sauce over each serving. Makes 1½ cups sauce, or about 5 or 6 servings.

FRUIT 'N GRANOLA PARFAITS

You also can eat the granola alone as a snack—

Ingredients for Making Granola:
  2 cups quick-cooking rolled oats
  ⅔ cup shredded coconut
  ½ cup plain wheat germ
  ½ cup peanut halves
  ¼ cup honey
  ¼ cup salad oil
  ¼ cup water
  ¼ teaspoon ground allspice
  ⅔ cup raisins

Ingredients for Fillings:
  Desired fresh fruit, such as
    strawberries, grapes,
    blueberries, raspberries,
    peach *or* banana slices, *or*
    pineapple, apple, pear, *or*
    melon chunks
  Flavored yogurt, such as lemon,
    lime, mandarin orange,
    raspberry, strawberry, *or*
    vanilla (optional)

Steps for Making Granola:
1. Collect all ingredients.
2. In a large bowl combine the oats, coconut, wheat germ, and peanuts.
3. In a jar with a lid combine honey, salad oil, water, and allspice. Cover the jar with lid and shake till ingredients are well blended.
4. Pour honey mixture over the oats mixture in bowl. Using a large spoon, stir the mixture very well to moisten all the ingredients.
5. Spread the granola on an ungreased 15x10x1-inch baking pan. Turn oven temperature to 300°.
6. Bake granola in a 300° oven for 25 minutes. Twice during the baking, use a big wooden spoon to carefully stir the mixture so it bakes evenly.
7. Using pot holders, remove the pan from the oven. Put the pan on a wire rack to cool. Stir in the raisins. When the granola is cool, put it in a plastic bag with a twist tie or in an airtight container. Makes 4 cups.

Steps for Making Parfaits:
1. Cut up the fruit you would like to use. Spoon some granola into the bottom of a parfait glass.
2. Cover with some fruit and more granola. Repeat with another layer of fruit and granola up to the top of the glass. Or, for a granola-yogurt-fruit parfait, top granola and fruit with a spoonful of yogurt. Repeat the layers with more fruit, granola, and yogurt up to the top of the glass.
3. Decorate the parfait with whipped cream and a few pieces of fruit, if desired. Serve immediately.

LOLLIPOP COOKIES

Each is just like a snack on a stick—

Ingredients You Will Need:
  1 package 3-dozen-size sugar,
    oatmeal, *or* peanut butter
    cookie mix
  12 to 14 wooden sticks
    Sugar
    Decorator candies, raisins,
    nuts, sunflower nuts, snipped
    dried fruit, *or* cut-up gum
    drops

Steps for Making Cookies:
1. Collect all ingredients (check cookie mix package for what you'll need to make the cookies).
2. Grease cookie sheets, if necessary (check cookie package).
3. Prepare cookie dough according to directions on package.
4. Roll dough with your hands into 1½-inch balls. Put on a cookie sheet. Insert a wooden stick halfway into each cookie. Press dough around stick on cookie sheet.
5. Dip a flat-bottomed glass in some sugar, then press down cookies with bottom of glass to flatten.
6. Preheat oven to 375°. Decorate cookies with desired decorations.
7. Bake in a 375° oven according to times given on cookie mix package. Remove from oven with pot holders.
8. With metal spatula, put cookies on wire rack. Cool. Makes 12 to 14.

FRESH FRUIT SNOW

You can use just one fruit or a combination of your favorites—

Ingredients You Will Need:
2 tablespoons water
1 teaspoon unflavored gelatin
4 cups cubed honeydew melon *or* cantaloupe, sliced strawberries, orange sections, *or* canned pineapple chunks, drained (juice pack)
2 tablespoons lemon juice
2 tablespoons honey

Steps for Making Snow:
1. Collect ingredients.
2. Measure water into a glass measuring cup; sprinkle the gelatin over. Stir in the gelatin. Set the measuring cup in the small saucepan.
3. Put saucepan on burner; turn heat to medium. Heat and stir mixture till gelatin is dissolved. Remove from heat.
4. In blender container put *1 cup* of the fruit, the lemon juice, the honey, and the gelatin mixture. Cover blender and blend at high speed for 30 seconds or till mixture is smooth.
5. Stop blender; uncover. Add remaining fruit; cover and blend again at high speed for 30 to 45 seconds more or till mixture is smooth.
6. Pour mixture into an 8x8x2-inch pan. Cover with foil. Put in freezer for 3 hours or till almost frozen.
7. With a fork, break the snow into chunks. Put *half* the chunks in the blender. Cover the container and blend at low speed for 15 seconds.
8. Turn speed to high and blend for a few seconds more. Stop blender; uncover and scrape down the sides with a rubber spatula. Cover blender and run again till smooth.
9. Pour mixture back into pan. Repeat with remaining snow chunks. Cover pan with foil and freeze several hours or till hard.
10. Let fruit snow stand on counter for 15 minutes before you plan to serve it. To serve, use a large spoon to scrape across the top of the snow. Spoon into serving dishes. Makes 6 servings.

ANIMAL BREADS

Use your imagination and create a whole barnyard or zoo of these cute critters—

Ingredients You Will Need:
Shortening
1 13¾-ounce package hot-roll mix
⅛ teaspoon ground tumeric (optional)
¾ cup warm water
1 egg
All-purpose flour
1 egg
1 tablespoon water
Assorted decorations: sesame seed, poppy seed, sunflower seed, slivered *or* sliced almonds, raisins, *or* currants
Honey Butter (optional)

Steps for Making Animals:
1. Collect all ingredients.
2. Grease two large baking sheets with shortening. Set aside.
3. Empty the contents of the hot-roll mix into a large mixing bowl. Remove the packet of yeast; set aside. Stir turmeric into flour mixture, if desired.
4. Run hot water till warm. Place the ¾ cup warm water in a small bowl. Sprinkle contents of the yeast packet over water. Stir till yeast is dissolved.
5. In a small bowl lightly beat the first egg. Add yeast mixture and beaten egg to flour mixture in bowl; stir with spoon till well blended. Cover bowl with plastic wrap.
6. Let rise for 30 to 45 minutes or till double.
7. Punch down dough. Sprinkle a little flour on a counter top or board.
8. Turn dough out onto floured surface. Knead for 1 to 2 minutes, adding more flour, if necessary, till dough is smooth and no longer sticky.
9. Divide dough in half. Cover half of the dough with plastic wrap and refrigerate till needed.

10. With your hands, pull off small pieces of dough to make animal shapes on baking sheet. Roll each piece of dough between the palms of your hands to shape it into a ball for a head or body, or long shapes for tails or legs. Use smaller pieces of dough to make wings, ears, or noses for animals.
To attach dough pieces, moisten them with a little water and press them together. Keep animals about 3 inches apart on baking sheet. Repeat with remaining dough.
11. Cover the animals with plastic wrap. Let them rise for 15 to 30 minutes or till double in size.
12. In a bowl beat the remaining egg with a fork, then beat in the 1 tablespoon water. Turn on the oven to 350°.
13. Press the desired decorations onto the animals, using raisins or nuts for eyes or sliced almonds for wings and feathers. Brush the egg mixture over the animals and decorations.
14. Bake the animals in a 350° oven about 15 minutes or till golden brown. Using pot holders, remove baking sheets from oven. With a metal spatula, transfer animals to wire rack. Cool. Serve animals with Honey Butter, if desired. Makes about 18 animals.

HONEY BUTTER

Makes your homemade Animal Breads or mini-bagels taste even better; it's good on hot toast, too—

Ingredients You Will Need:
½ cup butter *or* margarine, softened
1 tablespoon honey

Steps for Making Honey Butter:
1. In a small bowl stir together butter or margarine and honey till well blended.
2. Serve with warm or cool Animal Breads. Refrigerate leftovers in a covered container. Makes ½ cup.

THUMBPRINT SWEET ROLLS

If you have a favorite dried fruit you'd like to use, you can substitute it for the mixed dried fruit. Then add enough sugar to suit your taste—

Ingredients You Will Need for Rolls:
Shortening
1 13¾-ounce package hot-roll mix
2 tablespoons granulated sugar
¾ cup orange juice
1 egg
All-purpose flour

Ingredients for Filling:
1 cup mixed dried fruit, snipped
1¼ cups water
¼ cup chopped walnuts
3 tablespoons granulated sugar
1½ teaspoons butter *or* margarine
¼ teaspoon ground nutmeg

Ingredients for Icing:
1 cup sifted powdered sugar
¼ teaspoon vanilla
About 1½ tablespoons milk

Steps for Making Rolls:
1. Collect all ingredients.
2. Grease 2 large baking sheets with shortening. Set aside.
3. Empty contents of the roll mix into a large mixing bowl. Remove the packet of yeast; set aside. Stir the 2 tablespoons sugar into mixture in bowl.
4. In a small saucepan heat orange juice till warm. Use a cooking thermometer to measure the temperature; it should be between 115° and 120°. Remove pan from heat. Sprinkle the yeast from the mix over orange juice; stir to dissolve yeast completely.
5. Add orange juice mixture and the egg to flour mixture; stir with spoon till well blended.
6. Cover dough with plastic wrap. Let rise 30 to 45 minutes or till doubled.
7. Punch down dough. Sprinkle a little flour on board.
8. Turn dough out onto floured surface and knead for 1 to 2 minutes or till dough is smooth and no longer sticky. (Add a little additional flour, if necessary.)
9. Divide dough in half. Divide each half into 8 pieces. Shape into balls.
10. Place balls 3 inches apart on greased baking sheets. Flatten each ball into a 3-inch circle with the palm of your hand. Cover; let rise till nearly double (about 30 to 45 minutes).

11. Preheat oven to 375°. Prepare filling: in a saucepan combine the dried fruit and water. Heat mixture to boiling. Reduce heat; simmer, uncovered, for 10 minutes.
12. Pour fruit into a strainer to drain off water. Put fruit back into saucepan. Stir in the walnuts, the 3 tablespoons sugar, the butter or margarine, and nutmeg till well combined.
13. With your thumb, make a depression in each roll. Spoon some of the fruit filling into each hole.
14. Bake rolls in a 375° oven for 10 to 12 minutes or till golden brown. Remove from oven with pot holders. Use a spatula to put rolls onto a wire rack. Cool till just warm.
15. Make icing: in a small bowl stir together the sifted powdered sugar and vanilla. Stir in enough milk to make a thin glaze that drips off the spoon. Use a spoon to drizzle the glaze over warm rolls. Serve sweet rolls warm or cool. Makes 16.

SUNFLOWER CHEESE BALLS

Make these for an after-school or bedtime snack, or serve with soup or salad—

Ingredients You Will Need:
1 3-ounce package cream cheese
½ cup shredded cheese, such as brick, Monterey Jack, *or* American (2 ounces)
¼ cup sunflower nuts
2 tablespoons toasted wheat germ

Steps for Making Cheese Balls:
1. Take the cream cheese out of the refrigerator. Let the cheese stand at room temperature on the counter for 30 minutes to soften.
2. Collect all other ingredients.
3. In a medium bowl place the softened cream cheese and the desired shredded cheese. Mash the cheeses together with a fork till well blended.
4. Stir in the sunflower nuts. With your hands, mold the cheese mixture into 1-inch balls.
5. Sprinkle the wheat germ on a piece of waxed paper. Roll each cheese ball in wheat germ to coat.
6. Put cheese balls on a serving plate and serve. Or cover and store in refrigerator till serving time. Makes 12.

VEGETABLE BASKET WITH VERY CHEESY DIP

Ingredients You Will Need for Basket:
Assorted vegetables, such as cauliflower, broccoli, carrots, celery, mushrooms, zucchini, *or* cherry tomatoes

Ingredients for Dip:
1 cup cream-style cottage cheese
¾ cup parsley sprigs
2 tablespoons mayonnaise *or* salad dressing
¼ teaspoon celery seed
Parsley sprigs for garnish

Steps for Making Vegetable Basket:
1. Collect desired vegetables.
2. Rinse all vegetables in cool water; drain on paper toweling.
3. Using a sharp knife, cut up vegetables on cutting board. For cauliflower, remove green leaves and cut out stem. With your fingers, break the head into bite-sized flowerets. For broccoli, remove the outer leaves. Cut off about 3 inches of the stalks and discard. Cut broccoli lengthwise into stalks. For carrots and celery, cut off ends. (Peel carrots, if desired.) Cut both into long thin sticks. For zucchini and mushrooms, cut off the stem ends. Slice zucchini. Leave mushrooms and cherry tomatoes whole.
4. Arrange vegetables in basket or on serving tray.

Steps for Making Dip:
1. Collect dip ingredients.
2. In blender container or food processor bowl, place the cottage cheese, the ¾ cup parsley sprigs, mayonnaise or salad dressing, and celery seed.
3. Cover and blend till mixture is smooth. Stop the machine once. Uncover and check the mixture. Use a rubber spatula to scrape down the sides of the blender or food processor bowl. Cover and blend again if needed.
4. Pour dip into a small bowl. Garnish with more parsley sprigs, if desired. Serve dip with vegetables. Store dip in a covered container in refrigerator. Makes 1 cup.

CHEESY CHILI ROLL

This is great as a hot snack or a go-along for a main-dish soup or salad. Wrap any leftover slices in foil and refrigerate. Reheat in a 350° oven about 20 minutes or till hot—

Ingredients You Will Need:
    Shortening
    1 13¾-ounce package hot roll mix
    ¾ cup warm water
    All-purpose flour
    5 parsley sprigs
    1 15-ounce can chili with beans
    ½ cup peanut halves
    ⅔ cup shredded American *or* cheddar cheese
    Tortilla chips, cherry tomatoes, and parsley sprigs for garnish (optional)

Steps for Making Chili Roll:
1. Collect all ingredients.
2. Grease a large baking sheet with shortening. Set aside.
3. Empty the contents of the hot roll mix into a large mixing bowl. Remove the packet of yeast.
4. Place ¾ cup warm water in a small bowl. Measure the temperature of the water; it should be between 115° and 120°. Sprinkle the contents of yeast packet over the water. Stir till yeast is dissolved.
5. Add yeast mixture to flour mixture in bowl; stir till well blended.
6. Cover bowl with clear plastic wrap. Let dough rise for 30 to 45 minutes or till doubled.
7. Punch down dough. Sprinkle a little flour on a counter top or board.
8. Turn dough out onto floured surface and knead for 1 to 2 minutes or till dough is smooth and no longer sticky. (Add a little additional flour, if necessary.)
9. Tear off a large piece of waxed paper and wet one side of the paper with a few drops of water. Place paper, wet side down, on working area. Sprinkle some flour lightly over paper.
10. Divide dough in half. On waxed paper roll one half of dough to a 10x8-inch rectangle. With kitchen shears snip the parsley into small pieces.
11. Spread *half* the chili over dough, leaving a 1-inch edge of dough on all sides. Sprinkle *half* the peanuts and *half* the snipped parsley over chili.
12. Starting from one long side, roll up dough carefully to the end. With your fingers pinch together the edges on the sides and the end of the roll.
13. Using two spatulas, carefully lift roll onto a large greased baking sheet.
14. Repeat filling and shaping remaining dough. Transfer to baking sheet.
15. Cover the rolls with plastic wrap and let rise in warm place for 30 minutes or till doubled.
16. Preheat oven to 375°. Uncover rolls; using a sharp knife make four or five slashes in the top of the rolls (just deep enough so you can see the chili).
17. Bake rolls in a 375° oven for 25 minutes. With pot holders remove baking sheet from oven.
18. Sprinkle the top of each roll with half of the shredded cheese. With pot holders return rolls to oven; bake 5 minutes more or till cheese is melted.
19. Cut rolls crosswise into slices. Put slices on platter. Garnish platter with tortilla chips, tomatoes, and parsley, if desired. Serve hot. Refrigerate leftovers. Makes 14 to 16 servings.

CHUNKY PEANUT BUTTER SPREAD

This not only is a great snack spread on fruit and crackers, but also is a tasty filling for sandwiches—

Ingredients You Will Need:
    1 4-ounce package whipped cream cheese
    ½ cup chunky peanut butter
    2 tablespoons milk
    1 tablespoon honey
    ½ cup finely snipped raisins *or* dried apricots
    Flaked coconut (optional)
    Apple *or* pear slices
    Crackers

Steps for Making Spread:
1. Collect all ingredients.
2. In a small bowl stir together the cream cheese and peanut butter.
3. Add milk, 1 tablespoon at a time, stirring till blended. Stir in honey.
4. Stir in raisins or apricots. Using a rubber spatula, scrape mixture into a serving bowl.
5. If desired, sprinkle coconut on top. Arrange fruit slices and crackers on a serving plate with spread. Refrigerate any leftovers in a covered container. Makes 1½ cups.

SPAGHETTI SALAD

A great lunch for you and a friend—

Ingredients for Salad:
    2 ounces uncooked spaghetti, broken; macaroni; *or* other pasta (about 1 cup)
    4 to 6 large lettuce leaves
    1 small tomato
    ¼ medium cucumber
    4 slices bologna *or* lunch meat

Ingredients for Dressing:
    ¼ cup salad oil
    3 tablespoons vinegar
    ½ teaspoon salt
    ¼ teaspoon dried oregano, crushed
    Dash pepper

Steps for Making Salad:
1. Collect all ingredients.
2. Fill a 2-quart saucepan with water up to about 1 inch from the rim. Sprinkle in a dash of salt. Cover pan and put on burner of range top.
3. Heat over high heat till water boils. Add spaghetti or macaroni.
4. Turn the heat down to medium-high and cook the pasta, uncovered, for 7 to 12 minutes or till it's tender. To find out whether spaghetti is tender, remove a piece from the pan with fork. Rinse piece under cold water, then taste to see whether it is tender.
5. Drain the pasta in a strainer. Run some cold water over the pasta to cool it. Drain it again, and let it stand while preparing salad.
6. In a large bowl tear up the lettuce into bite-size pieces with your fingers.
7. Cut out core from tomatoes; cut the tomato into wedges. Slice the cucumber thinly and add it to the lettuce along with the tomato.
8. Cut up the lunch meat into long thin strips; sprinkle over salad.
9. Sprinkle the cooked spaghetti or macaroni over the salad.

Steps for Making Dressing:
1. In a jar with a lid, place the salad oil, vinegar, salt, oregano, and pepper. Cover the jar and shake well till the ingredients combine.
2. Uncover the jar and pour dressing over the salad. Using a big spoon and fork or two big spoons, toss salad to coat with the dressing.
3. Spoon salad onto two plates. Serve. Makes 2 servings.

FRESH FRUIT COOKIE TARTS

Ingredients You Will Need:
 1 roll refrigerated oatmeal raisin, peanut butter, *or* sugar cookie dough
 1 29-ounce can vanilla *or* tapioca pudding
   Desired fruit, such as strawberries, bananas, seedless grapes, oranges, kiwi, *or* apples
   Decorations, such as halved peanuts, raisins, *or* toasted coconut (optional)

Steps for Making Tarts:
1. Collect all ingredients.
2. Turn oven on to 350°.
3. With a sharp knife, cut roll of cookie dough into 9 slices. Arrange 4 inches apart on ungreased baking sheets.
4. Bake the cookies in a 375° oven for 12 to 15 minutes or till cookies are light golden brown.
5. Using pot holders, remove cookie sheets from oven. With a metal spatula, transfer cookies carefully to a wire rack. Cool thoroughly.
6. Spoon some pudding over each cookie, spreading it to the edges with the back of your spoon. If any pudding is left over, cover and refrigerate it for another dessert.
7. With a sharp knife, cut up desired fruits. For strawberries, cut out stems and slice. For bananas, peel and slice. For grapes, cut in half. For oranges, cut off outer peel and white part of peel. Divide orange into sections by pulling apart with fingers. For kiwi, peel fruit and slice off ends. Slice fruit. For apples, cut in half, then in quarters. Cut off stem and seeds. Slice apple.
8. Decorate cookies with slices of your favorite fruit. Add extra decorations, if desired.
9. Serve immediately. Makes 9.

MINI-BAGELS

Ingredients for Bagels:
   Shortening
 1 13¾-ounce package hot-roll mix
 ⅓ cup plain wheat germ
 ½ cup warm water
 2 eggs
   All-purpose flour
 1 tablespoon sugar

Ingredients for Topping:
 1 egg
 1 tablespoon water
   Sesame seed

Steps for Making Bagels:
1. Collect all ingredients.
2. Grease 2 large baking sheets with shortening. Set aside.
3. Empty the contents of the hot-roll mix into a large mixing bowl. Remove the packet of yeast and set aside. Stir the wheat germ into mixture in bowl.
4. Place ½ cup warm water into a small bowl. Measure the temperature of the water; it should be between 115° and 120°. Sprinkle the contents of yeast packet over water. Stir till dissolved.
5. In a small bowl beat the 2 eggs lightly with a fork. Add eggs and yeast mixture to flour mixture. Stir till well blended.
6. Cover bowl with plastic wrap. Let rise 45 to 60 minutes or till doubled.
7. Punch dough down. Sprinkle a little flour on counter top or board.
8. Turn dough out onto floured surface and knead for 1 to 2 minutes or till dough is smooth and no longer sticky. (Add a little additional flour, if necessary.)
9. Divide dough into 4 equal pieces. Divide each piece into 8 pieces. Shape each piece into a ball.
10. Make a hole in each ball by dipping your finger into some flour, then poking your finger through the center of each ball. Pull dough gently around the hole to make a smooth opening, making a ring shape.
11. Place bagels on greased baking sheets. Cover bagels with plastic wrap and let rise in a warm place for 25 to 35 minutes or till almost double.
12. Fill a large kettle or Dutch oven with 1 gallon water and add sugar. Bring water to boiling. Turn down the heat to simmering.
13. Using a big slotted spoon, slip 5 or 6 bagels gently into simmering water. Cook the bagels for 5 minutes, turning them once with the slotted spoon after 2½ minutes. Make sure bagels do not touch each other.
14. Drain bagels on paper toweling. Repeat with remaining bagels.
15. Put bagels back on the baking sheets. Preheat oven to 375°.
16. Make the topping: in a small bowl beat the remaining egg and the 1 tablespoon water with a fork. Use a pastry brush to brush the egg mixture over the tops of the bagels. Sprinkle bagels with some sesame seed.
17. Bake in a 375° oven for 20 to 25 minutes or till golden brown. Using pot holders, remove baking sheets from oven. With metal spatula put bagels on a wire rack to cool. Makes 32.

SNACK-IN-A-GLASS

Ingredients You Will Need:
 1 8-ounce carton fruit-flavored yogurt, such as strawberry, raspberry, cherry, orange, lemon, lime *or* boysenberry
 1 cup milk
 1 cup fresh *or* frozen unsweetened blueberries, raspberries, strawberries, orange sections; *or* peach slices
 1 egg
 2 teaspoons sugar
 ¼ teaspoon vanilla *or* almond extract
 2 or 3 ice cubes
   Extra pieces of fruit for garnish (optional)

Steps for Making Drink:
1. Collect all ingredients.
2. In blender container place the yogurt, the milk, fruit pieces, egg, sugar, and vanilla or almond extract.
3. Cover blender and turn on high speed till mixture is frothy (bubbly).
4. While blender is running, add ice cubes, one by one, through hole in lid of blender. Blend till smooth.
5. Pour into glasses; garnish each serving with an extra piece of fruit, if desired. Serve at once. Serves 4.

FROM THE RANGE TOP
•
OVEN
•
PRESSURE COOKER
•
MICROWAVE
•
CROCKERY COOKER

BY MARLENE BROWN

Cooking up a hearty dinner for family or company needn't force you into a pan-juggling act. If you follow along, we'll show you how to prepare six great dinners, each in one pot, with delicious results! Not only does one-pot cooking eliminate pre-dinner hassles; it also streamlines serving and after-dinner cleanup. And you can use the technique whether you opt for a Dutch oven, skillet, roaster, crockery cooker, pressure cooker, or microwave casserole. Cooking times for each are given in the recipes so you can choose the method that best suits your timetable.

For starters, try hearty **Sombrero Ribs With Tortillas.** These Mexican-style pork spareribs with sausage get their colorful appeal from zucchini and tomatoes, and their spunky flavor from garlic, chili peppers, and oregano. Serve the ribs with the rich gravy and warm flour tortillas.

Photographs: William Sladcik.
Food stylist: Fran Paulson

WONDERFUL

ONE-POT MEALS

WONDERFUL ONE-POT MEALS

•

I f you've been serving chili or beef stew to simplify family dinners, you've already adopted the one-pot meal idea. But a mix of meat and vegetables is just the beginning. With a little imagination and some ingredients borrowed from good cooks around the globe, you can create a variety of one-pot entrées. Each of the ones shown here is just as delicious made atop the range as it is in a crockery cooker, microwave dish, or pressure saucepan.

Bacon, white wine, and spices flavor the robust broth in **Rabbit Stew With Carrot Dumplings** *(top left)*. Your choice of domestic rabbit or chicken, plus carrots and onions, simmer under fluffy carrot dumplings.

Sausage and Vegetables Paprikash *(top right)* is a Hungarian-style medley of spaetzle, Polish sausage, yellow squash, lima beans, and tomatoes laced with paprika.

However you choose to cook it, **Curried Chicken in a Pot** *(center right)* will be a sensation on your table. The dish is spiced with cinnamon and curry along with Indonesian condiments like chutney, currants, and almonds. Sweet potatoes, mandarin oranges, and bananas complete the platter.

Uniquely seasoned **Szechwan .Lamb Soup With Wontons** *(front right)* is an Oriental meal in a bowl. Marinated lamb or beef strips, shrimp- and cabbage-filled wontons, and Oriental vegetables cook up quickly in a pepper-spiked broth.

Meatball Soup With Spinach Pistou *(bottom left)* has all the makings of a gourmet meal. Meatballs, pasta, and mushrooms fill this hearty soup to the brim, but it's the well-seasoned spinach puree you add that produces the unbeatable flavor.

CURRIED CHICKEN IN A POT

Cooking times: Range top—50 minutes; Oven—55 to 65 minutes; Crockery cooker—6½ to 8 hours; Pressure cooker—25 minutes; Microwave oven—26 minutes—

- 1 2½- to 3-pound broiler-fryer chicken, cut up
- 2 tablespoons cooking oil *or* butter *or* margarine
- 1 cup orange juice
- ⅓ cup currants *or* raisins
- ½ cup slivered almonds
- 3 tablespoons chutney, chopped
- 1 to 2 teaspoons curry powder
- ½ teaspoon ground cinnamon
- 5 or 6 medium (2 pounds) sweet potatoes, peeled and sliced crosswise into 1-inch pieces

Range-top method: In a 12-inch skillet brown chicken slowly in hot oil about 10 minutes; drain. Sprinkle with salt and pepper. Mix orange juice, currants, almonds, chutney, and spices. Add potato to skillet; pour orange juice mixture over all. Bring to boiling; reduce heat. Simmer, covered, for 30 to 40 minutes. Remove chicken and potatoes from pan; arrange on a warm platter. Garnish with bananas, oranges, and parsley, if desired. Skim fat from pan juices. Spoon some sauce over platter; pass remaining. Makes 6 servings.

Oven method: Arrange chicken in a shallow roasting pan. Dot with the 2 tablespoons butter; sprinkle with salt and pepper. Bake, uncovered, in a 425° oven 25 minutes. Drain. Mix orange juice, currants, almonds, chutney, and spices. Add potato pieces to roasting pan; pour orange juice mixture over all. Reduce heat to 350°. Bake, covered, for 30 to 40 minutes more. Continue and serve as directed for range-top method.

Crockery-cooker method: Cut sweet potatoes into 1-inch chunks; place in bottom of a 3½- to 4-quart crockery cooker. Top with chicken. Dot chicken with the 2 tablespoons butter; sprinkle with salt and pepper. In bowl combine ½ *cup* orange juice, currants, almonds, chutney, and spices. Pour over chicken in pot. Cover; cook on low for 6½ to 8 hours. Serve as directed for range-top method.

Pressure-cooker method: In pressure saucepan brown chicken as directed in range-top method. Drain. Mix orange juice, currants, almonds, chutney, and spices. Add potato pieces to pan; pour orange juice mixture over all. Cover pan; set control at 15 pounds pressure and place over high heat till control jiggles. Reduce heat (control should still rock back and forth); cook 15 minutes. Remove from heat; immediately run cold water over cooker to reduce pressure. Serve as for range-top method.

Microwave method: In a 3-quart nonmetal casserole micro-cook *1 tablespoon* butter or margarine, uncovered, on HIGH for 30 seconds or till melted. Roll chicken in butter to coat; season with salt and pepper. Arrange chicken in dish with sweet potatoes. Mix ⅔ *cup* orange juice, currants, almonds, chutney, and spices. Pour orange juice mixture into casserole. Micro-cook, covered, 25 minutes rearranging every 5 minutes. Serve as directed for range-top method.

SOMBRERO RIBS WITH TORTILLAS

Cooking times: Range top—1½ hours; Crockery cooker—7¾ hours; Pressure cooker—50 minutes—

- 8 ounces pork sausage links, cut up
- ½ cup sliced onion
- 1 clove garlic, minced
- 2½ pounds pork loin back ribs, cut into 2-rib sections
- 1 16-ounce can whole tomatoes
- 2 tablespoons chopped canned green chili peppers
- 2 teaspoons instant beef bouillon granules
- 2 teaspoons dried oregano, crushed
- 4 medium zucchini, cut into ½-inch-thick slices
- 1 large red *or* green sweet pepper, cut into bite-size pieces
- 3 tablespoons all-purpose flour
- ½ cup shredded cheddar cheese
- 8 warm flour tortillas, rolled

Range-top method: In Dutch oven brown sausage pieces, onion, and garlic; remove from pan. Drain. In same pan brown the ribs, half at a time. Return sausage mixture and ribs to pan. Add tomatoes, green chili peppers, bouillon granules, oregano, and 1 cup *water*. Cover; simmer 50 minutes. Add zucchini and the sweet pepper pieces; cover and simmer 15 minutes more. Remove meats and vegetables to platter; keep warm. Skim off fat from pan juices; measure juices. Add water if necessary to make 2 *cups* liquid; return to pan. Blend ⅓ cup *cold water* into the flour; stir into liquid. Cook and stir till bubbly; cook 1 minute more. Pour some sauce over meat on platter; sprinkle with cheese. Pass remaining sauce and warm tortillas. Serves 8.

Crockery-cooker method: In a 3½- to 4-quart crockery cooker combine onion, garlic, tomatoes, green chili peppers, bouillon granules, oregano, and ½ cup *water*. Top with sausage, then ribs; cover and cook on low for 6 hours. Uncover; remove ribs. Add zucchini and sweet pepper to cooker, covering with liquid; place ribs atop vegetables. Cover and cook 1 hour more. Remove meat and vegetables to platter; keep warm. Skim off excess fat from juices; measure juices. Add water to juices if necessary to make 2 cups liquid; pour into saucepan. Stir ⅓ cup *cold water* into ¼ cup flour; stir into liquid. Cook and stir for 1 minute or till mixture is bubbly; cook 1 minute more. Serve as directed for range-top method.

Pressure-cooker method: In pressure saucepan brown sausage, onion, garlic, and ribs as directed for range-top method. Remove from pan. In same pan combine tomatoes, green chili peppers, bouillon granules, oregano, and 1 cup *water*. Return sausage mixture and ribs to pan. Cover pan tightly; set control at 15 pounds pressure. Place pan over high heat till pressure control jiggles. Reduce heat (control should still rock back and forth); cook 15 minutes. Remove from heat; let stand 5 minutes. To finish reducing pressure, run cold water over cooker. Remove ribs to platter; keep warm. Bring pan juices to boiling; add zucchini and sweet pepper to pan. Simmer, uncovered, 5 to 10 minutes more. Arrange vegetables and sausage on platter; keep warm. Prepare gravy in pressure saucepan as directed for range-top method. Serve as directed for range-top method.

SZECHWAN LAMB SOUP WITH WONTONS

Cooking times: Range top—18 to 20 minutes; Crockery cooker—4 hours—

- 1¼ pounds boneless lamb *or* beef, cut in thin bite-size strips
- 3 tablespoons hoisin sauce
- 1 clove garlic, minced
- 1 beaten egg yolk
- ¼ cup finely chopped water chestnuts *or* celery
- 2 tablespoons finely chopped onion
- 1 teaspoon grated gingerroot *or* ¼ teaspoon ground ginger
- 1 4½-ounce can shrimp, drained, rinsed, and chopped
- ½ cup coarsely chopped Chinese cabbage
- 24 wonton skins
- 6 cups beef *or* chicken broth
- ⅛ teaspoon Szechwan pepper *or* ground red pepper
- 2 cups chayote melon, peeled, seeded, and cubed, *or* coarsely chopped, peeled apple
- 4 green onions, bias-sliced into 1½-inch lengths
- 1 tablespoon cornstarch
- 1 6-ounce package frozen pea pods

Range-top method: Combine meat strips with hoisin sauce, 1 tablespoon *water,* and garlic; toss to coat. Set aside. meanwhile, prepare wontons: in bowl combine egg yolk, water chestnuts, onion, gingerroot, and ⅛ teaspoon *pepper.* Stir in shrimp and cabbage; mix well. Position one of the wonton skins with one point toward you. Place a rounded spoonful of filling just below center of skin. Fold bottom point of skin over filling; tuck point under filling. Roll up skin and filling, leaving about 1 inch at top of skin. Moisten corners of skin with water. Grasp two upper corners of the triangle; bring these corners toward you below filling. Overlap the corners so wontons resemble nurses' caps; press to seal. Repeat to make 24 wontons. Cover and set aside.

In a 4-quart saucepan or Dutch oven bring broth to boiling. Add meat mixture and Szechwan pepper. Simmer, covered, for 10 minutes. Stir in cubed chayote and green onion. Cook, covered, 5 minutes. Combine corn-starch and 2 tablespoons cold *water;* stir into soup along with frozen pea pods and wontons. Cook 3 minutes more or till bubbly. Makes 8 servings.

Crockery-cooker method: Prepare lamb or beef as directed in range-top method; place in a 3½- to 4-quart crockery cooker with only *5 cups* of broth, Szechwan pepper, melon, and green onion. Cover; cook on low for 3½ hours. Meanwhile, prepare wontons as directed for range-top method; cover and set aside. Switch control to high. Combine cornstarch and 2 tablespoons cold *water;* stir into soup with pea pods. Cook on high for 30 minutes. Cook wontons, uncovered, in simmering water for 3 minutes; add to soup. Serve in soup bowls.

RABBIT STEW WITH CARROT DUMPLINGS

Cooking times: Range top—1¾ hours; Crockery cooker—6½ to 7½ hours; Pressure cooker—25 minutes—

- 1 2½- to 3-pound rabbit *or* chicken, cut up
- ¼ cup all-purpose flour
- 4 slices bacon
- 1½ cups chicken broth
- ½ cup dry white wine
- 8 to 12 whole boiling onions
- 6 juniper berries *or* whole allspice
- 1 bay leaf, crushed
- 5 medium carrots, cut into sticks
- 1 cup all-purpose flour
- 2 teaspoons baking powder
- ¼ teaspoon ground allspice
- ½ cup milk
- 2 tablespoons cooking oil
- ⅓ cup finely shredded carrot
- 1 teaspoon snipped parsley

Range-top method: Coat rabbit or chicken pieces with a mixture of the ¼ cup flour, ¼ teaspoon *salt,* and dash *pepper;* set aside. In a 4- or 5-quart kettle or Dutch oven, cook bacon slices till crisp; drain, reserving drippings in pan. Crumble bacon; set aside. Brown rabbit or chicken pieces in reserved drippings about 5 minutes per side. Drain off fat. Add broth, wine, onions, juniper berries or whole allspice, crushed bay leaf, and bacon. Bring to boiling. Reduce heat; simmer, covered, for 50 to 60 minutes. Add carrot sticks; cover and simmer about 25 minutes more.

Meanwhile, prepare dumplings: In medium bowl thoroughly combine the 1 cup flour, the baking powder, ¼ teaspoon *salt,* and ground allspice. Combine milk and oil; add all at once to flour mixture along with shredded carrot. Stir just till moistened. Drop the dumpling dough from a table-spoon, making 6 to 8 mounds atop bubbling stew. Sprinkle dumplings with parsley. Cover kettle tightly; simmer 15 minutes (do not lift cover). Serves 5 or 6.

Crockery-cooker method: Place carrot sticks and onions in bottom of a 3½- to 4-quart crockery cooker. Sprinkle rabbit or chicken pieces with salt and pepper (omit coating with flour). Place rabbit or chicken pieces over vegetables in pot. Dice the *un-cooked* bacon; combine with the broth, wine, juniper berries or whole all-spice, and crushed bay leaf. Pour mixture over meat in pot. Cover; cook on low for 6 to 7 hours or till meat is tender. Turn control to high. Prepare dumpling batter as directed for range-top method; drop dough from a table-spoon to make 6 to 8 mounds around edge of pot. Sprinkle dumplings with parsley. Cover; cook on high 30 minutes (do not lift cover). Serve.

Pressure-cooker method: In pressure saucepan prepare recipe as directed in range-top method through browning the rabbit or chicken in ba-con drippings. Drain off excess fat. Add broth, wine, carrot sticks, onions, jun-iper berries or whole allspice, crushed bay leaf, and crumbled bacon to pan. Cover pan; set control at 15 pounds pressure and place over high heat till control jiggles. Reduce heat (control should still rock back and forth); cook 15 minutes. Remove pan from heat; immediately run cold water over cooker to finish reducing pressure. Uncover pan. Prepare dumpling batter as di-rected in range-top method; return pan to heat. Bring stew to simmering. Drop dough from a tablespoon to make 6 to 8 mounds atop bubbling stew. Sprin-kle dumplings with parsley. Simmer, uncovered, for 5 minutes. Remove pressure gauge from lid; cover pan. Place over heat. Allow a small stream of steam to escape from vent tube for 5 minutes more. Remove pan from heat. Serve.

SAUSAGE AND VEGETABLE PAPRIKASH

Cooking times: Range top—20 minutes; Crockery cooker—3½ to 4½ hours; Pressure cooker—20 minutes—

- **1 10-ounce package spaetzle or small shell or bow macaroni (about 3 cups)**
- **2 tablespoons paprika**
- **½ teaspoon instant chicken bouillon granules**
- **Few drops bottled hot pepper sauce**
- **1 10-ounce package frozen lima beans**
- **½ cup chopped onion**
- **1 pound fully cooked Polish sausage or bratwurst, bias-sliced into ½-inch-thick slices**
- **3 small yellow squash or zucchini, cut into bite-size chunks**
- **12 cherry tomatoes, halved or 1 large tomato, cut into wedges**

Range-top method: In a 3-quart saucepan cook spaetzle in boiling salted water according to package directions; cover. Remove from heat; let stand 5 minutes. Drain in colander. (If using macaroni, cook according to package directions; drain immediately.) In same pan bring 1½ cups *water,* the paprika, chicken bouillon granules, and hot pepper sauce to boiling. Cook lima beans and onion in bouillon mixture according to bean package directions; do not drain. Add Polish sausage or bratwurst, yellow squash or zucchini, and drained spaetzle or macaroni to pan. Cover and cook about 10 minutes or till vegetables are nearly tender and mixture is hot. Stir in tomato pieces; heat through. Makes 6 servings.

Crockery-cooker method: In a 3½- to 4-quart crockery cooker combine spaetzle or macaroni and 2 quarts boiling salted water. Cover and cook on high about 15 minutes or till spaetzle are nearly tender. Drain and cool. Cover spaetzle; set aside. Run hot water over beans to separate; drain. Place beans, sausage or bratwurst, and squash or zucchini in pot. Combine the water, paprika, bouillon, and pepper sauce; pour over. Cover and cook on

low for 3 to 4 hours. Turn control to high. Stir in cooked spaetzle or macaroni; cover and cook 15 minutes more. Stir in tomatoes. Serve.

Pressure-cooker method: In pressure saucepan without pressure gauge, prepare spaetzle as directed for range-top method; set aside. In same pan combine the water, paprika, bouillon granules, and pepper sauce. Run hot water over beans to separate; drain. Add beans, sausage, and squash to pan. Cover pan; set control at 15 pounds pressure. Place over high heat till control jiggles. Reduce heat (control should still rock back and forth); cook 3 minutes. Run cold water over cooker to reduce pressure. Uncover; stir in spaetzle and tomatoes. Heat through and serve.

MEATBALL SOUP WITH SPINACH PISTOU

Cooking times: Range top—20 minutes; Crockery cooker—4½ to 5 hours; Pressure cooker—15 minutes; Microwave oven—36 minutes—

- **Spinach Pistou**
- **1 egg**
- **¼ cup milk**
- **¼ cup fine dry bread crumbs**
- **1 pound ground veal or ground beef**
- **2 tablespoons cooking oil**
- **6 cups beef broth**
- **1 cup celery, bias-sliced ¼-inch thick**
- **4 ounces fettuccine or linguine, broken into pieces**
- **2 cups sliced fresh mushrooms**
- **Shredded Gruyère cheese**

Range-top method: Prepare Spinach Pistou; set aside. Combine egg, milk, bread crumbs, and ½ teaspoon *salt.* Add veal; mix well. Shape into twenty-four 1½-inch meatballs. In a 4-quart Dutch oven brown meatballs, half at a time, in hot oil. Drain. Return the meatballs to Dutch oven. Add broth, celery, and ¼ teaspoon *pepper;* bring to boiling. Add pasta; cover and cook 5 minutes. Add Spinach Pistou and mushrooms; cook 5 minutes more or till hot. Serve with cheese. Serves 6.

Crockery-cooker method: Prepare and shape meatballs as directed for range-top method *except* omit the milk. Place in a 3½- to 4-quart crockery

cooker with beef broth, celery, and ¼ teaspoon *pepper.* Cover and cook on low for 4 hours. Add pasta; turn control to high and cook, covered, for 30 minutes more or till pasta is tender. Meanwhile, prepare Spinach Pistou; stir into soup with mushrooms. Turn cooker off; let stand, covered, 10 minutes. Serve as directed for range-top method.

Pressure-cooker method: Prepare Spinach Pistou. Prepare and shape meatballs as directed in range-top method. In pressure saucepan brown meatballs, half at a time, in hot oil; drain. Return all meatballs to pan. Add broth, celery, pasta, and ¼ teaspoon *pepper.* Bring to boiling; cover. Set control at 15 pounds pressure and place over high heat till control jiggles. Reduce heat (control should still rock back and forth); cook 8 minutes. Remove from heat; cool 5 minutes. Run cold water over cooker to finish reducing pressure. Uncover; add mushrooms and Spinach Pistou. Cook, uncovered, 2 minutes more or till hot. Serve as directed for range-top method.

Microwave method: Prepare and shape meatballs as directed for range-top method. In a 3-quart nonmetal casserole place *half* meatballs; micro-cook, uncovered, on MEDIUM for 5 minutes, turning meatballs over and rearranging twice. Set aside. Repeat with remaining meatballs. Drain off fat. Return all meatballs to dish. Add only *5 cups* beef broth, celery, and ¼ teaspoon *pepper;* micro-cook, covered, on HIGH 14 minutes or till mixture comes to boiling. Add pasta: cover and cook 10 minutes more or till pasta is nearly tender. Remove from oven; let stand 5 minutes. Meanwhile, prepare Spinach Pistou; stir into soup with mushrooms. Micro-cook, covered, for 2 minutes more. Serve as directed for range-top method.

SPINACH PISTOU

Dissolve ¼ teaspoon *instant beef bouillon granules* in 1 cup boiling *water.* Thaw one 10-ounce package frozen chopped spinach; drain well. In blender container or food processor bowl place bouillon mixture, spinach, ½ cup grated *Gruyère cheese,* ¼ cup *olive oil,* 2 cloves *garlic,* and 1 teaspoon *lemon juice.* Cover and blend till smooth.

MAY

By Joy Taylor

Tried-and-true tuna casserole isn't the only money-saving fish entrée you can serve your family! Follow our three cost-cutting strategies, and you'll have a world of delicious options to choose from, as we'll demonstrate on the next few pages. The lineup ranges from tempting Crab Artichoke Appetizers to exotic Tabouli-Seafood Salad to elegant Fish à la Diable. What all these dishes have in common is that they're as thrifty as they are tasty. Fish fanciers and bargain hunters never had it so good!

STRETCH FANCY-FISH FLAVOR

Lobster, scallops, crab, shrimp, sole! Any one of these delicacies is a seafood lover's delight, but a budget watcher's dilemma. To enjoy big flavor without big spending, just supplement a small quantity of the costly fish or shellfish with less expensive ingredients. These four seafood-stretching recipes show you how.

With **Seafood Thermidor** *(front right)* you can multiply two lobster tails to four generous servings. A wine-flavored stuffing, resplendent with lobster and fish, is piled into the halved tails. Each serving adds up to one lobster "tail," with extra stuffing served on the side.

Call on **Crab Artichoke Appetizers** *(front left)* when you want an elegant and economical first course. You can produce 12 of these extraordinary hors d'oeuvres from just one can of crab meat and three artichokes. To do it, simply stretch the classy ingredients with hard-cooked egg and sour cream.

To make a thrifty pasta salad company-special, add seafood. Our citrus-seasoned version, **Scallop Pasta Salad** *(back right),* won't scuttle your food budget because only a few scallops are required. To make them go far, you slice them, then add protein-rich beans and almonds.

The same seafood-stretching technique even lets you indulge in costly sole without a qualm. For **Sole Patties Paprikash** *(back left),* you deflate the cost by flaking the sole and mixing in gingered rice instead of serving the fillets whole. Garnish each fried patty with a halved shrimp and you have an impressive, yet low-priced, main dish.

Photographs: William Sladcik. Food stylist: Fran Paulson

D o you habitually buy the same high-priced fish because you aren't sure how other varieties will taste? If so, you're missing out on some great eating and significant savings. Those unfamiliar varieties, like shark, buffalo fish, and rockfish, are just as delicious as costlier halibut or salmon, and here are five recipes (plus another on page 73) to prove it.

For starters, try **Fish a la Diable** *(front right),* a simple yet very special entrée which you can make with several kinds of fish, including mullet, flounder, perch, whiting, and pollack. Cucumber strips (plus carrots, if you like) are tucked inside the fish roll-ups, and a yogurt-mustard sauce adds a tangy fillip. Besides being delicious, this dish is a dieter's delight!

No one will ever guess that this spectacular **Turban of Broccoli and Fish** *(front left)* evolved from such simple beginnings—namely croaker, turbot, or pollack fillets and pureed broccoli. Glazed carrots and lemony Hollandaise Sauce help glamorize this unusual main-dish ring.

To make inexpensive fish exotic, add lime juice and radishes, as was done with this **Oriental-Style Stuffed Fish** *(back left).* Stuff either one large fish, such as Spanish mackerel, or two small fish, such as ocean perch or catfish, with a brown rice mixture and then baste the fish with a soy sauce-sesame seed glaze.

Smoked Mussels Rockefeller *(back center)* is our modest (yet equally tasty) version of the well-known appetizer. Just before baking, a cheesy crumb mixture is sprinkled atop the smoked seafood-spinach combo.

You'll think you're eating lobster bisque when you taste **Monkfish-Zucchini Chowder** *(back right).* In fact, monkfish is nicknamed "poor man's lobster." This whole-meal soup is thickened with pureed vegetables and seasoned with pimiento, fresh parsley, and thyme.

DRESS UP CANNED &

FROZEN FISH

It's no news that canned and frozen fish are terrific bargains. But what *is* news is that these budget helpers now are available in many new forms, shapes, and flavors. Here are some main-dish and appetizer recipes to help you capitalize on these convenient and tasty fish items.

Tabouli-Seafood Salad *(front right)* is a meal-sized version of the Near Eastern bulgur-wheat favorite. What makes this modern-day main dish super-handy is that it features canned baby clams and frozen precooked shrimp. Mushrooms, onion, and dillweed add extra pizzazz.

Frozen breaded fish portions make short work of producing the **Italian Fish Platter** *(front left)*. The fish is topped with Swiss cheese and a lively tomato sauce, then served with cooked cabbage wedges. For extra savings, you can prepare this quick-to-make dish with other frozen products when they're on sale, such as batter-fried fish fillets, fish sticks, or shrimp sticks.

Once you try flaky **Seaside Bundles** *(back left)*, you'll be hooked on their mild flavor, convenience, and economy. Refrigerated roll dough encloses a creamy blend of canned fish, water chestnuts, and cheese. Our version features canned mackerel, but you could use tuna or salmon.

If you think of canned tuna solely in terms of salads and sandwiches, think again. It also can be the basis for tasty **Tuna- and Cheese-Stuffed Pasta** *(back center)*. The manicotti shells are packed with a tuna-vegetable mixture and topped with a cheese-olive sauce. To make the dish a real bargain, choose grated tuna in place of the costlier flaked version.

You can put another standby, salmon, to a new use, too, by building a **Tri-Level Salmon Tomato Appetizer** *(back right)*. It's bursting with springtime color and flavor. The pastry shell holds layers of cucumber-flavored rice, seasoned salmon, and a delicate tomato aspic. (A word to budget watchers: The redder the salmon, the higher the price.)

SEAFOOD THERMIDOR

2 6-ounce frozen lobster tails *or* 8
ounces frozen lobster meat
¾ cup water
¾ cup dry white wine
¼ cup chopped onion
¼ cup chopped celery
1 bay leaf
1 teaspoon dry mustard
1 teaspoon paprika
8 ounces fresh *or* frozen fish
fillets (flounder, haddock, *or*
turbot)
1 cup sliced fresh mushrooms
½ cup milk
3 tablespoons all-purpose flour
2 tablespoons snipped parsley
1 teaspoon instant chicken
bouillon granules
¾ cup soft bread crumbs
2 tablespoons grated Parmesan
cheese
2 tablespoons butter *or*
margarine, melted
Toasted triangles
Fresh dill (optional)
Lemon twists (optional)

Cook frozen lobster tails in enough
boiling salted water to cover for 8 minutes. Drain and cool slightly. Place
lobster, shell side down, on cutting
board. With a sharp knife, cut lobster
in half lengthwise. Remove meat; cut
meat into chunks. Clean and reserve
shells, keeping them intact. (Or, cook
frozen lobster meat in boiling water 1
to 3 minutes. Drain well.)

Meanwhile, in an 8-inch skillet
combine the water, wine, onion, celery, bay leaf, dry mustard, and paprika. Add fish fillets. Cover and simmer till fish flakes easily when tested
with a fork. (Allow 2 to 4 minutes for
½-inch-thick fillets.) Remove fish and
drain well. Cut fish into cubes. Strain
poaching liquid through cheesecloth.
Return liquid to skillet; bring to boiling. Boil, uncovered, for 6 to 7 minutes
or till liquid is reduced to ¾ cup. Add
mushrooms; simmer 4 minutes or till
tender. Stir milk into flour; add to
skillet. Stir in parsley and bouillon
granules. Cook and stir over medium
heat till thickened and bubbly. Cook
and stir 1 minute more. Stir in lobster
and fish cubes. Heat through.

If you use lobster tails, place the
lobster shell halves on a baking sheet.
Lightly spoon the seafood mixture into
each shell half. Keep any remaining
mixture warm in skillet. (If using frozen lobster meat, spoon the mixture
into four individual casseroles.)

Combine bread crumbs, Parmesan cheese, and butter or margarine.
Sprinkle over each serving. Broil 5
inches from heat for 2 minutes or till
lightly browned. To serve lobster shells,
arrange with toast triangles on serving platter. Spoon any remaining seafood mixture into a bowl; place in center of platter. Garnish lobster shells or
individual casseroles with fresh dill
and lemon twists, if desired. Serve immediately. Makes 4 servings.

CRAB-ARTICHOKE APPETIZERS

3 medium artichokes
Lemon juice
⅔ cup dairy sour cream
2 tablespoons sliced green onion
1 tablespoon dry sherry
⅛ teaspoon celery seed
⅛ teaspoon salt
Few dashes bottled hot pepper
sauce
Dash pepper
1 6½-ounce can crab meat,
drained and cartilage
removed
2 hard-cooked eggs, chopped
Lettuce leaves

Wash and trim stems, then remove
loose outer leaves from artichokes. Cut
off 1 inch of tops; snip off sharp leaf
tips. Brush cut edges with lemon juice.
In Dutch oven simmer artichokes,
covered, in large amount of boiling
salted water for 20 to 25 minutes or
till a leaf pulls out easily. Remove artichokes; drain upside down on paper
toweling. Remove center leaves and
chokes; discard. Chill artichokes.

In bowl stir together sour cream,
onion, sherry, celery seed, salt, hot
pepper sauce, and pepper. Reserve a
few larger segments of crab meat for
garnish. Flake remaining crab meat.
Stir flaked crab meat and chopped egg
into sour cream mixture. Cover and
chill.

To serve, cut each artichoke into
fourths. Spoon crab mixture onto each
artichoke piece. Garnish with reserved crab meat. Serve on a lettuce-
lined plate. Makes 12 servings.

SCALLOP-PASTA SALAD

*Instead of tossing this main-dish salad,
you might arrange it on individual lettuce-lined plates. Marinate the pasta in
half the dressing; marinate the scallops, oranges, beans, and onion in the
remaining dressing. To serve, arrange
pasta on plate; arrange scallops, oranges, and vegetables atop—*

8 ounces fresh *or* frozen scallops
½ teaspoon salt
1½ cups water
6 ounces linguine *or* spaghetti,
broken
1 11-ounce can mandarin orange
sections, drained
1 cup garbanzo beans, drained
2 tablespoons finely chopped
green onion
¼ cup salad oil
¼ cup white wine vinegar
1 teaspoon finely shredded
orange peel
½ teaspoon dry mustard
Dash ground red pepper
1 6-ounce package frozen pea
pods, thawed
Spinach leaves
⅓ cup slivered almonds, toasted
(optional)

Let frozen scallops stand at room temperature 20 minutes. Halve any large
scallops. Add salt to water; bring to
boiling. Add scallops. Reduce heat;
simmer for 1 minute or till scallops are
opaque. Drain and cool scallops. Slice
scallops. Meanwhile, cook pasta according to package directions; rinse
with cold water. Drain and cool.

In bowl toss together the scallops,
cooked linguine, orange sections, garbanzo beans, and green onion. In screw-
top jar combine the oil, vinegar, orange peel, mustard, and pepper; shake
well. Pour over scallop mixture. Toss
to coat, being careful not to break orange sections. Cover and chill. At
serving time, stir pea pods into pasta
mixture. Spoon mixture into a spinach-
lined bowl; sprinkle almonds atop, if
desired. Makes 4 servings.

SOLE PATTIES PAPRIKASH

12 ounces fresh *or* frozen sole
    fillets
2 beaten eggs
¼ cup fine dry bread crumbs
2 tablespoons snipped parsley
1 tablespoon grated onion
½ teaspoon grated gingerroot
1½ cups cooked rice
½ cup fine dry bread crumbs
2 tablespoons cooking oil
¼ cup dry white wine
4 fresh *or* frozen large shrimp in
    shells, thawed, shelled, and
    halved lengthwise
1 tablespoon butter
1 tablespoon all-purpose flour
1 tablespoon snipped parsley
1 teaspoon paprika
½ cup light cream *or* milk

Thaw frozen fish for 20 minutes; cut into four pieces. Place a greased rack in a large skillet with a tight-fitting lid. Add water till it almost reaches rack. Bring to boiling. Sprinkle fish with salt. Place fish on rack; cover skillet and steam about 5 minutes or till fish flakes easily. Lift out rack. Remove fish from rack; cool. Flake fish.

In a bowl combine eggs, the ¼ cup bread crumbs, the 2 tablespoons parsley, the onion, and gingerroot. Stir in rice and flaked fish. Using about ⅓ cup fish mixture for each, shape mixture into eight ¾-inch patties. (Chill mixture for easier shaping.) Coat patties with the ½ cup bread crumbs. In skillet heat oil. Add patties; cook, uncovered, over medium-low heat about 6 minutes on each side.

Meanwhile for sauce, in saucepan combine the wine and ¼ cup *water*. Bring to boiling; reduce heat. Add shrimp. Simmer 1 minute or till shrimp are pink. Drain shrimp, reserving liquid; set liquid aside. In same saucepan melt the butter; blend in the flour, the 1 tablespoon parsley, and paprika. Add cream. Cook and stir till thickened and bubbly; cook and stir 1 minute more. Stir in the reserved liquid. Heat through. To serve, arrange patties on platter; spoon sauce over. Top each with a halved shrimp. Garnish platter with parsley, if desired. Serves 4.

TURBAN OF BROCCOLI AND FISH

1½ pounds fresh *or* individually
    frozen fish fillets (croaker,
    flounder, ocean perch,
    whiting, turbot *or* pollack)
2 cups chopped fresh broccoli
1 medium onion, chopped (½
    cup)
¼ teaspoon dried tarragon,
    crushed
3 eggs
⅓ cup dairy sour cream
¼ cup grated Parmesan cheese
½ cup fine dry bread crumbs
1 recipe Hollandaise Sauce

Thaw fish, if frozen. In saucepan cook the broccoli with the onion and tarragon, covered in ½ cup *boiling water* for 5 to 10 minutes or till broccoli is tender. Drain and cool slightly. In blender container combine broccoli mixture, eggs, sour cream and ⅛ teaspoon *pepper*. Blend till smooth, scraping sides. Finely chop *8 ounces* of the fish; stir into the broccoli mixture with the bread crumbs.

Meanwhile, cut the remaining 1 pound fish into strips about 2 inches wide and 6 to 8 inches long. Lay fish strips in a greased 5-cup ring mold at even intervals; overlap as necessary, letting ends hang over edges of mold. Spoon the broccoli mixture into the mold. Smooth top. Fold ends of fillets over broccoli mixture.

Place mold in a 13x9x2-inch baking dish pan. Add hot water to pan to come halfway up the sides of mold. Bake, uncovered, in a 350° oven for 35 to 40 minutes or till knife inserted near center comes out clean. Remove mold from water. Let stand 10 minutes.

To drain off liquid, place wire rack over mold; invert (do not unmold). After draining, unmold onto serving platter. Remove any liquid from platter with paper toweling. Spoon some Hollandaise Sauce over mold; pass remainder. If desired, fill center of mold with cooked carrots. Serves 8.

Hollandaise Sauce: Cut ½ cup *butter* into thirds; let come to room temperature. Place 4 *egg yolks* and one-third of the butter in the top of a double boiler. Cook, stirring rapidly, over but not touching boiling water till butter melts. Add one-third more of the butter; continue stirring rapidly. As butter melts and mixture thickens, add the remaining butter, stirring

constantly. When butter is melted, remove pan from water; stir rapidly for 2 more minutes. Stir in 9 teaspoons *lemon juice*, 1 teaspoon at a time; stir in a dash *salt* and dash *pepper*. Heat again over boiling water, stirring constantly for 2 to 3 minutes or till thickened. Remove at once from heat. Makes 1 cup.

FISH À LA DIABLE

2 large carrots
1 medium cucumber, seeded
1 cup sliced fresh mushrooms
⅓ cup sliced celery
½ cup plain yogurt
1 to 2 tablespoons Dijon-style
    mustard
4 fresh *or* frozen fish fillets,
    thawed (croaker, mullet,
    flounder, ocean perch,
    whiting, turbot, *or* pollack)
Butter *or* margarine, melted
1 teaspoon all-purpose flour
3 tablespoons milk
Paprika

Cut carrots into 8 long strips. Cut cucumber into 6-inch strips. In saucepan cook the carrots, mushrooms, and celery in ¼ cup water 5 minutes or till just tender. Drain. Combine the yogurt and mustard. Brush some yogurt mixture over one side of each fillet, reserving about half the mixture for sauce. Lay 3 or 4 cucumber and 2 carrot strips crosswise on yogurt side of each fillet. Roll fish around vegetables. Secure with wooden picks.

Arrange fish rolls, seam side down, in a 9x9x2-inch baking pan. Brush with melted butter or margarine. Bake, uncovered, in a 400° oven about 25 minutes or till fish flakes easily. Remove to serving platter; remove picks.

In small saucepan stir flour into remaining yogurt mixture. Stir in milk. Add reserved mushrooms and celery. Cook and stir over medium heat till thickened and bubbly. Spoon over fish rolls. Sprinkle with paprika. Garnish plate with fresh dillweed and halved lemon slices, if desired. Makes 4 servings.

ORIENTAL-STYLE STUFFED FISH

1 3- to 4-pound *or* two 1½-pound
  whole dressed fresh *or* frozen
  fish (whitefish, perch, trout, *or*
  catfish)
1 cup long grain brown rice
2 tablespoons snipped chives
1 clove garlic, minced
½ teaspoon grated gingerroot
2 tablespoons butter
½ cup sliced radishes
2 teaspoons lime juice
  Butter, melted
2 tablespoons soy sauce
1 tablespoon lime juice
1 teaspoon sesame seed

Thaw fish, if frozen. Prepare the rice
according to package directions. In
saucepan cook chives, garlic, and gingerroot in the 2 tablespoons butter just
till tender. Remove from heat. Add the
radishes and the 2 teaspoons lime juice.
Stir in rice.

Sprinkle fish cavity with salt.
Spoon rice mixture into cavity; place
fish in a greased shallow baking pan.
Brush with melted butter. Bake in a
350° oven till fish flakes easily: 45 to
60 minutes for large fish, 30 to 45 minutes for small fish. Cover stuffing with
foil, if necessary to prevent drying out.
Combine the soy sauce, the 1 tablespoon lime juice, and sesame seed.
Brush over fish. Place fish 4 inches from
broiler; broil 2 minutes or till sesame
seeds are lightly toasted. Transfer fish
to platter. Garnish fish with parsley
and additional sliced radishes, if desired. Serves 6.

SMOKED MUSSELS ROCKEFELLER

1 10-ounce package frozen
  chopped spinach
2 3¾-ounce cans smoked
  mussels
  Milk
2 beaten eggs
½ cup shredded American cheese
½ cup fine dry bread crumbs
2 tablespoons chopped onion
¼ cup grated Parmesan cheese
2 tablespoons butter, melted

Cook spinach according to package directions; drain well, pressing out excess liquid. Set aside. Drain mussels,
reserving liquid. Add milk to mussel
liquid to equal ½ cup. If desired, set
aside 8 mussels for garnish. Coarsely
chop remaining mussels. In bowl combine eggs, milk mixture, spinach,
American cheese, ¼ cup of the bread
crumbs, the onion, and chopped mussels. Spoon mixture into 8 equal shells
or 6-ounce custard cups. Place in shallow baking pan. Combine remaining
bread crumbs, Parmesan cheese, and
butter; sprinkle over mixture in shells.
Bake in a 350° oven for 20 minutes.
Garnish with the reserved mussels.
Makes 8 appetizer servings.

MONKFISH-ZUCCHINI CHOWDER

1 pound fresh *or* frozen monkfish
  fillets
1 medium onion, chopped
2 tablespoons butter *or*
  margarine
1½ cups chicken broth
3 small potatoes, peeled and
  sliced
1 cup milk
1 2-ounce can sliced pimiento,
  drained and chopped
2 tablespoons snipped parsley
¼ teaspoon dried thyme, crushed
  Dash pepper
1½ cups sliced zucchini

Let frozen fish stand at room temperature for at least 20 minutes. Cut fish
into ¾-inch cubes. In 3-quart saucepan cook the onion in the butter or
margarine till tender. Stir in broth and
potatoes. Bring to boiling. Reduce heat.
Cover and simmer for 25 minutes or
till potatoes are very tender. Place *half*
of the mixture in blender container or
food processor bowl. Cover; process till
smooth. Repeat with remaining mixture. Return all to saucepan. Stir in
milk, pimiento, parsley, thyme, and
pepper. Bring to boiling. Reduce heat.
Add fish cubes to soup. Cook about 5
minutes, stirring constantly, to prevent scorching. Stir in zucchini. Cook
and stir about 5 minutes more or till
fish flakes easily. Season to taste.
Makes 4 or 5 servings.

ITALIAN FISH PLATTER

1 7- *or* 8-ounce package (4) frozen
  breaded fish portions
1 medium onion, sliced
½ cup sliced celery
2 tablespoons butter
½ cup tomato juice
1 7½-ounce can tomatoes, cut up
2 tablespoons snipped parsley
¼ teaspoon dried basil, crushed
½ small head cabbage, cut into
  thin wedges
½ cup shredded Swiss cheese

Bake fish portions according to package directions. Meanwhile, in saucepan cook onion and celery in the butter till tender. Add tomato juice,
undrained tomatoes, parsley, and basil.
Boil gently, uncovered, 10 to 15 minutes or till slightly thickened.

In skillet cook cabbage wedges,
covered, in a small amount of boiling
water for 10 to 12 minutes. Drain well.

Sprinkle cheese over fish portions. Bake 2 minutes more or till
cheese is melted. To serve, arrange
cooked cabbage and fish portions on
cabbage leaf-lined platter, if desired.
Spoon sauce over all. Serves 4.

SEASIDE BUNDLES

1 cup sliced green onion
2 tablespoons butter
1 8-ounce can water chestnuts,
  drained and chopped
½ cup dairy sour cream
1 2-ounce jar sliced pimiento,
  drained and chopped
¼ cup fine dry bread crumbs
1 beaten egg
½ cup shredded American cheese
1 16-ounce can mackerel, drained
  and flaked
2 packages (8) refrigerated
  crescent rolls

Cook onion in butter. Stir in chestnuts, sour cream, pimiento, crumbs,
egg, cheese, and ¼ teaspoon *pepper*. Stir
in fish. Unroll dough; form into eight
6x4-inch rectangles, using two rolls for
each. Seal perforations. Spoon ⅓ cup
filling on each. Fold dough over; seal
with fork tines. Bake on ungreased
baking sheet in 425° oven 10 minutes.
Top with more shredded cheese, if desired. Makes 8.

VERACRUZ STEAKS

2 cloves garlic, minced
2 tablespoons butter
1 16-ounce can tomatoes, cut up
1 cup chopped, peeled eggplant
2 tablespoons snipped parsley
**1 teaspoon instant chicken
    bouillon granules**
**Few dashes bottled hot pepper
    sauce**
**1 pound fresh or frozen fish fillets
    or steaks (shark, mackerel,
    turbot, or pollack)**
**1 medium onion, cut into thin
    wedges**
**1 medium green pepper, cut into
    strips**
2 teaspoons cornstarch

In 10-inch skillet cook garlic in butter till tender. Add *undrained* tomatoes, eggplant, parsley, bouillon granules, pepper sauce, ¼ teaspoon *salt*, and ⅛ teaspoon *pepper*. Bring to boiling. Simmer, covered, 10 minutes. Add fish and onion. Cover and cook over low heat for 7 minutes. Add green pepper; cook 5 minutes more or till fish flakes easily. Remove fish and vegetables to platter; keep warm. Strain sauce. Return to skillet. Blend 2 tablespoons *cold water* into cornstarch; add to skillet. Cook and stir over medium heat till thickened and bubbly. Cook 2 minutes more. Serve with fish. Serves 4.

TABOULI-SEAFOOD SALAD

2 cups warm water
¾ cup bulgur wheat
**1 10-ounce can whole baby
    clams, drained**
**1 6-ounce package frozen cooked
    shrimp, thawed**
**2 red or green peppers, cut into
    ½-inch squares**
**1 4-ounce can sliced mushrooms,
    drained**
¼ cup olive or salad oil
2 tablespoons lemon juice
½ teaspoon dried dillweed
¼ teaspoon salt
Lettuce leaves
**2 medium tomatoes, sliced and
    halved**
½ of a small onion, thinly sliced

In a bowl combine the warm water and bulgur. Let stand 1 hour. Drain well; press excess water out of bulgur. Combine bulgur, clams, shrimp, peppers, and mushrooms. In screw-top jar combine oil, lemon juice, dillweed, and salt; cover and shake well. Pour dressing over bulgur mixture; toss. Cover and chill. To serve, spoon bulgur mixture into a lettuce-lined bowl; arrange tomato pieces around edge of bowl. Top bulgur mixture with a few onion rings. Makes 4 servings.

TUNA-AND-CHEESE-STUFFED PASTA

If you don't have au gratin dishes, bake all of the stuffed manicotti in a 12x7½ x 2-inch baking dish—

8 manicotti shells
3 small carrots, sliced
½ cup chopped onion
½ cup chopped celery
1 beaten egg
**1 9-ounce can tuna, drained and
    flaked**
¾ cup cream-style cottage cheese
½ teaspoon salt
**¼ teaspoon lemon-pepper
    seasoning**
1¾ cups milk
2 tablespoon all-purpose flour
**½ cup shredded process Swiss
    cheese (2 ounces)**
½ cup pitted ripe olives, sliced
Parsley sprigs (optional)

Cook pasta according to package directions; drain well. Meanwhile, in saucepan cook carrots, onion, and celery in small amount of boiling water 8 minutes or till tender. Drain well. To *half* of the vegetables add the egg, tuna, cottage cheese, salt, and lemon-pepper seasoning. Spoon about ⅓ cup filling into each manicotti shell. Using 4 individual au gratin dishes, arrange two filled shells in each dish.

For sauce: In saucepan blend milk into flour. Cook and stir over medium heat till thickened and bubbly. Stir in Swiss cheese till melted. Add remaining cooked vegetables and the olives. Pour sauce over pasta shells in each dish. Cover dishes with foil. Bake in a 350° oven for 30 minutes or till heated through. Garnish with parsley, if desired. Makes 4 servings.

TRI-LEVEL SALMON-TOMATO APPETIZER

For a light entrée, prepare this recipe in six individual tarts—

Pastry for one-crust 9-inch pie
½ cup long grain rice
1 cup water
**⅓ cup creamy cucumber salad
    dressing**
1 envelope unflavored gelatin
1½ cups vegetable juice cocktail
2 tablespoons lemon juice
½ teaspoon sugar
¼ teaspoon celery salt
**1 16-ounce can salmon, drained,
    boned, and flaked**
¼ cup chopped green onion
¼ cup finely chopped celery
**3 tablespoons creamy cucumber
    salad dressing**
Celery leaves (optional)
Pitted ripe olives (optional)

Prepare pastry. Line a 10-inch flan pan or pie plate with the pastry. Prick sides and bottom. Bake in a 450° oven for 10 to 12 minutes or till golden. Cool on a wire rack.

Cook rice in water, covered, for 15 minutes or till tender. Combine hot cooked rice with the ⅓ cup dressing; press into pastry shell. Chill.

In small saucepan soften the gelatin in ¾ cup of the vegetable juice cocktail. Heat over low heat, stirring constantly, till gelatin is dissolved. Remove from heat. Stir in the remaining vegetable juice cocktail, *1 tablespoon* of the lemon juice, the sugar, and celery salt. Chill till mixture is partially set (consistency of unbeaten egg whites).

For filling, combine the salmon, green onion, chopped celery, the 3 tablespoons salad dressing, and the remaining lemon juice.

To assemble, top rice mixture with the salmon mixture, pressing lightly. Spoon partially set tomato mixture atop. Chill till firm. To serve, garnish with celery leaves and pitted ripe olives; cut into thin wedges. Makes 12 appetizer servings.

SHOW-OFF CAKE

For Stained-Glass Window Cake, secure a waxed paper pattern onto the top of the frosted cake with pushpins or straight pins. Transfer the design onto the frosting using a tracing wheel (above). Pipe on icing through a pastry tube to make "leading" within the design. Spoon melted jelly into each portion of the design (below).

Here's how to make the telegram's lines on your Live Wire Cake. Place wooden picks in the frosted cake top to mark 6 sections. Use cardboard as a guide and mark lines between picks by pressing the edge of the cardboard into the frosting (below). Then, place licorice strips over the lines.

DECORATING *Made Easy*

BY MARLENE BROWN

Whatever the red-letter event—birthday, graduation, anniversary, or bon voyage party—you're sure to find a merrymaking cake on these pages to fit the occasion. There's even a cake patterned after a favorite piece of a child's artwork. What's more, you don't need a diploma from a cake decorating school or any unusual equipment to create these extra-special cakes. They're all as simple to make as they are spectacular.

The **Rainbow Cake** *(back left)* displays a colorful cascade of candies on a pink frosting background. To create the rainbow, you halve a single cake layer crosswise, stack the halves with frosting in between, then stand the layers on the cut sides.

Why not deliver an edible telegram to the party guest(s) of honor? Just fill in the appropriate name, date, occasion, and message atop this **Live Wire Cake** *(back right)*. Cover the cake with frosting and make the colorful lines with licorice whips. Use small tubes of decorator frosting to write your message.

Nut and Seed Cake *(front right)* features a crunchy mosaic fashioned from interesting nuts and seeds. Cut the sides of a two-layer cake for the hexagonal shape, then frost the cake. Spread preserves atop to provide a glistening background for the design.

Melted jams and jellies create a special effect for **Stained-Glass Window Cake** *(bottom left)*. Draw a design on waxed paper, then use a tracing wheel to transfer the design to the cake. Pipe on Royal Icing for the leading; fill in between the lines with jelly.

Turn the page and learn how to personalize a cake decoration by using your child's or your own drawing. **Coloring Book Cake** is child's play!

All of our cake decorating ideas have step-by-step directions. Just follow along and your celebratory treats will be a "piece of cake" to put together.

Photographs: Mike Dieter

FOOD NOTES

SHOW-OFF CAKE DECORATING
Coloring Book Cake

Michael proudly shows off *Coloring Book Cake,* **a delicious reproduction of his own drawing.**

Decorating gel fills in his design on top of the cake, and colorful candies finish off the sides.

COLORING BOOK CAKE
You'll find the decorating gel in the frosting section of large supermarkets—
Food and equipment you'll need:
Colored artwork
Tracing paper *or* **waxed paper**
1   13x9-inch baked cake layer
**1   recipe Buttercream Frosting
      (see recipe below)**
Straight pins *or* **pushpins**
Tracing wheel *or* **pastry wheel**
**Assorted colors of glossy cake
      decorating gel**
**Assorted colored gumdrops,
      cinnamon candies, and hard
      candies**

Take a picture of the drawing with a 35-mm camera using slide film; project the picture onto a wall to approximately 12x8 inches. Trace the picture onto a piece of waxed paper or tracing paper you've taped to the wall.

Place the cake layer on a serving tray; frost top and sides with *Buttercream Frosting.* Let stand 1 hour. Position the paper tracing atop cake; secure with pins. Using a tracing wheel or pastry wheel, retrace the design in the frosting. Remove pins and drawing.

Using appropriate colors of cake decorating gel, outline edges of design traced in frosting. Then fill in the outlines by squeezing the tube of gel back and forth in straight lines until the entire design is colored in. Decorate the sides of the cake with gumdrops, cinnamon candies, and hard candies.

BUTTERCREAM FROSTING
6   tablespoons butter *or* **margarine**
**1   16-ounce package powdered
      sugar, sifted (about 4¾ cups)**
Light cream *or* **milk (about ¼ cup)**
1½ teaspoons vanilla

Cream butter or margarine; gradually add about *half* the sugar, blending well. Beat in *2 tablespoons* cream and vanilla. Gradually blend in remaining sugar. Add enough cream to make of spreading consistency.

STEP BY STEP TO DECORATED CAKES

All of our decorated cakes call for common baking pans that you probably already own. To make the cake layers, use a cake mix or your favorite scratch cake recipe. Choose a cake that's not too tender, such as pound cake or sponge cake. Then follow the instructions to make the designs. Bake the cake at least several hours ahead of the time you decorate it so it will be completely cool.

LIVE WIRE CAKE

Food and Equipment You'll Need:
 1 13x9-inch baked cake layer
 1 12x8-inch piece of cardboard
    Stick pins *or* pushpins
 1 can chocolate fudge frosting
 1 can vanilla *or* lemon frosting
    Yellow food coloring
    Wooden picks
    Red licorice whips
 1 tube brown glossy cake
    decorating gel

Place cake layer on a board or serving tray; center the piece of cardboard atop cake to leave a 1-inch border around top of cake. Secure cardboard with stick pins or pushpins. Frost sides and top border of cake with the chocolate frosting up to the cardboard edge. Remove cardboard and pins.

Tint the white or lemon frosting a bright yellow with food coloring. Carefully spread the yellow frosting on top of cake up to chocolate border.

For the message portion, mark the yellow rectangle into 6 sections with wooden picks by placing a ruler alongside the short side and inserting picks at 1, 2, 3, 4, and 7 inches down from the top border.

Using the cardboard as a guide, place picks in corresponding positions on the opposite side of the border. Mark lines between picks by pressing the edge of the cardboard gently into the frosting. Remove cardboard and wooden picks; cut licorice into six 12-inch pieces. Make the first line a double line by placing 2 pieces of the licorice side by side over the first line marked on the frosting. Make remaining lines by placing single strips of licorice over rest of marked lines.

With a wooden pick trace the words "Live Wire" atop the double strip of licorice in the upper right-hand corner of the cake. In the second space trace "To: _____"; in the third space "City: _____"; in the fourth space "Date: _____"; in the fifth space "Message: _____"; and "From: _____" in the bottom space. Write over your tracings by piping on decorating gel.

NUT AND SEED CAKE

Food and Equipment You'll Need:
 1 recipe Buttercream Frosting
    (see recipe, left)
 ½ to 1 teaspoon maple flavoring
 2 8-inch round baked cake layers
    Waxed paper
    Compass (optional)
    Wooden picks
    Cloth tape measure
    Apricot preserves, melted
    Assorted nuts *or* nut snacks
       such as sesame sticks *or* nut
       crunch
    Dark raisins (optional)
    About 8 ounces whole
       unblanched almonds

Prepare Buttercream Frosting, adding maple flavoring to taste. Place one cake layer on a board or serving plate; place 3-inch-wide strips of waxed paper around cake and tuck under cake slightly to cover outer edge of plate. Frost the top with some of the frosting. Place second cake layer atop. Find the center of the top cake layer with a compass or by crisscrossing two 9x1-inch strips of waxed paper atop cake. Mark center of cake with a wooden pick; remove compass (or crisscrossed strips of waxed paper). Wrap a tape measure around outer edge of cake; mark cake at 6 even-spaced intervals with wooden picks, placing picks just inside the top edge of cake. With a sawtooth knife, cut cake into a hexagon shape by trimming off rounded sides between wooden picks. Set aside

trimmings; reserve for snacking. Remove wooden picks *except* for center marker.

Brush crumbs from cut sides of cake; frost sides with remaining frosting, forming a high edge. Remove waxed paper strips from under cake. Carefully spread melted preserves over top of cake just to frosted edge. Arrange your choice of nuts or nut snacks spoke fashion from center of cake to edge and running down sides of cake. With contrasting nuts or snacks form circular bands atop cake between spokes, starting from the center and working toward outside edge of cake. Remove center marker. If desired, add a few raisins to center of the design and leave the outer edge of preserves ungarnished. Press whole almonds in horizontal rows onto top and bottom of cake sides. Store the cake, covered, in a cool place.

RAINBOW CAKE

Food and Equipment You'll Need:
  1 recipe Buttercream Frosting
    (see recipe, page 76)
    Red *or* yellow food coloring
    Assorted small candies such as
      jelly beans in several colors
  1 9- or 10-inch round baked cake
    layer
    Canned decorator frosting
    (optional)

Prepare Buttercream Frosting; tint it pastel pink or yellow with food coloring. If candy colors are mixed, separate the candies into color groups. Cut the baked cake layer in half crosswise; place 1 half of the cake on a large piece of foil. Frost the top of the layer with some of the Buttercream Frosting; top with the second half of the cake. Press

layers together to secure. Using foil, stand the cake layers up on the cut sides. Using 2 spatulas, transfer standing cake to a serving tray.

Frost the top and sides of the cake with the remaining Buttercream Frosting. Press the brightest candies into the frosting in a border along the top edge of the cake on the side facing you. Repeat with another color of candy, making a band just under top border.

Continue making 7 to 10 bands with remaining candies, ending with the lightest color. Write a message on the rounded edge of cake with decorator frosting or decorate with candles or do both. Serve cake the same day.

STAINED-GLASS WINDOW CAKE

If you want to make your own design, experiment first with different jams and jellies on a white paper plate to achieve the effect you want. Some preserves, such as raspberry, need to be strained before using—

Food and Equipment You'll Need:
    White paper
    Marking pencil
    Waxed paper
  1 recipe Royal Icing (see recipe,
    below right)
  2 9-inch round baked cake layers
    Straight pins *or* pushpins
    Tracing wheel *or* pastry wheel
    Brown paste food coloring
    Pastry bag and tip
  ¼ cup *each:* mint-flavored, red
    currant, apple, and grape jelly
    Demitasse spoon *or* small
    spoon
  1 cup apricot preserves

To create your own design, draw an 8-inch circle using an ink pen on a piece of white paper. (Use an 8-inch round pan as a model.) Draw the design within the circle. Or, use the grid to duplicate the design pictured on page 74.

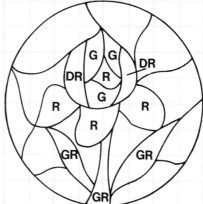

Color key: 1 square = 1inch
G = gold   DR = dark red
R = red   GR = green

To transfer design: On a piece of white paper draw an 8-inch square. Divide the square into 64 equal sections by drawing horizontal and vertical lines. Then draw an 8-inch circle within the square. Draw in the lines

of the design as shown on the grid. Using a marking pencil, trace the design onto a piece of waxed paper. Reserve about ⅓ cup of the icing; cover tightly with wet paper toweling and plastic wrap and set aside. Place 1 of the cake layers on a plate; cover plate edge with strips of waxed paper tucked slightly under the cake. Frost cake top with some of the Royal Icing. Top with second layer; quickly frost top and sides of cake. Remove waxed paper strips.

Let cake stand 20 minutes. Center waxed paper design on top of cake; secure with straight pins. Using tracing wheel, retrace the design in the frosting, pressing just enough to make a visible indentation. Remove paper and pins. Tint reserved Royal Icing a dark brown color with food coloring; place a pastry bag fitted with a small plain round tip. Push icing down into bag to remove air bubbles. Close pastry bag by flattening its sides above frosting. Fold in corners, then fold flap down. Roll top down a few inches toward tip. Holding the top edge of the cone in your hand, grasp the bottom of the cone near the tip and squeeze out icing over lines traced on cake. Allow cake to stand, uncovered, 10 minutes till dry.

Melt about ¼ cup mint-flavored jelly over low heat. Using a small spoon, fill in the stem-and-leaf portion of the design with the melted jelly. Repeat procedure with red currant, apple, and grape jellies; use to fill in petals of the flowers. Melt apricot preserves; push preserves through sieve to clarify. Use preserves to fill in around flower to outer edges of design. Let cake stand 1 hour to set. Cover cake tightly; store it in a cool place till serving time.

ROYAL ICING

  3 egg whites
  1 16-ounce package powdered
    sugar, sifted (about 3¾ cups)
  1 teaspoon vanilla
  ½ teaspoon cream of tartar

Combine the egg whites, sugar, vanilla, and cream of tartar. Beat on high speed of electric mixer for 7 to 10 minutes or till very stiff. Use immediately, covering the frosting in a bowl with wet paper towel at all times. Makes 3 cups.

JUNE

June 1982 ● $1.25

Better Homes
and Gardens

Housing costs: Reshaping the American Dream
New looks for old kitchens • Innovative attic conversions
Top performing arts festivals for vacationing families

·OUTDOOR LIVING·
Easy-does-it ideas for yard, deck, porch, and patio
Plus...Fabulous recipes to simplify summer entertaining

OUTDOOR LIVING

Open your doors to a sensational summer! Good friends and good food are key to summer fun, so we've filled these pages with delightful new ways to combine them. Our special party package includes a surprisingly simple barbecue for 60 . . . a help-yourself picnic for a dozen . . . and a summerized four-course progressive dinner that moves from backyard to backyard. And to take the hassle out of hot-weather entertaining, we've preplanned all three parties from start to finish. Menus, recipes, table (or lawn) settings, serving suggestions—everything you need is right here. All you do is pick your party, invite your friends, and follow our foolproof formula. Besides being super-simple to produce, our party scenarios are as flexible as your imagination. You can adapt them to any occasion, any setting under the sun (or moon). Have fun!

BRING ON THE GUESTS!

SIMPLIFIED SUMMER ENTERTAINING

By Marlene Brown

CO-OP COOKOUT

Yes! You can put on a barbecue for 60 handily, and without investing in a side of beef or going "whole hog." The trick is to make the barbecue a co-op cookout.

The co-op idea is a great way to pull off a church group gathering, neighborhood party, or family reunion. Simply divvy up the work load, recruiting each couple or family to contribute some of the food, utensils, or barbecue equipment. When the bash begins, everyone joins in the fun! This group *(top)* used a beach house for their afternoon cookout, but any park or big backyard works just as well.

The co-op menu *(right)* is designed to appeal to both children and adults. Another plus is that almost everything can be made ahead. The only exception is the main course, **Steak Pinwheel Pitas.** But don't worry—you don't have to wrestle with a special cut of meat to prepare them. Instead, you select simple beef round steaks, marinate them, and roll them around a spinach filling. When it's party-time, set up three barbecues with rotisseries and grill the meat rolls for just under an hour. Then slice and serve the meat so guests can assemble their own sandwiches with sprouts, onion, and a spicy sauce for embellishments.

Round out the menu with a bowl of **Hashed Browns Salad** and crowd-pleasing **Sweet-Sour Vegetables.**

For dessert *(top center),* set out trays of **Cheese 'n Chocolate Mini-Cakes** for the kids; luscious **Summer Fruit Tart** for the adults.

Throughout the festivities, keep cold pop and beer on hand in ice-filled buckets.

MENU

Steak Pinwheel
Pitas
•
Hashed Browns
Salad
•
Sweet-Sour
Vegetables
•
Cheese 'n
Chocolate
Mini-Cakes
•
Summer Fruit
Tart
•
Pop/Beer

Photographs:
George de Gennaro
Food stylist: Mable Hoffman
Field editor: Sharon Haven
Prop stylist: Jill Mead

81

GUESTS!

FUSS-FREE PICNIC

Summer just wouldn't be summer without care-free picnics, like the super-simple movable feast on these pages. It requires almost no cooking beforehand, and you don't have to strike up the coals at your open-air dining spot either. Plus, you can adjust the amount of food to the size of your group. The bill of fare is flexible, too, so you can cater to your picnickers' tastes, whether they run to gourmet fare or all-American standbys. In short, this picnic puts the emphasis where it belongs—on the pleasure of eating outdoors.

The basis of the self-service menu (shown on the buffet table and as a single serving, *above*) is the **Open-Faced Sandwich Buffet,** an attractive spread of meats, cheeses, and seafood of your choice. Accent the selection with a variety of toppers and condiments like **Zucchini Sandwich Filling** and **Tomato-Bacon Spread.** Then set out bread and let everyone design his own sandwich.

For the individual **Vegetable Salads Alfresco,** tie vegetable sticks in serving-sized bundles with green onion "strings," then chill. Use the vegetables as dippers for the creamy **Béarnaise Dip** and **Easy Guacamole.**

For a sweet ending, serve natural **Fruit Baskets**—papaya, melon, or pineapple shells filled with fresh fruit chunks. Pass **Orange Cream Cheese** for a tasty topper.

To simplify packing and unpacking your picnic basket, arrange the food in sturdy carriers that double as serving pieces. We used a sectional plastic tray, covered with foil, to transport and serve the sandwich makings. You might opt for foil- or napkin-lined wicker trays, colored metal containers, or acrylic serving pieces to house sandwich ingredients, the vegetables, or fruit. Also available are picnic baskets that have a removable shelf so you can pack crushables atop one another without mishap. Several containers with tight-fitting covers work well for the condiments.

For seating, you can spread a quilt on the ground, or use large beach towels.

MENU

Open-Faced
Sandwich Buffet
•
Vegetable Salads
Alfresco
•
Fruit Baskets
•
Punch/Lemonade

GUESTS!

PROGRESSIVE OUTDOOR DINNER

APPETIZER AND SALAD COURSES

Would you like to put on a special dinner for close friends, but you feel overwhelmed at the thought of a multi-course extravaganza? We have a fabulous solution! Invite three couples to participate in staging a progressive dinner—with a twist. Instead of traveling from one living room to the next for each course, this party moves from yard to yard. And with four couples pitching in, each gets a chance to play host without having to prepare a complete dinner.

Our four-course menu fea-tures foods that can easily be made ahead. We chose an international theme for this party, but an American theme would work equally well.

The opening course of this ethnic feast *(above)* consists of three intriguing appetizers: German-style **Fish in Sour Cream** *(back),* crispy **Fried Wonton Strips With Soy-Lemon Sauce** for a Far Eastern flavor *(center),* and slices of cold Italian **Tomato Pesto Tart** *(front).* Either wine or tea can be poured as an accompaniment.

To set the stage, we chose an Oriental theme for the table. Coffee tables were pulled outdoors, and large cushions were provided for seating.

For the next course *(right),* an ethnic salad bar was set up in another backyard. French **Artichoke-Mushroom Salad Remoulade** *(back right)* is a subtle complement to the piquant **Moroccan Orange Salad** *(front right)* that's garnished with olives and radishes. A medley of greens and feta cheese provides the makings for **Mideastern Green Salad** *(front left).* The **Tabbouli Bread** *(back left)* was sliced in thick wedges to show off the bulgur filling.

For the salad setup, the serving bar was covered with a checkered runner, and a basket was filled with the matching napkins. Serving pieces made of wicker, wood, and acrylic complete the bistro-style table setting.

MENU

Appetizer Course:

Fish in Sour Cream
•
Fried Wonton Strips With Soy-Lemon Sauce
•
Tomato Pesto Tart
•
Wine/Tea

Salad Course:

Artichoke-Mushroom Salad Remoulade
•
Moroccan Orange Salad
•
Mideastern Green Salad
•
Tabbouli Bread
•
Rosé Wine

GUESTS!

MAIN COURSE

Highlighting this novel progressive dinner is the delicious main course, **Indonesian Sâté** (sah-TAY). Despite the exotic-sounding name, the dish is simply the Southeast Asian version of grilled kabobs.

If you're the host for the main course, you can prepare this version of Sâté ahead. Just marinate chunks of chicken, lamb, and beef in a delightfully spicy mixture that's based on aromatic spices including mustard, coriander, turmeric, cumin, and garlic plus coconut milk.

Before you leave to enjoy the appetizer course, drain off the marinade and thread the meat on long skewers. Cover and refrigerate the meat till you return. Also prepare the spicy **Peanut Sauce.** It's used as a serve-with dipper for the grilled kabobs.

When it's time for the entrée course, fire up one or two hibachis till the coals are medium-hot and cook the **Turmeric Rice** accompaniment. Grill the kabobs for just 20 minutes, then serve them with the rice and sauce *(opposite)*. A robust red wine such as a cabernet sauvignon complements the spicy food. When you serve the rice, you can offer a couple of chutneys—one sweet and one hot. (They're sold in Oriental markets.)

For the serving setup, you have several options. These hosts *(pictured above)* rented a round table and chairs and set them up on their deck. They grilled the ka-bobs table-side over a large hibachi and passed the skewered meat with the bowls of rice and sauce. But you might set up two or three small low tables with pillows for seating, place a hibachi in the center of each table, and let your guests grill their own kabobs. And if the weather moves the party indoors, you can broil the Sâté on your conventional broiler or cooktop grill.

On party day, you can create some Southeast Asian ambience by covering the table with a colorful fabric. Brass candlesticks and serving pieces will enhance the main course setting. If you don't own any brass pieces, stoneware makes a great-looking alternative.

Main Course:

Indonesian Sâté
with Peanut
Sauce
•
Turmeric Rice
•
Red Wine

Dessert Course:

International
Coffees
•
Pizzelles
•
Baklava Tarts
•
Gugelhupf/
Apricot Sauce

GUESTS!

DESSERT COURSE

Though the coffee-and-dessert course marks the final stop for the traveling entourage, it's by no means the least important. This inviting dessert table, set out under the stars, is well worth an evening's wait.

First of all, let your guests choose from a variety of freshly brewed imported coffees, such as espresso, Turkish coffee, cappuccino, and spiced coffee. (They're available in the specialty sections of supermarkets and gourmet food shops.) Serve the brews in small coffee or demitasse cups. Provide a tray of liqueurs, such as crème de cacao,

orange liqueur, and apricot brandy; and a bowl of whipped cream to embellish each serving.

Then set out a tableful of exotic goodies and invite your guests to help themselves as they sip. The lineup pictured starts with Italian **Pizzelles** (pit-ZELLIES) *(left),* which are wafer-thin butter cookies that you make in a pizzelle iron. (If you don't own one, you can substitute a Scandinavian krumkake iron available in kitchen tool and gourmet shops.)

At center stage are dainty **Baklava Tarts,** traditional Greek treats. These almond-, walnut-, and apple-filled morsels are cradled in phyllo dough cups.

The Hungarian-style cake is called **Gugelhupf** *(right),* reput-

ed to be a favorite dessert of Marie Antoinette. Cut generous slices of this sweet yeast cake to serve with spoonfuls of the **Apricot Sauce.**

To give this late-night dessert course an elegant old-world look, we used an heirloom lace tablecloth, fine family china, and silver serving pieces. If you don't own a lace tablecloth, you might buy some inexpensive lace fabric or a pretty printed sheet to cover the table. Use pinking shears to cut some of the fabric into squares for tea napkins. Illuminate the yard with lanterns, gas lights, or tiny white Christmas lights strung across the lawn.

88

Co-Op Barbecue Plan

A barbecue for 60 guests is surprisingly easy if you use the divide-and-conquer approach—it works for any co-op project. Simply assign each couple or family to bring one menu item to the party. Since you'll need several batches of each dish to serve 60 guests, have several people bring the same item. Instruct each guest to bring the food/beverage in (or along with) its serving container, and to provide the necessary serving utensils. Don't forget to make arrangements for guests to bring eating utensils, grilling equipment, tables, and folding chairs or blankets.

Set out four or five large plastic buckets (or three plastic-lined garbage cans) filled with ice and an assortment of canned beverages. You also might rent or purchase self-dispensing stoneware crocks for lemonade or punch. If you like, provide trays and plastic bowls filled with cheese, crackers, and fruit for appetizers.

Set up four rotisserie grills in one area and assign two or three people to oversee the barbecuing. Be sure to equip each grill with oven mitts along with bowls of the marinade and basting brushes.

STEAK PINWHEEL PITAS

Multiply this recipe 4 times to make enough for 60 sandwiches—

- 2 beef round steaks (3½ to 4 pounds total)
- 1 32-ounce jar (3½ cups) extra-thick spaghetti sauce
- ¼ cup packed brown sugar
- ¼ cup lemon juice
- 2 tablespoons Worcestershire sauce
- 8 ounces fresh spinach with stems removed *or* two 10-ounce packages frozen chopped spinach, thawed and well drained
- Parsley sprigs (optional)
- Whole fresh mushrooms (optional)
- Pita bread rounds, kaiser rolls, hamburger buns, *or* thinly sliced French bread
- 2 8-ounce packages fresh alfalfa sprouts *or* wheat sprouts
- 2 cups chopped onion
- 8 ounces fresh mushrooms, sliced

Trim excess fat from meat. Without cutting meat, slash fat edges at 1-inch intervals. Pound meat with meat mallet to ¼-inch thickness. For marinade combine the spaghetti sauce, brown sugar, lemon juice, and Worcestershire sauce; stir to dissolve sugar. Place *half* the sauce in a large flat nonmetal baking dish. Place 1 steak in marinade, turning to coat. Add remaining sauce; repeat with second steak. Cover and marinate overnight in refrigerator. Drain meat; reserve marinade. Pat excess moisture from meat with paper toweling. If using fresh spinach, arrange 2 or 3 layers of leaves over each steak, overlapping as necessary so meat is completely covered. (If using frozen spinach, spread one 10-ounce package over each steak.) Roll up meat from the short side, jelly-roll fashion. Tie with string both lengthwise and crosswise.

Insert spit rod lengthwise through center of two steak rolls. Adjust holding forks; test balance. Insert meat thermometer near center of roast but not touching metal rod. Arrange *medium* coals on both sides of a drip pan in a grill with hood. Attach spit. Position drip pan under meat. Turn on motor; lower hood. Roast over *medium* coals 40 to 50 minutes or till meat thermometer registers 140° for rare or 160° for medium, basting occasionally with reserved marinade. Meanwhile, pour remaining marinade into saucepan. Place on side of grill and heat the last 15 to 20 minutes of roasting time.

To serve, remove strings from meat. Thinly slice meat crosswise; arrange it on platter. Garnish platter with parsley and whole fresh mushrooms, if desired. Serve with assorted breads, the heated sauce, sprouts, onion, and mushrooms so guests can assemble their own sandwiches. Makes 15 servings.

HASHED BROWNS SALAD

You won't need to peel and slice a mountain of potatoes to make this tasty takeoff on potato salad. Instead, simply use a package of timesaving frozen potatoes—

- 1 32-ounce package frozen loose-pack hashed brown potatoes
- 1 cup water
- ½ teaspoon salt
- 2 cups chopped celery
- 3 hard-cooked eggs, chopped
- ¼ cup sliced green onion
- 1 cup buttermilk salad dressing
- ½ cup plain yogurt *or* dairy sour cream
- 1 teaspoon celery seed
- ½ teaspoon salt
- 3 tomatoes, cut into wedges
- 2 green peppers, cut into julienne strips
- ½ cup chopped celery
- ¼ cup sliced green onion
- 1 hard-cooked egg, sliced

In Dutch oven place the potatoes, the water, and the first ½ teaspoon salt. Bring to boiling. Cook, covered, over low heat about 10 minutes or till potatoes are just tender, stirring occasionally to separate potatoes. Drain well. In the same Dutch oven combine the drained potatoes, the 2 cups celery, the chopped hard-cooked eggs, and the first ¼ cup green onion. Stir together the salad dressing, yogurt or sour cream, celery seed, and remaining ½ teaspoon salt. Pour over potato mixture, stirring gently to coat. In a large serving bowl spoon *half* of the potato salad. Top with *half* of the tomato wedges and green pepper strips. Spoon on remaining potato salad. Garnish with remaining tomato wedges, green pepper strips, ½ cup chopped celery, ¼ cup green onion, and hard-cooked egg slices in diagonal rows atop salad. Cover with clear plastic wrap and chill overnight. Makes 20 (½-cup) servings.

SWEET-SOUR VEGETABLES

2 16- *or* 20-ounce packages
  frozen loose-pack mixed
  vegetables (broccoli, carrot,
  and cauliflower blend)
4 medium cucumbers *or* zucchini,
  scored lengthwise and thinly
  sliced
2 medium onions, thinly sliced
  and separated into rings
1½ cups white wine vinegar
⅓ cup sugar
¼ cup salad oil
¼ cup soy sauce

Cook frozen vegetables, covered, in a small amount of boiling salted water for 3 minutes or till crisp-tender. Drain; run cold water over vegetables and drain again. In a large bowl combine the cooked vegetables, cucumber or zucchini, and onion. Combine vinegar, sugar, salad oil, and soy sauce. Stir till sugar is dissolved. Pour over the vegetables; toss the vegetables lightly to coat. Cover and chill 5 to 6 hours or overnight, stirring occasionally. Makes 20 (½-cup) servings.

CHEESE 'N CHOCOLATE MINI-CAKES

1 package fluffy white frosting
  mix (for 2-layer cake)
2 3-ounce packages cream
  cheese, softened
1 package 2-layer-size chocolate
  cake mix (pudding type)
1 can chocolate frosting
  Peanut halves (optional)

Prepare frosting mix according to package directions. In medium bowl beat softened cream cheese for ½ minute on medium speed; beat prepared frosting into cream cheese. Set aside. Prepare cake mix according to package directions. Fill paper bake cups in muffin pan ¼ full with cake batter (about 2 tablespoons each). Spoon about 1 tablespoon cream cheese mixture in center of each; fill cups half full with remaining batter (about 1 tablespoon each). Bake in 375° oven about 20 minutes or till done. Cool on wire racks. Frost with chocolate frosting; decorate with peanut halves, if desired. Makes about 30.

SUMMER FRUIT TART

You can bake the crust and prepare the filling for this tart up to a day ahead. Then assemble up to 6 hours before serving—

1 package piecrust mix (for 2-
  crust pie)
3 tablespoons sugar
1 tablespoon cornstarch
1 cup unsweetened pineapple
  juice
2 5-ounce jars Neufchâtel cheese
  spread with pineapple
1 cup sifted powdered sugar
⅓ cup finely chopped pecans
3 to 4 cups desired fruits: halved
  strawberries, blueberries,
  pineapple chunks, sliced
  banana, sliced peaches,
  sliced papaya, *or* halved
  grapes

Prepare pastry according to package directions. On floured surface roll dough out to a 15x10-inch rectangle. Fold pastry in half crosswise, then in half again. Transfer to a 15x10x1-inch baking pan; unfold pastry in bottom of pan. Prick surface of pastry well with fork. Bake in a 425° oven for 12 to 15 minutes or till golden. Cool in pan on a wire rack.

In saucepan stir together the sugar and cornstarch. Stir in pineapple juice. Cook and stir till mixture is thickened and bubbly; cook and stir 2 minutes more. Cover surface of mixture with waxed paper or clear plastic wrap; cool. In mixing bowl combine Neufchâtel cheese, powdered sugar, and pecans. To assemble tart, remove pastry from pan; place on large serving tray. Spread cheese mixture over pastry base to within ½ inch of edge. Arrange desired fruit over cheese. Carefully spoon cooled pineapple glaze over fruit to cover completely. Chill 2 to 6 hours. Makes 20 servings.

Totable Picnic

Invite one to 12 people to this portable party. The menu is flexible so you even can assemble the picnic on the spur of the moment. Just stop at the supermarket to pick up the makings, including purchased dips and spreads in place of the prepared recipes. Be sure to arrange for serving utensils (spreaders, spoons for the condiments, meat/cheese forks, and a knife for cutting the vegetables and fruit), serving trays, paper plates and cups, and a blanket for seating.

OPEN-FACED SANDWICH BUFFET

You'll need ¼ pound total of meat, cheese, and shrimp per person, and about ¼ cup deli salad to top each sandwich—

Assorted sliced cooked meats
  (ham, turkey, corned beef,
  roast beef, cold cuts)
Assorted sliced cheese
  (cheddar, Monterey Jack,
  Swiss)
Canned tiny shrimp, chilled,
  rinsed, and drained
Deli three-bean salad, coleslaw,
  and/or potato salad
Sliced tomatoes
Sliced cucumber
Leaf lettuce
Assorted sliced bread
  (pumpernickel, cracked
  wheat, firm-textured white,
  caraway-rye, flatbread)
1 recipe Zucchini Sandwich
  Filling
1 recipe Tomato-Bacon Spread
  Alfalfa *or* wheat sprouts
  Pickle slices
  Pitted whole *or* sliced ripe
  olives

Arrange meats, cheeses, shrimp, deli salads, tomato, cucumber, and leaf lettuce on a serving tray. Cover the tray with plastic wrap or foil and chill. At the picnic site, serve with assorted breads, Zucchini Sandwich Filling, Tomato-Bacon Spread, sprouts, pickles, and olives so guests can assemble their own sandwiches.

ZUCCHINI SANDWICH FILLING

Yogurt adds an interesting tang to this savory filling—

- 4 medium zucchini, finely shredded (4 cups)
- 1 8-ounce container plain yogurt
- ¼ cup sliced green onion
- 1 teaspoon sugar
- ½ teaspoon dried basil, crushed
- ½ teaspoon salt

Place shredded zucchini in sieve; press to remove excess liquid. In a mixing bowl stir together plain yogurt, sliced green onion, sugar, dried basil, and salt. Add drained zucchini; mix well. Place in a storage container that has a lid; chill. Stir well before serving. Makes 3 cups, or enough for 10 to 12 open-faced sandwiches.

TOMATO-BACON SPREAD

For extra zip, add a dash of bottled hot pepper sauce—

- ½ cup chili sauce
- ¼ cup tomato paste
- 6 slices bacon, crisp-cooked, drained, and crumbled
- 1 tablespoon sliced green onion

In bowl combine chili sauce, tomato paste, cooked bacon, and green onion; mix well. Transport spread in a covered container. Makes 1 cup.

VEGETABLE SALADS ALFRESCO

If you like, arrange the prepared vegetables on a platter rather than tying them into bundles—

- 4 large carrots, cut into long thin sticks
- ½ pound whole fresh green beans
- 1 pound broccoli, cut into narrow stalks
- 1 pound fresh asparagus spears
- 1 pint cherry tomatoes
- 8 to 12 green onions
- 1 bunch radishes
- 1 recipe Béarnaise Dip
- 1 recipe Easy Guacamole

Cook carrots and green beans separately, covered, in small amount of boiling salted water for 3 to 4 minutes; drain. Cook broccoli and asparagus separately, covered, in boiling salted water for 2 minutes; drain. Pour cold water over all vegetables; drain again. Wash and drain tomatoes.

To make ties for bundles, cut off green onion tops; slice tops lengthwise into eight to twelve ¼-inch-wide strips. (Save white portions for another use.) Immerse strips in boiling water for 1 minute; drain on paper toweling. To assemble bundles, tie an assortment of vegetable strips together carefully with a strip of the green onion. Place bundles, tomatoes, and radishes in plastic bags or airtight containers; chill till ready to serve.

At the picnic site, arrange vegetable bundles in serving basket or tray with tomatoes and radishes. Place containers of Béarnaise Dip and Easy Guacamole in center of tray. Makes 8 to 12 servings.

BÉARNAISE DIP

Packaged sauce mix makes easy work for this taste accompaniment—

- 1 1-ounce envelope hollandaise sauce mix
- ½ cup mayonnaise *or* salad dressing
- 2 tablespoons dry white wine
- ½ teaspoon dried tarragon, crushed
- Chicken broth (optional)

Prepare hollandaise sauce mix according to envelope directions. Stir in mayonnaise or salad dressing, wine, and tarragon; chill. (Thin with a little chicken broth, if necessary.) Makes about 1½ cups.

EASY GUACAMOLE

Lemon juice prevents the avocados from discoloring—

- 2 medium ripe avocados, seeded, peeled, and chopped
- ½ cup dairy sour cream
- 2 tablespoons lemon juice
- ¼ teaspoon onion salt
- Several dashes bottled hot pepper sauce

In blender container or food processor bowl combine chopped avocados, sour cream, lemon juice, onion salt, and bottled hot pepper sauce. Blend till mixture is smooth, scraping down sides of container as necessary. Turn mixture into a serving bowl. Cover and chill till needed. Makes about 1¾ cups.

ORANGE CREAM CHEESE

Use as a topping for the Fresh Fruit Baskets. To make the fruit baskets, hollow out melon, papaya, or grapefruit halves, or fresh pineapple quarters, reserving the scooped-out fruit. Cube reserved fruit; combine with other fruit, such as strawberries, grapes, or bananas, and spoon into the fruit shells to serve. Treat papaya and bananas with lemon juice or ascorbic acid color keeper to prevent discoloration—

- 1 8-ounce container soft-style cream cheese
- ⅓ cup orange marmalade

In small mixer bowl combine cream cheese and orange marmalade. Beat with electric mixer till combined. Turn into serving container. Makes 1⅓ cups.

Progressive Dinner

FISH IN SOUR CREAM

1 16-ounce package frozen fish
   fillets
16 ounces pickled herring
1 onion, thinly sliced
2 dill pickles, sliced (½ cup)
1 tablespoon capers
⅓ cup plain yogurt
⅓ cup dairy sour cream
⅓ cup mayonnaise *or* salad
   dressing
¼ teaspoon sugar
⅛ teaspoon dry mustard
⅛ teaspoon pepper
1 medium apple, cored and thinly
   sliced

Let frozen fish stand at room temperature for 20 to 30 minutes. Cut fish into 1-inch cubes. Place cubes of fish in greased skillet and add enough water to cover. Bring to boiling; reduce heat. Cover and simmer till fish flakes easily when tested with a fork, about 4 minutes. Drain and set aside.

Drain herring, reserving liquid. Cover and refrigerate reserved liquid. In a bowl combine fish cubes, drained herring, onion, pickles, and capers. Combine yogurt, sour cream, mayonnaise, sugar, mustard, and pepper. Add to fish mixture, stirring gently to coat. Cover and chill thoroughly. Before serving, if desired, stir a little of the reserved herring liquid into the fish mixture to make it thinner. Fold in apple. Turn mixture into serving dish; sprinkle with paprika, if desired. Makes 6 cups.

FRIED WON TON STRIPS WITH SOY-LEMON SAUCE

Fry the won ton strips and make the sauce the morning of the party (the strips will stay crisp stored in an airtight container)—

16 won ton skins (3-inch squares)
   or 4 egg roll skins
   Cooking oil for shallow-fat
   frying
¼ cup soy sauce
2 tablespoons red bean paste
2 tablespoons lemon juice
2 teaspoons brown sugar

Quarter egg roll skins. Cut won ton skins or quartered egg roll skins in ½-inch-wide strips. Fry strips, about 15 at a time, in shallow hot fat, for 30 to 60 seconds or till golden, separating pieces as they are added and stirring once. Remove with slotted spoon; drain on paper toweling. Serve with *Soy-Lemon Sauce:* In a small bowl blend soy sauce into bean paste; stir in lemon juice and sugar. Serve a small amount in individual sauce dishes or small bowls for dipping won ton strips. Makes ½ cup sauce.

TOMATO PESTO TART

For another easy appetizer, serve just the hollowed-out cherry tomatoes filled with Parsley Pesto. You need not bake the filled tomatoes, just cover and chill till serving time—

Pastry for 1-crust 9-inch pie
2 slightly beaten eggs
1 cup cream-style cottage
   cheese, sieved
½ cup dairy sour cream
½ teaspoon dried basil, crushed
6 cherry tomatoes, halved and
   seeded
1 recipe Parsley Pesto

On lightly floured surface roll out pastry to a 12-inch circle. Line a 9-inch pie plate or quiche dish with the pastry. If using pie plate, trim to ½ inch beyond edge; flute. If using quiche dish, trim to 1 inch up side of dish. Do not prick pastry. Line pastry shell with double thickness of heavy-duty foil. Bake in 450° oven 5 minutes. Remove foil. Bake 7 minutes more or till nearly done. Remove from oven. Reduce oven temperature to 325°.

Combine eggs, cottage cheese, sour cream, and basil; pour into warm pie shell. Arrange tomato halves, cut side up, atop filling. Bake in 325° oven for 20 to 25 minutes or till knife inserted off center comes out clean. Remove to wire rack. Place a teaspoon of Parsley Pesto in each tomato. Cool to room temperature. Serve at room temperature or chilled. Chill, covered, to store. Makes 12 appetizer servings.

PARSLEY PESTO

1 egg
2 tablespoons cooking oil
2 cups lightly packed fresh
   parsley sprigs
1 teaspoon dried basil, crushed
1 clove garlic, minced
¼ cup grated Parmesan cheese
3 tablespoons fine dry bread
   crumbs

In blender container or food processor bowl place the egg, cooking oil, parsley, basil, and garlic; cover and blend till pureed. Stir in grated Parmesan cheese and dry bread crumbs. Refrigerate in covered container till needed. Makes about ⅔ cup.

ARTICHOKE-MUSHROOM SALAD REMOULADE

This salad also would make an elegant first course—

2 9-ounce packages frozen
   artichoke hearts
⅔ cup mayonnaise *or* salad
   dressing
2 tablespoons dry white wine
2 tablespoons capers, chopped
1 tablespoon Dijon-style mustard
1 teaspoon dried tarragon,
   crushed
2 cups sliced fresh mushrooms
   Romaine leaves *or* Belgian
   endive
   Pimiento strips (optional)

Cook artichoke hearts according to package directions; drain. (Halve any large pieces lengthwise.) Stir together mayonnaise or salad dressing, wine, capers, mustard, and tarragon. Pour dressing mixture over warm artichokes; stir to coat. Cover and chill. To serve, add mushrooms to artichoke mixture; toss lightly to coat. Turn into lettuce-lined serving bowl; garnish with pimiento, if desired. Makes 8 servings.

MOROCCAN ORANGE SALAD

This unusual salad has a relish-like taste, so keep the servings small—

4 oranges
¼ cup lemon juice
1 tablespoon sugar
¼ teaspoon ground cinnamon
Dash salt
½ cup sliced radishes *or* white radishes
¼ cup pitted ripe olives, halved lengthwise

Cut off the peel and white membrane of oranges. Slice crosswise into very thin slices (or cut into sections). For marinade, combine lemon juice, sugar, cinnamon, and salt. Arrange orange slices on a serving dish, overlapping edges slightly. Top with sliced radishes and black olives; spoon marinade over all. Cover; chill till serving time. Serves 8.

MIDEASTERN GREEN SALAD

Before you leave for the appetizer course, wash the greens; then shake together the dressing and chill. At serving time, just assemble the ingredients—

2 cups torn spinach leaves
2 cups radish *or* lettuce leaves
1 bunch (2 cups) watercress
2 cups parsley sprigs
1½ cups feta cheese, crumbled
⅓ cup olive *or* salad oil
3 tablespoons lemon juice
1 teaspoon sugar
1½ teaspoons fresh mint leaves, finely chopped, *or* ½ teaspoon dried mint, crushed
⅛ teaspoon salt
⅛ teaspoon freshly ground black pepper
1 cucumber, seeded and coarsely shredded

Arrange greens and cheese separately on serving tray. For dressing, in screw-top jar combine oil, lemon juice, sugar, mint, salt, and pepper. Cover and shake well. Serve the assorted greens, cheese, shredded cucumber, and dressing separately; assemble individual servings, as desired. Makes 8 salads.

TABOULEH BREAD

1½ cups warm water
¾ cup bulgur
⅓ cup tomato sauce
1 medium tomato, peeled, seeded, and chopped
⅓ cup snipped parsley
2 tablespoons lemon juice
1½ teaspoons fresh mint leaves, finely chopped, *or* ½ teaspoon dried mint leaves, crushed
1 16-ounce loaf frozen white bread dough, thawed
2 teaspoons butter *or* margarine

In a bowl combine water and bulgur; let stand 1 hour. Drain, pressing out excess water. Combine drained bulgur, tomato sauce, chopped tomato, parsley, lemon juice, and mint; set aside.

On a floured surface roll dough out to a 20x10-inch rectangle. (If dough is too elastic to roll, cover and let rest for 5 to 10 minutes.) Spread bulgur mixture over dough to 1 inch from edges. Roll up dough, jelly-roll style, from long edge. Moisten and seal edge and ends. Starting from one end of roll, coil roll loosely (snail fashion) and place, seam side down, in a greased 9x1½-inch round baking pan. Cover and let rise in warm place till nearly double, about 45 to 60 minutes.

Bake in a 375° oven for 35 to 40 minutes or till done, covering with foil the last 15 minutes, if necessary, to prevent overbrowning. Remove from pan to wire rack; spread butter or margarine on top of hot loaf. Cool. Cut into wedges to serve.

INDONESIAN SÂTÉ WITH PEANUT SAUCE

If fresh coconuts are unavailable for the unsweetened coconut milk, look for canned coconut milk at an Oriental food market. Or, stir together 2 cups grated coconut and 1 cup boiling water. Let stand 5 minutes. Place mixture in blender container or food processor bowl. Cover; process 1 minute—

1 pound boneless beef round steak *or* sirloin steak, cut into 1-inch cubes
1 pound boneless lamb, cut into 1-inch cubes

1 pound chicken breasts, boned, skinned, and cut into 1-inch pieces
1 cup unsweetened coconut milk (2 coconuts)
1 small onion, grated
1½ teaspoons dry mustard
1½ teaspoons ground coriander
½ teaspoon ground turmeric
½ teaspoon salt
1 clove garlic, minced
¼ teaspoon ground cumin
Cherry tomatoes (optional)
1 recipe Peanut Sauce

Place cut-up meat in a shallow non-metal bowl. Combine coconut milk, onion, mustard, coriander, turmeric, salt, garlic, and cumin; mix well. Pour mixture over meat, tossing meat to coat. Cover and marinate meat overnight in refrigerator. Drain, reserving marinade. On skewers alternate meat cubes with chicken pieces. Grill over *medium-hot* coals about 20 minutes for medium doneness for beef and lamb, and well-doneness for chicken, basting frequently with reserved marinade. If desired, add a cherry tomato to the end of each grilled kabob before serving. Serve with Peanut Sauce. Makes 8 servings.

PEANUT SAUCE

2 tablespoons sliced green onion
1 small clove garlic, minced
2 teaspoons cooking oil
½ cup chicken broth *or* beef broth
¼ cup peanut butter
1 tablespoon soy sauce
½ teapoon finely shredded lemon peel
1 tablespoon lemon juice
1 teaspoon chili powder
½ teaspoon brown sugar
¼ teaspoon ground ginger

In a small saucepan cook green onion and garlic in hot oil till onion is tender but not brown. Stir in broth, peanut butter, soy sauce, lemon peel, lemon juice, chili powder, brown sugar, and ginger. Simmer, uncovered, about 10 minutes, stirring frequently. Remove from heat; cool. Serve sauce warm or at room temperature for dipping. Makes ¾ cup.

June

TURMERIC RICE

⅓ cup sliced green onion
1 tablespoon butter *or* margarine
1½ cups long grain rice
3 cups water
1 tablespoon lemon juice
1½ teaspoons instant beef bouillon granules
¼ teaspoon salt
¼ teaspoon ground turmeric
½ cup light raisins
Parsley sprig (optional)

In a large saucepan cook onion in butter or margarine till tender but not brown. Add rice; cook and stir over low heat till rice is golden. Add water, lemon juice, beef bouillon granules, salt, and turmeric; heat to boiling. Reduce heat; cover and simmer 15 minutes. Remove from heat and stir in raisins. Let stand, covered, for 10 minutes. Garnish with parsley, if desired. Makes 8 servings.

PIZZELLES

3½ cups all-purpose flour
2 tablespoons baking powder
3 eggs
1 cup sugar
½ cup butter *or* margarine, melted and cooled
1 teaspoon vanilla

Thoroughly stir together flour and baking powder. Beat eggs till foamy; stir in sugar. Add cooled melted butter or margarine and vanilla. Stir in flour mixture; mix well. Chill thoroughly.

Using about 2 tablespoons dough for each cookie, shape into balls. Heat seasoned pizzelle iron on top of range over medium-high heat. Place one ball of dough on iron. Squeeze lid to close; bake over medium-high gas flame or electric element about 1 to 2 minutes on each side or till golden brown. (Or, use an electric pizzelle iron according to the manufacturer's directions.) Turn wafers out onto wire rack to cool. Makes 2 dozen.

GUGELHUPF

1 package active dry yeast
¼ cup warm water (115° to 120°)
¼ cup butter *or* margarine
½ cup sugar
2 eggs
½ cup milk
2 teaspoons finely shredded lemon peel
2½ cups all-purpose flour
⅔ cup light raisins
3 tablespoons fine dry bread crumbs
Blanched whole almonds
1 recipe Apricot Sauce

Soften yeast in warm water. In small mixer bowl beat together butter or margarine, sugar, and 1 teaspoon *salt*. Add eggs; beat well. Add softened yeast, milk, and lemon peel; mix well. Add 1½ cups of the flour; beat at low speed of electric mixer for ½ minute, then beat at high speed for 2 minutes, scraping bowl constantly. By hand, stir in remaining flour. Stir in raisins. Turn mixture into a greased bowl. Cover and let rise in a warm place till double (about 2 hours).

Generously butter a 7- or 8-cup fluted tube pan. Sprinkle with bread crumbs, shaking to coat pan evenly. Arrange almonds in bottom of pan. Stir down batter; carefully spoon into prepared pan. Let rise in a warm place till almost double (about 1 hour).

Bake in a 350° oven 35 to 40 minutes or till golden. Cool 10 minutes; remove to wire rack. Cool. Serve with Apricot Sauce. Makes 1 cake.

APRICOT SAUCE

½ cup sugar
4 teaspoons cornstarch
1 12-ounce can apricot nectar
2 tablespoons butter *or* margarine
1 tablespoon lemon juice

In saucepan combine sugar and cornstarch. Stir in apricot nectar. Cook and stir over medium heat till mixture is thickened and bubbly; cook and stir 2 minutes more. Stir in butter till melted. Add lemon juice. Cover surface with waxed paper. Cool. Cover and refrigerate till serving time. Makes 1¾ cups.

BAKLAVA TARTS

The tartness from the shredded apple helps cut the richness of the sweet nut filling—

6 sheets frozen phyllo dough, thawed
1 egg white
¼ cup sugar
2 cups coarsely shredded, peeled apple
¾ cup ground walnuts
¾ cup ground almonds
⅓ cup unsalted butter *or* regular butter *or* margarine, melted
1 cup sugar
½ cup water
2 tablespoons lemon juice
1 tablespoon honey
2 inches stick cinnamon
12 whole almonds *or* walnut halves

Trim each phyllo sheet, if necessary, to a 16x12-inch rectangle. Cover phyllo with dampened towel. Beat egg white till soft peaks form (tips curl over). Gradually add the ¼ cup sugar, beating till stiff peaks form (tips stand straight). Set aside. Fold in apple and ground nuts.

Place one rectangle of the phyllo dough on a flat surface; brush with some of the melted butter or margarine. Top with a second rectangle of phyllo and brush again with butter. Repeat with remaining phyllo and butter. With long, sharp knife cut stacked phyllo lengthwise and crosswise to make twelve 4-inch squares. Place phyllo squares in buttered muffin pans, pressing gently in center to form muffin shape. Spoon about ¼ cup of the ground nut mixture into each cup. Bake in a 325° oven for 30 minutes or till golden.

Meanwhile, in a small saucepan combine the 1 cup of sugar, the water, lemon juice, honey, and stick cinnamon. Boil gently, uncovered, for 15 minutes. Remove from heat. Remove stick cinnamon. Cool syrup slightly. Spoon warm syrup over hot pastries. Cool pastries in muffin pan. Carefully remove pastries to shallow baking pan. Store, covered, in a cool place till serving time. To serve, top each pastry with a whole almond or walnut half. Makes 12 tarts.

JULY

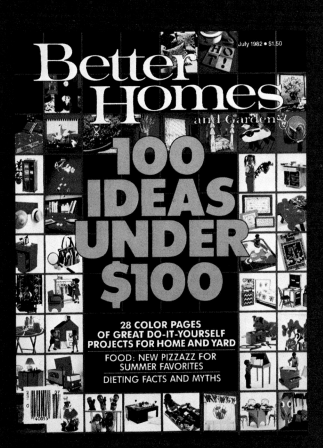

July 1982 • $1.50

Better Homes and Gardens

100 IDEAS UNDER $100

28 COLOR PAGES OF GREAT DO-IT-YOURSELF PROJECTS FOR HOME AND YARD

FOOD: NEW PIZZAZZ FOR SUMMER FAVORITES

DIETING FACTS AND MYTHS

NEW *Pizzazz*

FOR OLD FAVORITES

By Nancy Byal

Who says you can't improve on a good thing? With a bit of imagination and a dash of daring, you can make family-favorite dishes look and taste better than ever. To prove it, we selected a summer's worth of tried-and-true recipes—from anytime appetizers to company-special desserts—and made them seem brand-new and extra-special by introducing some surprising variations.

You can use this innovative approach to update and rejuvenate any old-faithful recipe in your repertoire, all through the year. And in the process, you'll make cooking more creative, more rewarding, and much more fun!

ADD A NEW *Flavor*

Even when the mercury rises, you don't have to settle for serving "the same old thing." Simply change or modify flavors in a standby, and you can stamp it "your specialty."

To give ever-popular shrimp cocktail a taste lift, try this variation. **Curried Shrimp and Cucumber Cocktail** *(left front)* combines the shrimp with savoy cabbage, cucumbers, and curry sauce.

There are as many ways to concoct daiquiris as there are fruits and liqueurs. For starters, make **Melon Daiquiri Slush** *(left back)* using cantaloupe and orange liqueur or honeydew and melon liqueur.

Chilled Spumoni Soufflé *(center back)* is a delicious spin-off on a classic Italian flavor combo—spumoni. Spoon each flavor into a separate compartment of a divided des-

sert dish, as shown; or layer the flavors in a soufflé dish.

Grilled hamburgers are good, of course, but **Great Caesar Burgers** *(right back)* are even better. To make this takeoff on the renowned salad, you accent the patties with Parmesan and anchovies, then serve them on **Caesar Toast.**

Bratwurst 'n Rye *(right center)* is a glorified version of hot dogs in a blanket. To "put on the dog," combine smoked sausage, Swiss cheese, Dijon-style mustard, and sauerkraut in a caraway-rye crust.

And for posh oven-fried chicken, try **Lahaina Chicken Rolls With Glazed Papaya** *(right front)*. Each chicken breast is all dressed up with coconut, papaya, and other Hawaiian ingredients.

Photographs: George de Gennaro. Food stylist: Mable Hoffman

STREAMLINE SUMMER Classics

While you're refurbishing your old favorites, why not make them quicker and easier at the same time? To do it, just short-cut the cooking steps and/or use time-saving ingredients.

The blender makes short work of **Pot de Crème Ice Cream** *(left front),* a frozen version of the chilled dessert classic. It doesn't even need to be beaten during the freezing!

Our **Fruit-Topped Cheese Tart** *(left center)* would do a French chef proud, but it's surprisingly easy to make. In fact, both the flaky puff-pastry crust and the velvety smooth cream cheese filling go together in just a fraction of the time it takes to make a cheesecake.

PDQ Pickles *(back)* definitely live up to their name. Most crispy bread-and-butter pickles are time-consuming to prepare, but these are an overnight wonder. Bring the spiced pickling brine to boiling, add fresh vegetables, let them steep overnight—and enjoy!

Shortcut Smoked Turkey *(right center)* is yet another time-saver. Instead of cooking the whole bird, you smoke a breast, cutting the grilling time in half. Spoon **Java Barbecue Sauce** over the servings and accompany them with **Orange Pilaf Peppers.**

Want to serve up a classic pasta dish pronto without sacrificing one iota of rich flavor? Try **15-Minute Pasta Primavera** *(right front).* It beats the clock by capitalizing on seasoned Oriental noodle mix and frozen mixed vegetables.

SERVE UP THE
Unexpected

Surprise your family and friends at mealtime *and* give them their favorite foods—simultaneously. The secret is to put the favorites together in unfamiliar ways, like the novel creations in the photograph at right.

Add cream or milk to guacamole dip, and you have glamorous **Guacamole Soup** *(left front)*. Easy-to-make **Taco Cups** are the unusual—and edible—containers for this chilly appetizer soup. To make them, simply press a clean can into the center of each flour tortilla as it fries in deep hot fat.

Antipasto Tuna Tray *(left center)* turns stylish Italian antipasto into a delectable summer main dish. Marinate tuna, plus your choice of fresh vegetables, in an herbed oil and vinegar dressing. Then arrange the ingredients on a tray or platter instead of stirring them together.

Strawberry Shortcake Alaska *(back)* is a show-off version of the all-time favorite dessert. A lightly toasted meringue conceals layers of fresh berries, shortcake, and strawberry ice cream.

Spoon the makings of a popular summer drink into an ambrosial coconut crust to create **Piña Colada Chiffon Pie** *(right center)*. It looks and tastes sensational, and it couldn't be simpler to make.

If you like eggs Benedict, you'll love **Wilted Salad Benedict** *(right front)*. It features poached eggs and **Mock Hollandaise** atop steamed spinach, broccoli, carrots, green onion, and optional Canadian-style bacon.

CHILLED SPUMONI SOUFFLÉ

You might make a raspberry sauce to spoon over each serving. Reserve ⅓ cup of the raspberry syrup and add 1 teaspoon cornstarch. Cook and stir till bubbly—

- ¼ cup sugar
- 1 envelope unflavored gelatin
- 1½ cups milk
- 4 beaten egg yolks
- ¼ cup rum
- 1 teaspoon vanilla
- 1 10-ounce package frozen raspberries, thawed
- 4 egg whites
- 2 tablespoons sugar
- 1 cup whipping cream
- ¼ cup chocolate-flavored syrup
- ¼ cup finely chopped pistachio nuts
  Few drops green food coloring (optional)
  Few drops red food coloring (optional)

Fold a 23x12-inch piece of waxed paper lengthwise in fourths. Oil one side; attach paper, oiled side in, around top of a 1-quart glass dessert dish with 3 separate sections or a 1-quart soufflé dish so the paper extends 2 inches above dish. In saucepan combine the ¼ cup sugar and the gelatin. Stir in milk; cook and stir over medium heat till gelatin dissolves. Gradually stir *half* of the hot mixture into beaten egg yolks; return to saucepan. Cook and stir 4 to 5 minutes more or till slightly thickened. *Do not boil.* Remove from heat; stir in rum and vanilla. Chill till partially set (the consistency of unbeaten egg whites), stirring occasionally. Meanwhile, drain raspberries. Reserve 3 of the berries for garnish, if desired; sieve remaining berries. Discard seeds. Beat egg whites till soft peaks form (tips curl over). Gradually add the 2 tablespoons sugar, beating till stiff peaks form (tips stand straight). Fold in partially set gelatin mixture. Beat ½ cup of the whipping cream to soft peaks; fold into mixture. Divide mixture into thirds. To one third, fold in chocolate syrup. Turn into one section of dessert dish (or bottom of soufflé dish). Fold nuts and, if desired, green food coloring into second third.

Spoon into second section of dish (or atop chocolate mixture). Fold sieved raspberries into remaining gelatin mixture. If desired, add a drop of red food coloring. Spoon into third section of dish (or over nut layer). Chill till firm, several hours or overnight. Carefully remove collar. Beat remaining cream; pipe or spread atop. Garnish with reserved berries, if desired. Makes 6 to 8 servings.

GREAT CAESAR BURGERS

Caesar Toast goes perfectly with a salad or alone as a snack cracker, too—

- 1 2-ounce can anchovy fillets
- 1 teaspoon Worcestershire sauce
  Dash pepper
- 1 pound lean ground beef
  Small romaine leaves
- 1 tablespoon grated Parmesan cheese
- 2 tablespoons sliced green onion
- 1 recipe Caesar Toast

Drain anchovy fillets. Remove 4 fillets; roll and set aside. Mash remaining anchovy fillets. Combine mashed anchovies, Worcestershire sauce, and pepper; add ground beef and mix well. Shape into four 4-inch patties. Grill over *medium-hot* coals for 5 to 6 minutes; turn and grill 4 to 5 minutes more or till desired doneness. For each serving, place one romaine leaf atop 2 or 3 pieces of Caesar Toast. Top with a meat patty, a little Parmesan cheese, green onion, and one rolled anchovy fillet. Makes 4 servings.

Caesar Toast: Cut 8 to 12 slices *French bread* ⅛ inch thick. Brush both sides of bread with *olive* or *salad oil.* Sprinkle with a little *garlic salt.* Halve crosswise. Place on baking sheet. Bake in 300° oven about 30 minutes or till slices are dry and crisp.

CURRIED SHRIMP AND CUCUMBER COCKTAIL

Thin the sauce with a little bit of milk to turn it into a wonderful vegetable or fruit salad dressing—

- 6 cups water
- 2 tablespoons salt
- 1 pound fresh *or* frozen shrimp in shells
- 1 cup sliced unpeeled cucumber
  Savoy *or* Chinese cabbage leaves
- 1 recipe Curried Cocktail Sauce

In large saucepan combine water and salt. Bring to boiling. Add shrimp. Simmer 1 to 3 minutes or till shrimp turn pink. Drain; cool slightly. Peel and devein, keeping tails intact. Cover and chill shrimp.

Arrange chilled shrimp and cucumber slices in 4 or 6 cabbage-lined dishes. Serve with *Curried Cocktail Sauce:* stir together ¼ cup *mayonnaise* or *salad dressing,* ¼ cup *plain yogurt,* and ½ to 1 teaspoon *curry powder.* Makes 4 main-dish servings or 6 appetizer servings.

MELON DAIQUIRI SLUSH

Use limeade and melon liqueur with the honeydew; lemonade and orange liqueur with the cantaloupe—

- 1½ cups cubed honeydew *or* cantaloupe melon
- ½ of a 6-ounce can (⅓ cup) frozen limeade *or* lemonade concentrate
- ⅔ cup light rum
- ⅓ cup melon liqueur *or* orange liqueur
- 3 cups ice cubes
  Melon balls (optional)
  Mint leaves (optional)

In blender container combine cubed melon with juice concentrate, rum, and liqueur. Cover and blend till smooth. With blender running, add ice cubes one at a time through hole opening in lid. (If mixture becomes too thick, add a little water.) Pour into stemmed glasses. If desired, garnish with melon balls on wooden picks and mint leaves. Store any unused slush in freezer. Makes 6 to 8 servings.

BRATWURST 'N RYE

The rye-dough wraps have a biscuit-like texture—

  8 smoked bratwurst (1½ pounds)
  1 cup all-purpose flour
  ½ cup rye flour
  2 teaspoons baking powder
  ¾ teaspoon salt
  ½ teaspoon onion powder
  ½ teaspoon caraway seed
     (optional)
  ½ cup milk
  ¼ cup cooking oil
  1 tablespoon Dijon-style mustard
  2 slices process Swiss cheese,
     cut in 8 strips
  ½ of an 8-ounce can sauerkraut,
     rinsed and drained
     Pickles (optional)
     Celery leaves (optional)
     Cherry tomatoes (optional)

In 10-inch skillet brown bratwurst; set aside. In mixing bowl combine all-purpose flour, rye flour, baking powder, salt, onion powder, and caraway seed. Add milk and oil all at once. Stir till the dough clings together in a ball. Turn out onto a lightly floured surface. Knead 10 to 12 times. Roll to a 20x10-inch rectangle; cut into eight 5-inch squares. Slit each bratwurst lengthwise, cutting just to center but not through. Spread the cut surfaces of bratwurst with a little of the mustard. Insert one strip of Swiss cheese and 1 tablespoon sauerkraut into each bratwurst. Place one bratwurst diagonally atop a square of dough; bring two opposite corners of the dough up around bratwurst. Place, seam side down, on baking sheet. Bake in a 450° oven for 10 to 12 minutes. Garnish each serving with a pickle slice, celery leaves, and cherry tomatoes, if desired. Makes 8 servings.

LAHAINA CHICKEN ROLLS

If you can't find the grated coconut, also called cookie coconut, in your supermarket, grate ½ cup shredded coconut in a blender or food processor—

  2 whole large chicken breasts (1½
     pounds), skinned, boned, and
     halved lengthwise
  ¼ cup butter *or* margarine,
     softened
  ½ cup finely chopped macadamia
     nuts *or* almonds, toasted
  2 tablespoons parsley
  1 tablespoon sliced green onion
     with tops
  ½ cup grated coconut
  ½ cup day-old bread crumbs
  1 beaten egg
  1 recipe Glazed Papaya

Place chicken, boned side up, between two pieces of clear plastic wrap. Pound out from center with meat mallet to ⅛-inch thickness. Remove wrap. Combine the butter or margarine and the chopped nuts; stir in parsley and onion. Spoon mixture into center of each chicken piece. Fold in two sides, fold over other two sides, overlapping the ends (to resemble a bundle). Press ends to seal. Combine coconut and bread crumbs. Dip chicken in egg; roll in crumb mixture. Cover; chill at least 1 hour. Place chicken, seam side down, in ungreased shallow baking pan. Bake in 375° oven for 40 minutes or till tender. Do not turn. Serve with Glazed Papaya. Serves 4.

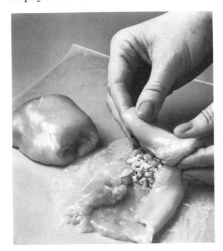

Microwave method: Pound, fill, coat, and chill chicken as directed at left. Place chicken, seam side down, in a 10x6x2-inch baking dish. Micro-cook, uncovered, on MEDIUM 10 minutes. Turn chicken over. Micro-cook, uncovered, 10 to 12 minutes or till chicken is cooked through, rotating a half-turn after 6 minutes.

GLAZED PAPAYA

  1 papaya, seeded and cut
     lengthwise into eighths
  ¼ cup guava *or* apple jelly
  2 teaspoons lime juice

Place papaya pieces, skin side down, in shallow baking pan. Melt jelly over low heat; stir in lime juice. Brush *half* the mixture over papaya. Bake in 375° oven for 8 to 10 minutes. Remove from oven; brush with remaining glaze. Makes 4 servings.

  Microwave method: Place papaya in 9-inch pie plate. Prepare glaze as directed above. Brush papaya with glaze. Micro-cook, uncovered, on HIGH for 2 minutes. Brush with remaining glaze. Cook 2 to 3 minutes more or till heated through.

PDQ PICKLES

The turmeric gives these pickles their bright yellow color—

  1 tablespoon mixed pickling spice
  ¾ cup vinegar
  ½ cup sugar
  ½ teaspoon salt
  ¼ teaspoon ground turmeric
  4 cups desired vegetables, such
     as zucchini *or* cucumber
     slices, whole cherry tomatoes
     or tomato wedges, small
     onion rings, carrot sticks

Tie mixed pickling spice in cheesecloth. In saucepan combine pickling spice bag, vinegar, sugar, salt, and turmeric; bring to boiling. Simmer 5 minutes. Remove from heat; pour over desired vegetables. Cool to room temperature. Store in covered container in refrigerator. Remove spice bag before serving. Makes about 4 cups.

FRUIT-TOPPED CHEESE TART

Choose your favorite fruits to decorate the top of this spectacular dessert—

  1 10-ounce package frozen patty
      shells, thawed
  1 8-ounce package cream cheese,
      softened
  1 1½-ounce envelope dessert
      topping mix
  ⅓ cup milk
  2 tablespoons Amaretto
  ½ teaspoon vanilla
  1 to 1½ cups fresh *or* canned
      fruit, such as sliced peaches,
      halved seedless grapes,
      sliced pears, *or* mandarin
      orange sections
  ¼ cup apricot jam
  1 tablespoon water
      Toasted sliced almonds
      (optional)

On lightly floured surface stack 2 of the patty shells and roll out to an 8-inch circle. Transfer to the bottom of a 9-inch springform pan. Trim edges to fit pan bottom. Prick well with a fork. Halve the remaining patty shells crosswise. Moisten bottoms with water to secure pastry in pan and arrange, cut-side inward, around edge of the circle; push pieces up against sides of pan slightly. Place in 450° oven; immediately reduce oven temperature to 400°. Bake 25 minutes or till puffed and golden. Carefully remove sides of pan; slide puff onto wire rack. While the puff is hot, carefully remove the center and doughy portion of each semicircle. Cool.

For filling, whip cream cheese on medium speed of electric mixer till fluffy; beat in dry topping mix. Gradually blend in milk, Amaretto, and vanilla; beat on high speed till fluffy (about 7 minutes). Turn into prepared pastry. Cover; chill 5 to 6 hours or overnight. To serve, arrange desired fruit atop tart. Combine apricot jam and water; spoon over fruit. Sprinkle with the toasted sliced almonds, if desired. Cut into wedges to serve. Makes 6 servings.

SHORTCUT SMOKED TURKEY WITH ORANGE PILAF PEPPERS

Coals are of medium-slow hotness when you can hold your hand, palm side down, about 4 inches above them for 5 seconds—

      Hickory chips
  1 3½- to 4-pound frozen turkey
      breast, thawed
      Cooking oil
  1 recipe Orange Pilaf Peppers
  1 recipe Java Barbecue Sauce

About 1 hour before cooking soak hickory chips in enough water to cover. Drain chips. In covered grill place *medium-slow* coals on both sides of a drip pan. Place a small pan of water at one end of firebox for moisture. Sprinkle coals with some dampened chips. Insert meat thermometer in center of meat, not touching bone. Place turkey breast on grill over drip pan; lower grill hood or cover with foil tent. Grill over *medium-slow* coals till meat thermometer registers 185°, about 2¼ hours. Brush meat frequently with oil. Sprinkle dampened chips over coals every 30 minutes. Add Orange Pilaf Peppers to grill over drip pan the last hour of grilling. Slice turkey; serve with Java Barbecue Sauce and Orange Pilaf Peppers. Makes 4 servings plus turkey leftovers.

ORANGE PILAF PEPPERS

  1 cup quick-cooking rice
  1 cup orange juice
  ¼ teaspoon salt
  ¼ cup sliced green onion
  ¼ cup slivered almonds, toasted
  2 teaspoons butter *or* margarine
  ½ teaspoon finely shredded
      orange peel
  2 large green peppers

Prepare rice according to package directions using the orange juice instead of water and the ¼ teaspoon salt. Stir the green onion, almonds, butter or margarine, and orange peel into the cooked rice. Remove tops from green peppers. Cut peppers in half lengthwise; remove seeds and membrane. Fill peppers with rice mixture. Wrap each vegetable in a square of heavy-duty foil. Place on grill over drip pan the last hour of smoking.

POT DE CRÈME ICE CREAM

Small servings are appropriate for this rich dessert—

  ½ cup water
  1 6-ounce package (1 cup) semi-
      sweet chocolate pieces
  3 egg yolks
  1 4-ounce container frozen
      whipped dessert topping,
      thawed
      Fresh strawberries (optional)

In small saucepan heat water to boiling. *Immediately* pour over chocolate pieces in blender container or food processor bowl. Cover and blend till chocolate is melted. Add egg yolks; cover and blend till thickened and smooth, stopping occasionally to scrape sides of blender. Remove mixture to a mixing bowl; fold dessert topping into chocolate mixture. Turn into a 9x5x3-inch loaf pan or an 8x8x2-inch pan. Cover and freeze firm. Scoop into small balls or cut into small squares to serve. Garnish each serving with a fresh strawberry, if desired. Serves 8 to 10.

JAVA BARBECUE SAUCE

¾ cup catsup
½ cup water
¼ cup chopped onion
1 clove garlic, crushed
2 tablespoons brown sugar
1 tablespoon Worcestershire
   sauce
1 teaspoon instant coffee crystals
⅛ teaspoon ground pepper

In medium saucepan combine catsup, water, onion, garlic, sugar, Worcestershire sauce, coffee crystals, and pepper. Simmer, uncovered, for 30 minutes or till desired consistency. Pass sauce with sliced turkey. Makes about 1½ cups.

15-MINUTE PASTA PRIMAVERA

The frozen vegetables may be packaged under a variety of names, such as Milan-style or Italian-style—

1 3-ounce package Oriental
   noodles with chicken flavor
1 tablespoon butter *or* margarine
3 cups frozen loose-pack mixed
   vegetables (carrots,
   cauliflower, green beans,
   zucchini, butter beans)
¼ cup water
¾ cup light cream
2 teaspoons cornstarch
   Dash pepper
   Grated Parmesan cheese

Cook Oriental noodles in boiling water according to package directions *except* do not add seasoning packet. Drain; toss with butter or margarine. Keep noodles warm over hot water. In medium saucepan combine frozen vegetables and water. Bring to boiling; reduce heat. Cover and cook 3 to 4 minutes or till just barely tender. Do not drain. Combine cream, cornstarch, pepper, and the seasoning packet from the noodle mix; add to vegetables. Cook and stir over medium heat till thickened and bubbly; cook 2 minutes more. Turn noodles onto platter or individual serving plates. Spoon vegetable mixture over. Pass Parmesan cheese to sprinkle atop. Serve at once. Makes 4 servings.

GUACAMOLE SOUP

Use a 3½-inch-diameter can to help shape the tortillas as they fry—

1 13¾-ounce can chicken broth
2 medium avocados, seeded,
   peeled, and cut into chunks
1 4-ounce can green chili
   peppers, rinsed and seeded
1 slice onion
2 tablespoons lemon juice
½ teaspoon salt
1 cup light cream *or* milk
1 large tomato, peeled, seeded,
   and chopped
1 recipe Taco Cups
   Chopped tomato (optional)

In blender container or food processor bowl combine chicken broth, avocados, chili peppers, onion, lemon juice, and salt. Cover; blend till smooth. Pour into a mixing bowl. Stir in cream and tomato. Cover; chill well. Serve in Taco Cups. Garnish with additional chopped tomato, if desired. Makes 6 servings.

Taco Cups: In saucepan or deep-fat fryer, heat 3 inches of *cooking oil* to 365°. For each taco cup place a 7- or 8-inch *flour tortilla*, one at a time, in hot oil. Using tongs, hold a clean 3½-inch-diameter can atop tortilla and press it against the bottom of the pan for 20 to 30 seconds or till tortilla is golden. Lift can and tortilla from oil; drain the shaped tortilla well on paper toweling. Repeat to make 6 cups total.

ANTIPASTO TUNA TRAY

Have your guests choose their favorite vegetables to go with the tuna and assemble their own salads—

1 cup celery bias-cut into ½-inch
   pieces
1 cup sweet red *or* green peppers,
   cut into chunks
1 small onion, sliced and
   separated into rings
½ cup tarragon vinegar
¼ cup dry white wine
2 tablespoons salad oil
2 tablespoons sugar
1 clove garlic, minced
½ teaspoon paprika
¼ teaspoon salt
¼ teaspoon dried basil, crushed
   Dash pepper
1 bay leaf
1 6½-ounce can tuna (water
   pack), drained
2 medium tomatoes, seeded and
   cut into thin wedges
1 cup whole fresh mushrooms

Cook celery in small amount of boiling, lightly salted water for 5 minutes; drain. Set aside. Cook red or green pepper chunks and onion, separately, in boiling, lightly salted water for 3 minutes; drain. Set aside. For marinade, in small saucepan combine tarragon vinegar, white wine, salad oil, sugar, garlic, paprika, salt, basil, pepper, and bay leaf; bring to boiling. Remove from heat.

Meanwhile, arrange all the vegetables in a 12x7½x2-inch dish. Place the drained tuna in a shallow bowl; pour the marinade over the vegetables and the tuna. Cover and refrigerate for several hours or overnight, spooning the marinade over occasionally. Remove the vegetables and the tuna from the marinade with a slotted spoon and arrange on a serving tray or a platter. Makes 4 servings.

STRAWBERRY SHORTCAKE ALASKA

Framboise is a raspberry liqueur—

- 1 pint strawberry ice cream, softened
- 2 cups all-purpose flour
- 2 tablespoons sugar
- 1 tablespoon baking powder
- ½ teaspoon salt
- ½ cup butter *or* margarine
- 1 beaten egg
- ⅔ cup milk
- ¼ cup framboise, orange liqueur, *or* fruit juice
- 3 cups sliced fresh strawberries
- 5 egg whites
- ½ teaspoon cream of tartar
- ½ teaspoon vanilla
- ⅔ cup sugar

Foil-line an 8-inch round pan; spoon in ice cream, spreading evenly. Freeze firm. Thoroughly stir together flour, the 2 tablespoons sugar, the baking powder, and salt. Cut in the butter or margarine till the mixture resembles coarse crumbs. Combine beaten egg and milk; add all at once to dry ingredients and stir just till moistened. Spread evenly in a greased 9x1½-inch round baking pan. Bake in 450° oven for 15 to 18 minutes or till done. Cool in pan 10 minutes; remove from pan. Cool completely on wire rack. Split in half horizontally. Sprinkle cut sides of shortcake with liqueur or fruit juice. Place bottom of shortcake on wood board, pizza baker, or baking sheet. Place ice cream atop; remove foil. Place *half* the berries and remaining shortcake on top. Arrange remaining berries atop shortcake. Return to freezer just while preparing egg whites. Beat egg whites, cream of tartar, and vanilla till soft peaks form (tips curl over). Gradually add remaining sugar; beat till stiff peaks form (tips stand straight). Remove cake and ice cream from freezer. Spread meringue over cake, sealing to bottom of board or pan. Bake in 500° oven for 3 to 4 minutes. Serve immediately. Makes 10 to 12 servings.

WILTED SALAD BENEDICT

The mock hollandaise doubles as a sauce for the eggs and a dressing for the vegetables—

- ½ cup broccoli flowerets
- ½ cup bias-sliced carrots
- 2 tablespoons sliced green onion
- 4 cups torn fresh spinach
- 4 eggs
- ¼ cup dairy sour cream
- ¼ cup mayonnaise *or* salad dressing
- 1 teaspoon lemon juice
  Dash bottled hot pepper sauce
- ½ cup diced, fully cooked ham *or* Canadian-style bacon (optional)
  Shredded carrot (optional)

Place broccoli flowerets and sliced carrots in steamer basket; place over, but not touching, boiling water. Cover; reduce heat. Steam 8 minutes; add sliced green onion and steam 2 minutes more or till vegetables are barely tender. Add the spinach, steam 1 to 2 minutes more or till spinach begins to wilt (leaves should still hold their shape).

Meanwhile, poach eggs in greased poacher cups 4 to 5 minutes or till desired doneness. Meanwhile, for mock hollandaise, in a small saucepan combine the dairy sour cream, the mayonnaise or salad dressing, the lemon juice, and the bottled hot pepper sauce. Cook and stir over low heat till heated through. *Do not boil.*

To serve, divide vegetable mixture among 2 individual steamer baskets or dinner plates; sprinkle with diced, fully cooked ham or Canadian-style bacon, if desired. Top each with 2 of the eggs. Spoon some of the mock hollandaise over. Garnish eggs with shredded carrot, if desired. Serve immediately. Makes 2 servings.

PIÑA COLADA CHIFFON PIE

For this recipe, don't use fresh pineapple juice because it will keep the gelatin from setting—

- 1 envelope unflavored gelatin
- ¼ cup sugar
- ⅛ teaspoon salt
- ¾ cup unsweetened pineapple juice
- 2 teaspoons lemon juice
- 3 slightly beaten egg yolks
- ¼ cup light rum
- 3 egg whites
- 2 tablespoons sugar
- 1 cup whipping cream
- 1 recipe Coconut Crust, baked and cooled
  Crushed pineapple (optional)
  Chopped candied cherries (optional)

In medium saucepan combine unflavored gelatin, the ¼ cup sugar, and the salt. Add pineapple juice, lemon juice, and egg yolks; mix well. Cook and stir over medium heat till gelatin dissolves and mixture is slightly thickened. Remove from heat; cool slightly. Stir in rum. Chill till consistency of corn syrup, stirring occasionally. Remove gelatin mixture from refrigerator while beating egg whites. Immediately beat egg whites till soft peaks form (tips curl over). Gradually add the remaining sugar, beating till stiff peaks form (tips stand straight). When gelatin is partially set, fold in egg whites. Beat cream to soft peaks; fold whipped cream into gelatin mixture. Chill mixture till it mounds when dropped from a spoon. Turn into cooled *Coconut Crust.* Chill overnight or till firm. Garnish with a ring of crushed pineapple and chopped cherries, if desired.

Coconut Crust: In mixing bowl combine 2 cups flaked *coconut* and 3 tablespoons *butter* or *margarine,* melted. Turn coconut mixture into a 9-inch pie plate. Press mixture evenly onto bottom and up sides to form a firm, even crust. Bake in 325° oven about 20 minutes or till golden. Cool thoroughly on wire rack.

AUGUST

See recipe page 187.

FRESH·FROM·THE·FARM FRUIT & VEGETABLE RECIPES

BY JOY TAYLOR, DORIS EBY, AND NANCY BYAL

The summer crops are in, and produce bins everywhere —from roadside markets to gourmet food shops—are overflowing with melons, berries, corn, and more! Since capitalizing on these healthful and versatile foods calls for some know-how, we decided to consult the experts—families who grow and sell fruits and vegetables for their livelihood. The families we chose not only are produce pros, but they also are past masters at cooking their crops. On the next few pages the Kozlowskis, the Youngses, the Redmans, and the Wilsons share their expertise and favorite recipes to help you cook up the freshest-tasting meals ever!

Photographs: Fred Lyon. Field editor: Helen Heitkamp

FRUIT SPECIALTIES FROM SONOMA COUNTY

"The only way a small ranch can survive is for all the family to work together." This commitment has proved successful for Tony and Carmen Kozlowski on their 26-acre ranch in Sonoma County, California.

Several generations of the Kozlowskis work on their apple and berry ranch—from Carmen's 76-year-old mother, Julia, to her 12-year-old granddaughter, Tracy. Carmen and her married daughter, Carol Every, manage the colorful produce stand where the ranch's harvest is sold, while Carmen's husband, Tony, and son, Perry, oversee the ranch's operation.

The Kozlowskis grow several apple varieties—Gravenstein, Rome, Jonathan, Red Delicious, Granny

Smith—but their favorite summer apple is the Gravenstein. "The Gravenstein was called the ugly apple for years," Perry says, "because it did not have a long shelf life. But it's our favorite all-around apple for eating and cooking because of its sweetness and juiciness, and its thin skin."

In addition to selling apples, the Kozlowskis stock their produce stand with the raspberries, blueberries, boysenberries, and blackberries that grow amongst the apple trees; the vegetables from Julia's garden; walnuts and vegetables from Perry's farm; and the family's homemade jams and ciders.

The Kozlowskis are creative when it comes to cooking their abundant crops. Carol even assembled the family's favorite recipes to share with customers, and some of the best are featured here.

The Kozlowski clan often show off their various fruits in delectable desserts. *Opposite page (clockwise from the top right):* **Raspberry Meringue, Raspberry-Almond Tart, Red Raspberry Crepes, Raspberry-Apple Pie,** plus **Sonoma Sangria.**

Above right: **Zucchini Bread** and **Zucchini Pickles** are two ways the family uses the abundant squash crop. The Kozlowskis' **Raspberry-Apple Cider** has celebrity status in Sonoma County. Try our version on page 117.

Above center: Julia's Spanish heritage has influenced many family recipes including this **Favorite Pepper Salad** and **Gazpacho.**

FRUIT & VEGETABLE RECIPES

Jo-Hana and Paula set high standards for all the big-batch foods they prepare at the farm. "We carefully select quality ingredients just as a home cook would do," says Jo-Hana. Here's a sampling of their irresistible sweets *above (clockwise from left)*: **Peach and Brown Sugar Muffins** and **Blueberry Corn Muffins**; **Peach Jam Bread** (in basket); **Rhubarb Bread**; **Strawberry-Pineapple Jam**; **Thumbprint Cookies**; **Blueberry Pie**. *Opposite page:* For home-style eating, the Youngs rely on their vegetable crops. **Hot Red Cabbage** and **Cucumber Relish** are family standbys. **Tomato Quiche** shows off abundant tomatoes.

BAKERY BONANZA ON LONG ISLAND

John and Vivian Youngs' pioneering spirit continues to revitalize their 91-year-old family farm. For decades, the bounty from this six-generation farm was transported to produce markets in New York City. But in 1960, John and Vivian built a farm stand on their 80 acres. Then, seven years ago, a new dimension was added to their produce stand—"fresh baked goods with homemade flavor"—thanks to the enterprising spirit of their daughters, Jo-Hana and Paula. The two women started making and selling fresh-made jams plus a few baked goods to make use of overripe fruit that would otherwise be thrown away. The innovation was an instant success and led to a full-time bakeshop that enlisted all the Youngses in a common effort.

Paula and Jo-Hana have enjoyed collecting recipes and cooking for years.

Photographs: Bradley Olman. Field editor: Bonnie Maharam

They grew up watching the skilled hands of their grandmother at work in the kitchen. Then Paula reinforced her interest in cooking by earning a bachelor's degree in home economics.

The sisters get their recipe ideas from several sources, including friends and old cook books. "We'll try a recipe and we'll change it till it's perfected," says Jo-Hana. "Most recipes are too sweet for our taste so we invariably reduce the sugar."

John and Vivian now supervise the farm's produce stand, while Jo-Hana and Paula mix up batches of goodies in their assembly-line kitchen. With the help of four employees, they bake 60 to 100 pies a day, in addition to bakery-casefuls of muffins, breads, and cookies.

This family cooperation has resulted in one of the finest produce stands and bake shops on Long Island. And, says Jo-Hana, "It's nice to work and have all the family around."

FRUIT & VEGETABLE RECIPES

Photographs: Fred Lyon

Many Redman recipes feature peaches and nectarines. **Opposite page** (clockwise from front right): **Glazed Nectarine Pie, Peach Kuchen, Peach Custard Crunch,** and **Peaches and Cream Pie.** When the fresh fruits aren't in season, the Redmans use preserved fruits. **Top** (clockwise): **Nectarine-Pear Jam, Brandied Applesauce, Dried Cherries, Cherry Vinegar,** and **Dried Cherry Bread.**
Left: Nectarine-Cherry Chicken Salad is a fresh summer main dish.

ORCHARD FAVORITES FROM WASHINGTON STATE

The Redman family of Wapato, Washington, are celebrating big this year. It's the 50th anniversary of the Redmans' life on their farm. In 1932, Ray Redman, Sr., and his wife, Elizabeth, purchased a modest 20-acre peach, pear, and apricot orchard. In the years that followed, they were joined by their son, Ray, Jr.; grandson, Ray III (Gip); and their respective families in building one of the largest and most successful tree fruit ranches in the famed Yakima Valley. This three-generation family business today includes 350 acres of sweet cherries, peaches, nectarines, apples, and pears, plus wholesale packing facilities and a roadside market.

The Redmans attribute their success to "down-to-earth" ideas. First and foremost, the family is dedicated to growing and selling only the best fruit. Throughout the years of expansion, the Redmans have managed to maintain high quality, and be innovators in fruit growing and processing. The second reason for their success, as Carol Redman sees it, is that the family genuinely enjoy their common enterprise. "We may complain a lot from time to time," she says, "but we all love what we do."

The Redmans have another interest in common: cooking. Pat, Ray, Jr.'s wife, is an avid recipe collector. She's noted for creating the unexpected and never wasting ripe fruit. Ray, Jr., has acquired a reputation for his luscious **Peach Daiquiris.** And Carol is always seeking new fresh fruit desserts. The Redmans shared a few of their favorite summer recipes with us so we could pass them along to you.

FRUIT & VEGETABLE RECIPES

Lynne's creative way with recipes pays off, as you'll discover when you try her inventions. *Right (clockwise from top right):* **Pasta With Broccoli and Sausage, Vegetable Rutabaga Soup, Celeriac Soup, Mixed Summer Vegetables,** and **Spinach Frittata.** When Alan had a bumper crop of vegetables, Lynne came up with these salads. *Above (clockwise from top):* **Fresh Cauliflower Salad, Marinated Green Beans,** and **Parsnip Slaw.**

HOME-STYLE COOKING IN MASSACHUSETTS

Family commitment, team spirit, and the highest quality product and service—these components spell success for Wilson Farms in Lexington, Massachusetts.

First cousins Alan Wilson and Donald Wilson run this 98-year-old family farm where almost every imaginable fruit and vegetable is grown. Donald oversees the cultivation of the 35 acres in Lexington and a 250-acre family farm in New Hampshire, with help from his wife, Betty, and their sons, Jimmy and Calvin.

Alan manages the retail end of the operation which includes stocking their rustic produce stand. And when Alan's children, Lesley and Scott, are home from college, they work as field hands side by side with several cousins.

Lynne Wilson, Alan's wife, is responsible for the produce stand's most

Photographs: Bradley Olman. Field editor: Estelle Guralnick

popular customer service—free recipes featuring the farm's crops. When a fruit or vegetable crop is prolific, Lynne creates a new recipe around it. "I improvise on old recipes, substituting this for that," says Lynne. Once a recipe is tested and perfected, it's offered at the produce stand. "I sell the produce, and

Lynne tells people how to prepare it," is how Alan describes their joint effort to provide complete customer service.

"Customer demand has determined our growth," reflects Alan. New crops are planted every year to satisfy buying trends, too. When fresh herbs became popular, for example, the Wilsons

devoted several acres to basil, tarragon, dill, and oregano plants. Basil is even grown hydroponically in a greenhouse to ensure a year-round supply.

To the Wilsons, "Satisfaction Guaranteed" is not an idle slogan but a serious commitment that they take pride in fulfilling.

August

RASPBERRY MERINGUE

4 egg whites
¾ teaspoon cream of tartar
¼ teaspoon salt
1⅓ cups sugar
2 cups fresh *or* frozen
    unsweetened raspberries,
    thawed
¼ cup sugar
½ teaspoon unflavored gelatin
½ cup water
1 tablespoon lemon juice
2 3-ounce packages cream
    cheese, softened
¼ cup sugar
1 teaspoon vanilla
2 cups whipping cream
1 cup miniature marshmallows

In large mixer bowl beat the egg whites, cream of tartar, and salt till soft peaks form (tips curl over). Gradually add the 1⅓ cups sugar, beating till stiff peaks form (tips stand straight). Cover baking sheet with plain brown paper. Using the rim of a 9-inch pie plate, draw a circle on paper. Spread meringue over circle on paper. Build up the sides with the back of a spoon to form a shell. (Make the bottom ½ inch thick and sides about 2 inches high.) Bake meringue in a 275° oven for 1 hour. Turn off oven; let meringue stand in oven with door closed for 1 hour more. Remove from oven. Peel off paper. Cool on rack.

Mash and sieve ½ cup of the berries. In saucepan combine the first ¼ cup sugar and the gelatin; stir in mashed berries, the water, and lemon juice. Stir over low heat till gelatin is dissolved. Remove from heat. Cool to room temperature. Add remaining raspberries. Cover and chill.

In mixing bowl beat together cream cheese, the remaining sugar, and the vanilla. Beat whipping cream till soft peaks form (tips curl over). Fold a small amount of whipped cream into cream cheese mixture; fold in remaining whipped cream and the miniature marshmallows.

To assemble, fill meringue with cream mixture; spread mixture over outside of entire shell. Chill 5 hours or overnight. At serving time, top with fruit mixture. Cut into wedges using a wet knife. Makes 10 servings.

RED RASPBERRY CREPES

1 4-ounce container whipped
    cream cheese
10 Dessert Crepes
2 tablespoons toasted slivered
    almonds
3 tablespoons sugar
1 tablespoon cornstarch
    Dash salt
1 cup cranberry juice cocktail
1 tablespoon butter *or* margarine
1 tablespoon orange liqueur
1 tablespoon lemon juice
1 pint fresh raspberries *or* one
    10-ounce package frozen red
    raspberries, thawed and
    drained
¼ cup toasted slivered almonds

Spread cheese over unbrowned side of each Dessert Crepe, leaving a ¼-inch rim around edge. Sprinkle each crepe with a portion of the 2 tablespoons almonds. Fold each crepe into a triangle by folding in half, then in half again. Cover crepes; set aside.

For sauce: In a 10-inch skillet combine the sugar, cornstarch, and salt. Stir in cranberry juice and butter or margarine. Cook and stir till thickened and bubbly. Cook and stir 2 minutes more. Stir in liqueur, lemon juice, and berries. Add crepes to sauce; heat through. Sprinkle the ¼ cup almonds atop. Serve immediately. Serves 10.

Dessert Crepes: In mixing bowl combine 1 cup *all-purpose flour,* 2 tablespoons *sugar,* and ⅛ teaspoon *salt.* Add 2 *eggs,* 1½ cups *milk,* and ¼ cup melted *butter* or *margarine.* Beat with a rotary beater till well mixed. Heat a lightly greased 6-inch skillet. Remove from heat. Spoon in 2 tablespoons batter; lift and tilt skillet to spread batter. Return to heat; brown on one side (do not turn). Invert pan over paper toweling; remove crepe. Repeat with remaining batter, greasing skillet as needed. Makes about 16 crepes.

RASPBERRY-ALMOND TART

6 cups fresh *or* frozen
    unsweetened raspberries
¾ cup sugar
1 tablespoon lemon juice
2 inches stick cinnamon
    (optional)
2 cups all-purpose flour
2 cups finely ground unblanched
    almonds
½ teaspoon baking powder
⅔ cup butter *or* margarine
⅔ cup sugar
1 egg
½ teaspoon vanilla
½ teaspoon finely shredded
    lemon peel

In saucepan combine the raspberries, the ¾ cup sugar, the lemon juice, and cinnamon. Boil gently, stirring frequently, about 45 minutes or till mixture is reduced to 2 cups. Discard cinnamon. Set mixture aside to cool.

Meanwhile, stir together the flour, ground almonds, and baking powder; set aside. In a large mixer bowl beat the butter or margarine on medium speed of electric mixer about 30 seconds. Add the ⅔ cup sugar and beat till light and fluffy. Add egg, vanilla, and lemon peel; beat till blended. Gradually add the flour mixture to the creamed mixture, beating well. Cover and chill for 30 minutes or till firm.

Reserve one-third of the dough for the lattice top. On floured surface roll remaining dough to a 14-inch circle; line the bottom and sides of an 11-inch quiche dish with dough. Spread cooled fruit mixture evenly over crust. On a lightly floured surface roll the reserved dough to an 8x5½-inch rectangle. Cut into eight 1-inch wide strips. Using a long spatula, carefully transfer dough strips, one at a time, to the top of tart. Place strips in a spoke fashion, meeting all in the center of the tart. Press strips to edges of crust to seal. Bake tart in a 350° oven about 35 minutes or till crust is lightly browned. If necessary, cover edge of tart with foil to prevent overbrowning. Makes 12 servings.

RASPBERRY-APPLE PIE

Pastry for 2-crust 9-inch pie
¾ cup sugar
3 tablespoons quick-cooking
    tapioca
⅛ teaspoon ground cinnamon
⅛ teaspoon ground nutmeg
3 tablespoons butter or
    margarine, melted
3 cups thinly sliced, peeled
    apples
3 cups fresh or frozen
    unsweetened red raspberries,
    thawed

Prepare and roll out half the pastry to
a 12-inch circle. Line a 9-inch pie plate
with the circle of pastry; trim to edge
of pie plate. Mix the sugar, tapioca,
cinnamon, nutmeg, and butter. Add
apples and raspberries; toss to coat. Let
mixture stand 15 to 20 minutes. Turn
berry mixture into pastry-lined pie
plate. Roll out remaining pastry. Cut
slits in top crust for escape of steam;
place pastry atop filling. Seal and flute
edge. Cover edge of pie with foil. Bake
in 375° oven 20 minutes. Remove foil;
bake 20 to 30 minutes. Cool on rack.

FAVORITE PEPPER SALAD

4 sweet red or green peppers
1 small red onion, sliced and
    separated into rings
3 stalks celery, thinly sliced
    (1 cup)
2 tablespoons snipped parsley
⅓ cup olive or salad oil
¼ cup red wine vinegar
1 clove garlic, crushed
¼ teaspoon salt
Lettuce

Place whole peppers on a baking sheet.
Roast in a 500° oven, turning peppers
every 2 to 3 minutes till all sides are
roasted evenly. Put hot roasted peppers into a covered container. Let stand
30 minutes. Peel off skins. Slice peppers into thin strips or cube.
    In a small bowl combine the pep-
pers, onion, celery, and parsley. Mix
together the oil, vinegar, garlic, and
salt; pour over vegetables. Toss lightly
to coat. Cover and chill. Drain vegetables before serving. Serve in a lettuce-lined bowl. Serves 8.

SONOMA SANGRIA

In large pitcher combine 4 cups *dry red
wine,* 2 cups *apple cider* or *apple juice,*
and 1 cup *carbonated water.* Add 1 medium *apple,* cored and sliced; 1 medium *peach,* pitted and sliced; and 1
medium *orange,* sliced. Stir in 1 cup
brandy, if desired. Serve over ice.
Serves 10 to 12.

RASPBERRY-APPLE CIDER

Thaw one 12-ounce package frozen
loose-pack lightly sweetened *raspberries.* Crush by pressing against the side
of a bowl with the back of a spoon. Add
4 cups *apple cider* or *apple juice* to
crushed berries and juice. Cover and
chill. Strain liquid through double-
thickness cheesecloth; discard seeds.
Serve chilled over ice. Makes 4½ cups.

GAZPACHO

1 medium sweet red pepper
½ of a medium red onion
1 medium cucumber
1 46-ounce can tomato juice
3 tablespoons vinegar
2 tablespoons olive or salad oil
2 cloves garlic, minced
1 teaspoon salt
    Condiments, such as chopped
    pimientos, chopped red
    onion, chopped cucumber,
    and croutons

In blender container or food processor
bowl blend the red pepper till chopped.
Remove from container. Blend the ½
onion in blender container or food processor bowl till chopped. Remove from
container. Blend the 1 medium cucumber in blender container or food
processor bowl till chopped. In large
bowl combine the chopped red pepper,
onion, and cucumber; stir in the tomato juice, vinegar, olive oil, garlic, and
salt. Cover and chill. To serve, spoon
soup into individual bowls. Pass condiments to sprinkle atop each serving.
Serves 8 to 10.

PEACH AND BROWN
SUGAR MUFFINS

4 cups all-purpose flour
⅔ cup packed brown sugar
2 tablespoons baking powder
½ teaspoon baking soda
¼ teaspoon ground allspice
2 eggs
2 cups dairy sour cream
½ cup milk
½ cup cooking oil
1 cup chopped fresh, frozen, or
    canned peaches

Stir together the flour, sugar, baking
powder, baking soda, allspice, and 1
teaspoon *salt.* Make a well in the center. Combine eggs, sour cream, milk,
and oil; stir in peaches. Add peach
mixture all at once to the flour mixture. Stir just till moistened; batter
should be lumpy. Grease muffin pans
or line with paper bake cups; fill ⅔ full.
Bake in a 400° oven for 20 to 25 minutes. Serve warm. Makes about 24
muffins.

ZUCCHINI BREAD

1½ cups all-purpose flour
1 cup whole wheat flour
2 teaspoons ground cinnamon
1 teaspoon baking soda
½ teaspoon baking powder
3 eggs
2 cups packed brown sugar
2 cups finely shredded unpeeled
    zucchini
¾ cup cooking oil
2 teaspoons finely shredded
    lemon peel
1 teaspoon vanilla
½ cup sunflower nuts (unsalted)
    or 1 cup pinenuts

Stir together the flours, cinnamon,
baking soda, baking powder, and 1
teaspoon *salt.* In mixer bowl beat the
eggs, brown sugar, and zucchini. Add
oil, lemon peel, and vanilla; mix till
well blended. Stir flour mixture into
zucchini mixture. Fold in nuts. Turn
batter into two greased 8x4x2-inch loaf
pans. Bake in a 350° oven about 50
minutes. Cool in pan 10 minutes; cool
on wire rack. Wrap; store overnight
before slicing. Makes 2 loaves.

ZUCCHINI PICKLES

    3 pounds firm zucchini
    2 pounds small onions
    ¼ cup pickling salt
    3 cups vinegar
    2 cups sugar
    2 teaspoons mustard seed
    1 teaspoon celery salt
    1 teaspoon ground turmeric

Thinly slice zucchini. Quarter onions; thinly slice. In large bowl add enough water to cover zucchini and onions; stir in pickling salt. (For crisper vegetables, add ice.) Let stand at room temperature for 2 hours. Drain; rinse and drain thoroughly.

In large saucepan combine the vinegar, sugar, mustard seed, celery salt, and ground turmeric. Bring to boiling. Remove from heat. Add zucchini and onion. Let stand 2 hours. Bring to boiling. Reduce heat; simmer, uncovered, 5 minutes. Pack vegetables and liquid into hot, clean pint jars; leave a ½ inch headspace. Wipe rims. Adjust lids; process in boiling water bath for 15 minutes (start timing when water boils). Makes 6 pints.

BLUEBERRY CORN MUFFINS

Be careful not to mash the berries when folding them into the batter—

    1½ cups all-purpose flour
    1½ cups cornmeal
    ½ cup sugar
    1 tablespoon baking powder
    ¼ teaspoon salt
    2 beaten eggs
    1 cup milk
    ½ cup cooking oil
    2 cups fresh *or* frozen
        blueberries, thawed

In large mixing bowl stir together the flour, cornmeal, sugar, baking powder, and salt. Make a well in the center. Combine the eggs, milk, and oil; add all at once to flour mixture. Stir just till moistened; batter should be lumpy. Fold in fresh or frozen berries. Grease muffin pan or line with paper bake cups; fill each about ⅔ full. Bake in a 400° oven for 20 to 25 minutes or till golden. Remove from pans. Serve warm. Makes 18 muffins.

PEACH JAM BREAD

    1½ cups all-purpose flour
    ¾ teaspoon salt
    ½ teaspoon baking soda
    ½ teaspoon ground cinnamon
    ½ teaspoon ground nutmeg
    ¾ cup sugar
    ⅓ cup shortening
    2 eggs
    ¾ cup peach jam
    ½ teaspoon vanilla
    ½ cup buttermilk

In mixing bowl stir together the flour, salt, soda, cinnamon, and nutmeg; set aside. In large mixer bowl beat the sugar and shortening on high speed of electric mixer till light and fluffy. Beat in the eggs, one at a time, beating 1 minute after each. Add peach jam and vanilla; mix well. Add flour mixture and buttermilk alternately to creamed mixture, beating well after each addition. Pour batter into two greased and floured 7½x3½x2-inch loaf pans. Bake in a 350° oven for 40 to 45 minutes or till wooden pick inserted near center comes out clean. Cool in pans 10 minutes. Remove from pans. Cool thoroughly on wire racks. Makes 2 loaves.

STRAWBERRY-PINEAPPLE JAM

    3½ cups crushed strawberries
        (6 cups whole berries)
    1½ cups chopped fresh pineapple
        (8 ounces)
    1 1¾-ounce package powdered
        fruit pectin
    7 cups sugar

In an 8- or 10-quart kettle combine the crushed strawberries, pineapple, and pectin. Bring to a full rolling boil. Stir in sugar. Return to a full rolling boil. Boil hard, uncovered, for 1 minute, stirring constantly. Remove from heat; quickly skim off foam with a metal spoon. Ladle jam at once into hot, clean half-pint jars, leaving a ¼-inch headspace. Wipe jar rims; adjust lids. Process in boiling water bath for 15 minutes (start timing when water boils). Makes 7½ half-pints.

CUCUMBER RELISH

    2 medium cucumbers, seeded
    ¼ cup mayonnaise *or* salad
        dressing
    ¼ cup vinegar
    2 tablespoons chopped pimiento
    2 teaspoons grated onion
    ½ teaspoon salt
        Few dashes pepper

Coarsely shred cucumbers; wrap in cheesecloth and press out excess liquid. Place cucumbers in bowl; stir in the mayonnaise, vinegar, pimiento, onion, salt, and pepper. Cover and chill. Drain well before serving. Spoon cucumber mixture into a lettuce-lined bowl. Makes about 2½ cups.

RHUBARB BREAD

    2¾ cups all-purpose flour
    1½ cups packed brown sugar
    1 teaspoon baking soda
    1 teaspoon salt
    1 beaten egg
    1 cup buttermilk
    ½ cup cooking oil
    1 teaspoon vanilla
    1 cup finely chopped fresh *or*
        frozen rhubarb, thawed and
        drained
    2 tablespoons all-purpose flour
        Butter *or* margarine
        Granulated sugar

Grease four 6x3x2-inch loaf pans, three 7½x3½x2-inch loaf pans, or two 8x4x2-inch loaf pans; set aside.

Stir together the 2¾ cups flour, the brown sugar, baking soda, and salt. Combine egg, buttermilk, oil, and vanilla. Stir into dry ingredients; mix well. Toss rhubarb with the 2 tablespoons flour; fold rhubarb into batter. Pour batter into prepared pans. Dot each loaf with two to three teaspoons butter; sprinkle each with two to three teaspoons granulated sugar. Bake in a 350° oven till a wooden pick inserted near the center comes out clean. Bake the 6x3x2-inch loaves about 40 minutes; bake the 7½x3½x2-inch loaves about 45 minutes; or bake the 8x4x2-inch loaves about 55 minutes. Cool in pans 10 minutes. Remove from pans; cool thoroughly on wire rack. Makes 2 to 4 loaves.

THUMBPRINT COOKIES

You can buy the nut butter or make your own with a food processor—

1½ cups butter *or* margarine
1¼ cups sugar
1 egg
¾ cup (6 ounces) almond butter, cashew butter, *or* peanut butter
3½ cups all-purpose flour
Jam *or* preserves

In mixer bowl beat butter on medium speed of electric mixer for 30 seconds. Add the sugar; beat till creamy. Add egg and nut butter; beat well. Add flour; beat till well blended. Cover and chill about 1 hour. Using 1 tablespoon dough for each, shape into 1¼-inch balls; place on ungreased cookie sheets. Press down centers with thumb. Fill centers with desired jam or preserves. Bake in a 350° oven for 10 to 12 minutes or till done. Remove to wire rack; cool. Makes about 7 dozen cookies.

Nut Butter: Place steel blade in food processor work bowl. Add 2 cups blanched whole almonds, toasted, or 2 cups raw cashews, toasted, or 2 cups cocktail peanuts. Process till butter forms, stopping to scrape sides of bowl occasionally to make sure mixture is evenly blended. (This will take 3 to 5 minutes.) Continue processing about 2 minutes or till smooth. Makes 1¼ cups. (Store remaining nut butter in covered container in refrigerator.)

BLUEBERRY PIE

Pastry for 2-crust 9-inch pie
¾ cup sugar
¼ cup all-purpose flour
4 cups fresh *or* frozen blueberries
2 tablespoons lemon juice
1 to 2 teaspoons sugar

On floured surface roll out *half* of the pastry to a 12-inch circle. Line a 9-inch pie plate with pastry circle. Trim pastry to edge of pie plate. In a mixing bowl combine the ¾ cup sugar and the flour. Add berries; toss gently. Let berry mixture stand for 10 minutes, stirring occasionally. Stir in lemon juice. Turn berry mixture into pie plate.

For top crust, roll out remaining pastry to a 12-inch circle. Cut a 2-inch circle out of the center of the top crust; place pastry atop filling. Seal and flute edge. Sprinkle with the 1 to 2 teaspoons sugar. To prevent the pastry from overbrowning, cover edge of pie with foil. Bake in a 375° oven for 20 minutes. Remove foil and bake for 25 to 30 minutes more or till golden. Cool pie on wire rack before serving. Serve slightly warm or cool.

TOMATO QUICHE

It's important to use light cream, not milk, in this brunch-style entrée—

Pastry for 1-crust 9-inch pie
1 tablespoon chopped green onion
1 tablespoon butter *or* margarine
1 cup coarsely chopped, peeled, and seeded tomatoes (2 medium)
1 cup shredded Swiss cheese
2 tablespoons grated Parmesan cheese
4 beaten eggs
1 cup light cream
¼ teaspoon salt

Prepare pastry. On floured surface roll out pastry till dough is ⅛ inch thick. Line a 9-inch quiche dish or pie plate with pastry. Trim pastry; flute edge. *Do not prick.* Line pastry with double thickness of heavy-duty foil. Bake in a 450° oven for 5 minutes. Carefully remove foil. Bake 5 to 7 minutes more or till golden. Remove from oven; reduce oven temperature to 325°. (Pastry shell should still be hot when you add filling; do not partially bake ahead of time.)

Meanwhile, in skillet cook onion in butter or margarine till tender. Remove from heat. Stir tomato and cheese into onion. Spoon tomato mixture into pastry shell. Beat together eggs, cream and salt; pour over tomato mixture in dish. Bake in a 325° oven 30 to 35 minutes or till almost set in center. Let stand 5 minutes. Makes 8 servings.

GLAZED NECTARINE PIE

⅔ cup sugar
3 tablespoons cornstarch
Dash salt
3 ripe medium nectarines, peeled, pitted, and mashed
⅓ cup water
1 9-inch baked pastry shell, cooled
6 medium nectarines, pitted and diced *
2 medium nectarines, pitted and sliced *or* quartered
Whipped cream

In a small saucepan combine sugar, cornstarch, and salt. Stir in the mashed fruit and water. Cook and stir till mixture is thickened and bubbly. Cook and stir 2 minutes more. Remove from heat; cover surface with clear plastic wrap. Set aside to cool.

Spread about ¼ cup of the cooled mixture in the bottom of the baked pastry shell. Reserve ⅓ cup of the cooled mixture; set aside. Combine diced fruit with remaining mixture, stirring to coat fruit well. Turn into the pastry shell.

Top with sliced or quartered fruit; spoon the reserved ⅓ cup mixture over pie. Cover and chill several hours. To serve, fill center of pie with whipped cream. If using the quartered fruit, cut wedges of pie between the quarters.

*Note: To prevent the nectarines from turning brown, dice and slice or quarter them into a prepared solution of ascorbic acid color keeper or lemon juice mixed with water; drain the nectarines well before using.

PEACH DAIQUIRIS

3 large ripe peaches *or* nectarines, peeled and pitted
2 tablespoons fresh lime juice
½ cup light rum *or* vodka
3 tablespoons sugar
3 cups crushed ice

Place fruit and juice in blender. Cover; blend till smooth. Add liquor and sugar. Cover; blend. With blender running, add ice through opening in lid; blend till slushy. Serves 9.

HOT RED CABBAGE

1 medium head red cabbage,
  shredded (about 7 cups)
  Water
2 tablespoons butter *or*
  margarine
1 beaten egg
¼ cup vinegar
3 tablespoons sugar
2 teaspoons prepared mustard

In saucepan cook cabbage in a small amount of boiling salted water for 8 to 10 minutes or till tender. Drain well. In the same pan melt the butter or margarine. Combine egg, vinegar, sugar, and mustard; stir into melted butter. Add cabbage. Cook and stir for 1 to 2 minutes or till cabbage is coated and heated through. Turn into cabbage-leaf-lined serving bowl. Serve immediately. Makes 6 servings.

PEACH KUCHEN

1½ cups all-purpose flour
¼ cup sugar
1 tablespoon baking powder
¼ teaspoon salt
1 slightly beaten egg
½ cup milk
⅓ cup shortening, melted
1 slightly beaten egg
1 8-ounce carton dairy sour
  cream
⅓ cup sugar
3 peaches, peeled, pitted, and
  quartered *or* sliced
  Ground cinnamon

In mixing bowl stir together the flour, the ¼ cup sugar, the baking powder, and salt. Combine the first egg, milk, and melted shortening; add to flour mixture. Mix well. Spread in a greased 9x9x2-inch baking pan. Bake in a 350° oven for 15 minutes. Remove from oven. In bowl combine the remaining egg, sour cream, and the ⅓ cup sugar. Spread evenly over partially baked kuchen. Arrange peach quarters or slices atop. Sprinkle cinnamon over peaches. Continue baking 15 minutes more. *Do not overbake.* Cool on wire rack. Serve warm or chilled. Serves 10.

PEACHES AND CREAM PIE

2½ cups all-purpose flour
1 teaspoon salt
6 tablespoons butter *or*
  margarine
⅓ cup lard
6 to 8 tablespoons ice water
½ cup sugar
3 tablespoons all-purpose flour
¼ to ½ teaspoon ground nutmeg
4 cups peeled, sliced peaches
  (8 medium)
½ cup whipping cream
½ teaspoon vanilla

For pastry, in mixing bowl stir together the 2½ cups flour and the salt. Cut in butter and lard till pieces are the size of small peas. Sprinkle in ice water, one tablespoon at a time, stirring with a fork just till dough forms a ball. Wrap and chill at least 1 hour. On floured surface roll *half* the pastry to a 12-inch circle. Ease pastry into a 9-inch pie plate, being careful to avoid stretching pastry. Trim pastry even with rim.

Combine sugar, the 3 tablespoons flour, and nutmeg; add peaches. Toss to coat. Stir in cream and vanilla. Pour filling into pastry-lined pie plate. Roll out remaining pastry for top crust. Place over top of pie. Trim top crust ½ inch beyond edge of pie plate. Fold extra pastry under bottom crust; flute edge. Cut slits for escape of steam.

Cover edges of pie with foil to prevent overbrowning. Bake in a 450° oven for 20 minutes. Reduce heat to 350°; continue baking 45 to 50 minutes, removing foil after 15 minutes.

CHERRY VINEGAR

Substitute this for ordinary vinegar in vegetable salads—

1 cup fresh dark sweet cherries,
  pitted
2 cups vinegar

Place the pitted cherries in a glass jar or bottle; pour in the vinegar. Cover tightly. Let stand at room temperature at least 2 weeks before using. Makes about 2 cups.

PEACH CUSTARD CRUNCH

4 egg yolks
1 cup light cream
¼ cup packed brown sugar
½ teaspoon finely shredded
  orange peel
⅛ teaspoon salt
¼ cup muscatel wine
3 large peaches, peeled, halved,
  and pitted
  Coarsely crushed peanut brittle
  or chopped nuts

In a heavy saucepan beat the egg yolks slightly; blend in the cream, brown sugar, orange peel, and salt. Cook and stir over medium heat till mixture just comes to a boil. Remove from heat and stir in the wine. Turn into a bowl; cover and chill thoroughly.

To serve, pour some of the custard mixture into each of six stemmed glasses. Place one peach half in each glass; sprinkle peanut brittle or nuts over the top. Makes 6 servings.

NECTARINE-PEAR JAM

2 cups finely chopped, ripe
  nectarines (about 1 pound)
2 cups finely chopped, peeled,
  ripe pears (about 1 pound)
4 teaspoons finely shredded
  orange peel
¼ cup orange juice
3 tablespoons lemon juice
7½ cups sugar
1 6-ounce package (2 foil
  pouches) liquid fruit pectin

In an 8- or 10-quart kettle combine nectarines, pears, orange peel, orange juice, and lemon juice. Stir in sugar. Bring mixture to a full rolling boil; boil hard, uncovered, for 1 minute, stirring constantly. Remove from heat; stir in the pectin. Quickly skim off foam with a metal spoon. Ladle jam at once into hot, clean half-pint jars, leaving ¼-inch headspace. Wipe jar rims; adjust lids. Process in boiling water bath for 15 minutes (start timing when water returns to boiling). Makes 7 to 8 half-pints.

DRIED CHERRIES

2 pounds fresh dark sweet
    cherries

Wash cherries; remove stems. Place cherries in steamer basket over boiling water; steam 2 minutes. Let cherries stand in basket till cool enough to handle. Halve cherries; remove pits. Use food dehydrator according to manufacturer's directions. *Or,* place cherries on stainless steel racks in a single layer. Preheat oven to 200°. (If broiling element of oven comes on, put a cookie sheet on rack in uppermost shelf position.) Place rack with cherries in oven at least 8 inches from heat source. Allow space between racks for air to circulate freely. Dry fruits 5½ to 6 hours, rotating racks with cherries once or twice. Turn off oven the last hour if necessary to prevent scorching. Cool fruit completely. (Dried fruit should be leathery yet sticky when cool.) Store in a tightly covered container. Makes 1½ cups.

NECTARINE-CHERRY
CHICKEN SALAD

½ cup mayonnaise
2 tablespoons vinegar
2 tablespoons honey
1 teaspoon lemon juice
½ teaspoon curry powder
⅛ teaspoon ground ginger
3 cups cubed cooked chicken
1½ cups thinly sliced celery
3 medium nectarines, pitted and
    sliced (1½ cups)
1½ cups dark sweet cherries,
    halved and pitted
1 tablespoon thinly sliced green
    onion
½ cup toasted, slivered almonds
    Leaf lettuce

For dressing, combine mayonnaise, vinegar, honey, lemon juice, curry powder, ginger, and ⅛ teaspoon *salt;* set aside. Combine the cooked chicken, celery, nectarines, cherries, and green onion. Pour the dressing over chicken mixture; toss lightly to mix. Chill several hours. At serving time, add the toasted almonds and toss with salad. Serve in a lettuce-lined bowl. If desired, garnish with a few nectarine wedges. Serves 6.

DRIED CHERRY BREAD

3 eggs
2 cups chopped, peeled apples
1 cup cooking oil
1 cup sugar
½ cup milk
1 teaspoon vanilla
2 cups all-purpose flour
1 cup whole wheat flour
⅓ cup wheat germ
2 teaspoons baking soda
1 teaspoon baking powder
1 teaspoon salt
1 teaspoon ground cinnamon
1 recipe Dried Cherries *or*
    snipped raisins
⅔ cup chopped pecans

In mixer bowl beat eggs, apples, oil, sugar, milk, and vanilla on medium speed of electric mixer for 1 minute. Stir together flours, wheat germ, baking soda, baking powder, salt, and cinnamon. Blend into egg mixture. Beat on high speed for 40 seconds. Stir in cherries and nuts. Pour batter into two greased 8x4x2-inch loaf pans. Bake in a 350° oven for 45 to 50 minutes or till wooden pick inserted near center comes out clean. Cool in pans 10 minutes. Remove from pans; cool thoroughly on wire racks. Wrap; store overnight before slicing. Makes 2 loaves.

BRANDIED APPLESAUCE

8 to 10 cups peeled and coarsely
    chopped Golden Delicious
    apples
1 cup water
⅓ to ½ cup packed brown sugar
⅓ cup brandy

In a large heavy saucepan combine the chopped apples, water, and brown sugar. Bring to boiling. Reduce heat; cover and simmer 35 to 40 minutes or till of desired consistency, stirring frequently. Add more water, if necessary, to keep mixture from sticking. Add brandy and cook, covered, 5 minutes longer. Cool. Store in refrigerator. Or, if desired, spoon into 1-pint moisture-vaporproof freezer containers, leaving ½-inch headspace; seal, label, and freeze. Makes about 5 cups.

CELERIAC SOUP

3½ cups chopped celeriac
1 cup sliced leeks
½ cup chopped onion
3 cups chicken broth
½ teaspoon salt
2 cups light cream

In 3-quart saucepan combine celeriac, leeks, and onion; add chicken broth and *salt.* Bring to boiling; reduce heat. Simmer, covered, for 25 to 30 minutes or till vegetables are very tender. Transfer *half* of the vegetable mixture to blender container or food processor bowl; cover and blend till smooth. Repeat with remaining vegetable mixture. Return pureed mixture to saucepan. Gradually add the light cream. Heat through. Season to taste. Serve hot or cold. Garnish with parsley sprigs, if desired. Serves 10.

Cauliflower-Leek Soup: Prepare Celeriac Soup as directed above, *except* substitute 3½ cups *sliced cauliflower* for the celeriac and use only *2 cups* chicken broth.

VEGETABLE RUTABAGA SOUP

1½ pounds lean beef stew meat,
    cut into ½-inch cubes
6 cups water
2 cups beef broth
1 medium onion, quartered
2 cloves garlic, minced
2 teaspoons salt
½ teaspoon dried basil, crushed
⅛ teaspoon pepper
1 bay leaf
2 cups peeled, cubed rutabaga
1 cup sliced carrot
1 cup sliced celery
1 onion, sliced
1½ cups peeled, chopped tomato
2 tablespoons tomato paste
1 cup elbow *or* shell macaroni

Combine meat, water, beef broth, quartered onion, garlic, salt, basil, pepper, and bay leaf. Bring to boiling; reduce heat. Cover; simmer for 45 minutes. Stir in rutabaga, carrot, celery, sliced onion, tomato, and tomato paste. Return to boiling; reduce heat. Simmer, covered, for 45 minutes. Add macaroni. Simmer 15 minutes more. Remove bay leaf. Sprinkle with Parmesan cheese, if desired. Serves 9.

PASTA WITH BROCCOLI AND SAUSAGE

⅓ cup whipping cream
3 eggs
1½ pounds Italian sweet sausage links, sliced into ¼-inch pieces
1 cup sliced fresh mushrooms
1 clove garlic, minced
2 tablespoons butter or margarine
3 cups broccoli flowerets
1½ cups (6 ounces) elbow macaroni or shell macaroni
1 cup grated Romano or Parmesan cheese
⅛ teaspoon pepper

Let cream and eggs come to room temperature. In a small skillet cook the sausage slices till browned and cooked through. Drain off fat. Remove sausage; keep it warm. In same skillet cook the mushrooms and garlic in the butter or margarine till tender. Meanwhile, cook the broccoli, covered, in a small amount of boiling salted water about 8 minutes or till tender. Drain. Cook macaroni according to package directions; keep hot.

Beat whipping cream, eggs, cheese, and pepper. Stir. Toss macaroni and cream mixture; stir in mushrooms. Arrange on serving platter. Spoon broccoli and sausage atop. Toss; serve at once. Serves 6.

PARSNIP SLAW

3 cups peeled, shredded parsnips
¾ cup chopped celery
½ cup finely chopped green pepper
½ cup thinly sliced radishes
½ cup mayonnaise or salad dressing
3 tablespoons Italian salad dressing

Combine the parsnips, celery, green pepper, and radishes. Combine mayonnaise, Italian salad dressing, ¼ teaspoon *salt*, and ⅛ teaspoon *pepper*; add to vegetables. Stir gently to coat. Cover; chill thoroughly. Garnish salad with whole radishes, if desired. Makes 8 side-dish servings.

MIXED SUMMER VEGETABLES

½ cup chopped onion
1 clove garlic, minced
2 tablespoons butter or margarine
2 cups coarsely chopped zucchini
2 cups fresh corn kernels
2 cups peeled, seeded, and chopped tomato
2 to 3 tablespoons fresh snipped basil or 2 to 3 teaspoons dried basil, crushed

In a 10-inch skillet cook the onion and garlic in the butter or margarine till tender but not brown. Add the zucchini; cook and stir over medium heat about 3 minutes. Stir in the corn; cook and stir 2 to 3 minutes more. Stir in the tomato and basil. Cook 1 minute more or till vegetables are heated through, but tomatoes are still firm. Season to taste with salt and pepper. Makes 8 servings.

FRESH CAULIFLOWER SALAD

4 cups sliced cauliflower flowerets (1 small head)
½ cup chopped green pepper
¼ cup chopped onion
⅔ cup dairy sour cream
3 tablespoons mayonnaise or salad dressing
1 teaspoon dry mustard
1 teaspoon sugar
1 tablespoon snipped fresh dill or 1 teaspoon dried dillweed
Few dashes bottled hot pepper sauce
2 medium tomatoes, seeded and chopped

In large bowl stir together the cauliflower, green pepper, and onion. Combine the sour cream, mayonnaise or salad dressing, mustard, sugar, dill, and hot pepper sauce. Season to taste with salt and pepper. Gently stir dressing into vegetable mixture. Cover and chill several hours. Just before serving, carefully stir tomato into salad. Makes 10 servings.

SPINACH FRITTATA

10 ounces fresh spinach leaves
⅓ cup thinly sliced green onion
2 tablespoons butter or margarine
6 beaten eggs
¼ cup light cream or milk
½ teaspoon salt
⅛ teaspoon pepper
1 cup shredded Swiss cheese

Wash and trim spinach. Cook spinach over medium-low heat, covered, just till wilted. Drain well. Chop and set aside.

In a 10-inch oven-going skillet cook onion in butter. Spread spinach evenly in bottom of skillet. Beat together eggs, cream, salt, and pepper; pour over spinach. Cook over medium-low heat. As eggs set, run a spatula around the edge of skillet, lifting egg mixture to allow uncooked portion to flow underneath. Continue cooking and lifting edges till almost set (surface will be moist). Place skillet under broiler 5 inches from heat; broil for 1 to 2 minutes or just till top is set. Sprinkle with cheese before serving. Serves 4.

MARINATED GREEN BEANS

1 pound fresh green beans
½ cup salad oil
½ cup wine vinegar
1 tablespoon snipped fresh dill or 1 teaspoon dried dillweed
1 clove garlic, minced
½ teaspoon dry mustard
½ teaspoon sugar
½ teaspoon salt
⅛ teaspoon pepper
1 small onion, thinly sliced

Wash beans; remove ends and strings. Cook beans, covered, in a small amount of boiling salted water for 20 to 30 minutes; drain well. Meanwhile, mix oil, vinegar, dill, garlic, mustard, sugar, salt, and pepper. Combine cooked beans and onion. Pour marinade over vegetables. Cover; chill several hours or overnight. Drain before serving. Makes 8 servings.

SEPTEMBER

HOW TO MAKE MEALS
MORE
NUTRITIOUS

BY NANCY WALL

It sometimes seems that we Americans are on a culinary collision course. Our interest in creative cooking has never been higher. But simultaneously, we're keenly aware of the importance of eating nutritious meals. What's a person to do?

The answer: adapt your planning and cooking habits so you can enjoy fun-to-fix foods and a nutritionally balanced diet. And to make that adaptation easy, we provide ten practical guidelines for nutritious eating and illustrate them with 25 wonderful recipes. Happy and healthful eating!

▶ FOCUS ON LOW-FAT DAIRY PRODUCTS

Did you know that most Americans consume six to eight tablespoons of fat a day yet need only the equivalent of one tablespoon? Fats are necessary in our diet for energy, but enough is enough! An easy way to start a fat-curbing program is to substitute low-fat dairy products—such as low-fat cottage cheese, skim milk or low-fat milk, cheeses made with part-skim milk, Neufchâtel cheese, and part-skim ricotta cheese —for dairy products that are higher in fat. Case in point: **Spaghetti Pizza** features both low-fat farmer cheese and part-skim mozzarella cheese. In keeping with the low-fat idea, we also used lean ground turkey as a meaty topper.

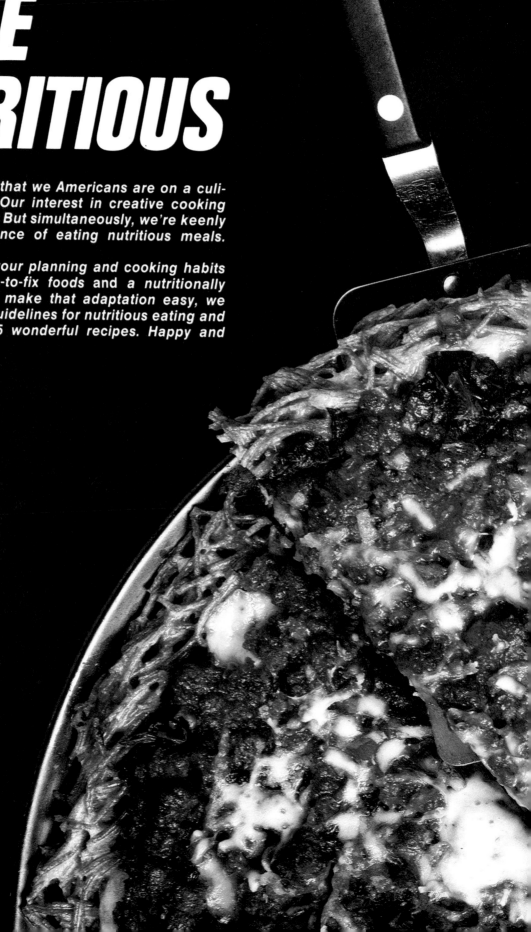

▲ CAPITALIZE ON VEGETABLES IN SNACKS AND DESSERTS

Pack extra nutrition into nibbles and desserts by incorporating raw, cooked, pureed, or shredded vegetables into your recipes. Vegetables supply fiber, vitamins, minerals, and add flavor to everyday treats. **Surprise Cake Roll** gets a nutritional lift from mashed sweet potatoes.

Photographs: William Sladcik. Food stylist: Fran Paulson

▲ ENJOY NATURALLY SWEET DESSERTS

Sugar is America's number one flavor booster. In fact, we consume enough sugar to add about 600 calories per day to the diet. Most of the sugar we consume is in desserts. But that doesn't mean you have to swear off all desserts if you're counting calories.

You can still have "sweets" in your menus if you capitalize on the sweetness that's naturally found in many foods. *Pearadise Pie*, for example, gets all its deliciousness from the sugars found in bananas, strawberries, pears, and cantaloupe.

More than 70 percent of the protein we eat comes from meat, fish, poultry, egg, dairy sources. In some cases, more of the calories in these foods come from their fat t from their protein. The trick is to limit your fat intake by searching out the leanest cut meat, fish, and poultry, and trimming any visible fat before you cook them.

For *Teriyaki Marinated Steak With Sweet-Sour Vegetables,* we chose a lean bone round steak, trimmed the visible fat, marinated the meat for extra juiciness, and t broiled it—all without adding any additional fat.

▶ DOUBLE UP ON EGG WHITES

Eggs are a high-quality source of protein. Unfortunately, the yolk contains fat and cholesterol. If you're watching your fat intake, monitor the number of yolks you eat. But take advantage of the egg whites—they're an excellent low-fat source of protein. *Cheese and Onion Popovers,* wisely substitute egg whites for the traditional whole eggs.

◀ ADD VARIETY WITH WHOLE GRAINS

Whole grains pack fiber that aids in digestion and makes you feel satisfied. The filling in *Bulgur Salad Pockets* is one hearty example.

▶ DRIZZLE ON LOW-FAT SALAD DRESSINGS

You may think you're doing your figure a favor when you have a salad for lunch or dinner. But because most salad dressings are oil-based, you may have added unnecessary and unwanted calories the second you splashed the dressing on. The alternative? Eliminate the oil. Here are some tasty examples.

Plain yogurt, tofu, and chopped spinach are blended to give **Tofu Dressing** its creamy texture. A dillweed, basil, and garlic combination gives **Zesty Salad Dressing** its zippy flavor. Our **Mock Mayonnaise** will taste almost like the real thing, but it's made without the oil. Another low-calorie wonder is **Gingered-Poppy Seed Dressing.** It gets a nutrition lift from orange juice.

▲ IMPROVISE WITH UNIQUE FLAVOR SEASONINGS

We consume two to four teaspoons of salt every day, yet we need only about $1/10$ teaspoon. Besides posing a threat to health, too much added salt overpowers the natural flavor of the foods being prepared. What's the solution? Try seasoning foods with an herb or spice combination or wine, vinegar, or lemon juice. Bitters, an aromatic blend of herbs and spices, were used to season **Orange-Sauced Chicken.**

▶ COMBINE A SIDE DISH AND DESSERT

There's no need to skip a nutritious side dish to allow for a rich dessert. Simply combine a side dish and a dessert into one course. That way, you save calories while still providing a well-balanced meal. For after dinner, plan a slightly sweet bread or a whole grain pudding. We combined the bread and dessert portion of a meal in **Banana Surprise Muffins.**

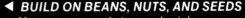

◀ BUILD ON BEANS, NUTS, AND SEEDS

Yes, you need to replenish your protein stockpile every day to build and repair tissues. But that doesn't mean all of your protein should come from the same kinds of foods. Although you probably get more than two-thirds of your protein from meats and dairy products, you don't need more than about one-third of your protein from those sources. For better variety, call on beans, nuts, and seeds to supply some of your daily quota of protein. Try **Hearty Vegetable Stew** for starters. It gives you as much protein as you would get from a regular meat entrée—and all the protein comes from kidney beans and garbanzo beans, plus crunchy peanuts.

SPAGHETTI PIZZA

8 ounces whole wheat spaghetti
1 tablespoon cooking oil
2 beaten eggs
1 cup shredded farmer *or* mozzarella cheese (4 ounces)
1 pound raw ground turkey
½ cup chopped onion
¼ cup chopped green pepper
1 clove garlic, minced
1 7½-ounce can tomatoes, cut up
1 6-ounce can tomato paste
1½ teaspoons dried basil, crushed
1 teaspoon dried marjoram, crushed
¼ teaspoon salt
⅛ teaspoon ground nutmeg
1 cup low-fat cream-style cottage cheese, drained *or* part-skim ricotta
4 slices mozzarella cheese (4 ounces)
1 10-ounce package frozen chopped spinach, thawed and well drained

For crust: Cook spaghetti in boiling salted water according to package directions; drain. Stir together the drained pasta, the oil, eggs, and ¼ *cup* of the shredded farmer cheese. Press spaghetti mixture into a greased 14-inch pizza pan, building edges high, to form a crust. Bake in 400° oven for 10 minutes.

For filling: In skillet cook the turkey, onion, green pepper, and garlic till meat is browned and vegetables are tender. Stir in *undrained* tomatoes, tomato paste, basil, marjoram, salt, and nutmeg. Spread cottage cheese or ricotta cheese over bottom of spaghetti crust. Layer mozzarella cheese slices atop. Spoon thawed spinach atop, then the turkey mixture. Cover pizza with foil. Bake in a 400° oven for 12 to 15 minutes. Uncover; sprinkle with remaining shredded farmer cheese. Bake 2 minutes longer or till cheese is melted. Makes 8 servings.

Per serving: 329 calories, 26 g protein, 31 g carbohydrate, 11 g fat, 412 mg sodium.

SURPRISE CAKE ROLL

¾ cup all-purpose flour
1 teaspoon baking powder
1 teaspoon ground ginger
¼ teaspoon ground nutmeg
3 eggs
¾ cup granulated sugar
⅔ cup mashed, cooked sweet potatoes
1 teaspoon lemon juice
¾ cup finely chopped pecans
¾ cup sifted powdered sugar
1 15-ounce carton part-skim ricotta cheese (about 2 cups)
1 teaspoon vanilla
Skim milk
Pecan halves

Grease and lightly flour a 15x10x1-inch jelly-roll pan. Mix flour, baking powder, ginger, and nutmeg. In a small mixer bowl beat eggs at high speed of electric mixer 5 minutes or till thick and lemon colored. Gradually add granulated sugar, beating till sugar dissolves. Stir in mashed sweet potatoes and lemon juice. Fold dry ingredients into sweet potato mixture. Spread evenly in prepared pan. Sprinkle with the finely chopped nuts. Bake in a 375° oven for 12 to 15 minutes or till done. Immediately loosen edges of cake from pan and turn out onto a towel sprinkled lightly with *1 tablespoon* of the sifted powdered sugar. Starting with narrow end of cake, roll warm cake and towel together so nuts are on outside of cake. Cool, seam side down, on a wire rack.

For filling: In small mixer bowl beat together ricotta cheese, the remaining powdered sugar, and vanilla till smooth. If mixture becomes too stiff, beat in 1 to 2 tablespoons additional skim milk. Set aside one-third of the filling (about ⅔ cup). Unroll cake; spread with the remaining filling. Roll up cake. Transfer to platter. Using a pastry bag, pipe the reserved filling atop cake to decorate. Garnish top of cake roll with nut halves. Pipe the remaining filling between additional pecan halves, if desired. Place filled nuts alongside cake roll. Serves 10.

Per serving: 284 calories, 9 g protein, 38 g carbohydrate, 12 g fat, 113 mg sodium.

PEARADISE PIE

Each serving of this light and luscious dessert has only 233 calories—

3½ cups flaked whole grain cereal
¼ cup wheat germ
6 tablespoons butter *or* margarine, melted
1 12-ounce can pear nectar
1 tablespoon cornstarch
1 teaspoon vanilla
2 small bananas, sliced
2 tablespoons lemon juice
1 tablespoon water
2 cups sliced fresh pears
2 cups fresh strawberries, sliced
½ of a small cantaloupe, seeded, sliced, and peeled

For crust: Place cereal in a plastic bag or between 2 sheets of waxed paper. Crush into fine crumbs; measure 1¼ cups crumbs. Place crumbs in medium mixing bowl; stir in wheat germ and melted butter or margarine. Toss to thoroughly combine. Turn into a 9-inch pie plate. Press onto bottom and up sides to form a firm, even crust. Bake in a 375° oven for 4 to 6 minutes. Cool thoroughly on wire rack.

Meanwhile, in saucepan combine pear nectar and cornstarch. Cook and stir over medium heat till thickened and bubbly. Cook and stir 2 minutes longer. Stir in vanilla. Set aside.

To assemble pie: In small bowl combine lemon juice and water. Dip banana and pear slices in lemon juice mixture, being careful not to mash bananas. Layer ¼ cup of the glaze, all the banana slices, another ¼ *cup* of the glaze, all the strawberries, and another ¼ *cup* of the glaze. Next, arrange pear and cantaloupe slices atop glaze, alternating every three pear slices with one cantaloupe slice. Top with remaining glaze mixture. Chill 2 to 4 hours. Before serving, garnish with additional strawberries. Serves 8.

Per serving: 233 calories, 4 g protein, 37 g carbohydrate, 10 g fat, 247 mg sodium.

ZESTY SALAD DRESSING

    1 tablespoon cornstarch
    1 teaspoon sugar
    ½ teaspoon dried dillweed
    ¼ teaspoon dried basil, crushed
    ⅛ teaspoon garlic powder
    ¼ cup catsup
    3 tablespoons tarragon vinegar
  1½ teaspoons Worcestershire
        sauce

Mix the cornstarch, sugar, dillweed, basil, garlic powder, and ¼ teaspoon *salt.* Add 1 cup *cold water,* catsup, vinegar, and Worcestershire. Cook and stir till bubbly; cook and stir 2 minutes more. Cover; chill. Makes 1⅓ cups.

Per tablespoon: 6 calories, 2 g carbohydrate, 64 mg sodium.

MOCK MAYONNAISE

    ½ teaspoon unflavored gelatin
    3 tablespoons vinegar
    2 egg yolks
    1 egg
    ½ teaspoon sugar
    ¼ teaspoon dry mustard
    ¼ teaspoon paparika

In saucepan soften gelatin in ¼ *water* and vinegar. In blender container place egg yolks, egg, sugar, mustard, paprika, and ½ teaspoon *salt.* Cover; blend 5 seconds. Bring gelatin mixture to boiling. With lid ajar and blender running at high speed, slowly pour in hot gelatin mixture. Blend 60 seconds. Cover; chill. Beat smooth with rotary beater. Makes ¾ cup.

Per tablespoon: 18 calories, 1 g protein, 1 g fat, 96 mg sodium.

GINGERED POPPY-SEED DRESSING

Combine ½ of a 1¾-ounce package *powdered fruit pectin,* 1 teaspoon *poppy seed,* and ⅛ teaspoon *ground ginger.* Stir in 1 cup *orange juice,* 2 tablespoons *honey,* and 2 tablespoons *lemon juice.* Cover; chill. Stir well before serving. Makes 1½ cups.

Per tablespoon: 13 calories, 3 g carbohydrate.

TERIYAKI MARINATED STEAK WITH SWEET-SOUR VEGETABLES

    ½ cup dry sherry
    1 tablespoon soy sauce
    1 tablespoon grated gingerroot or
        1 teaspoon ground ginger
    1 clove garlic, minced
  1½ pounds boneless beef round
        steak, cut 1½ inches thick and
        trimmed of separable fat
    1 cup sliced cauliflower flowerets
    ½ cup water
    1 8-ounce can pineapple chunks
        (juice pack)
    1 2-ounce jar sliced pimiento
    1 tablespoon cornstarch
    1 medium green pepper, cut into
        1-inch squares
    1 tablespoon vinegar
    1 teaspoon paprika
    ½ teaspoon instant beef bouillon
        granules

For marinade: Combine sherry, soy sauce, gingerroot, and garlic. Pierce all surfaces of meat with a long-tined fork. Place meat in plastic bag; set it in shallow dish. Add marinade to bag; close bag. Turn bag to coat all surfaces of meat. Refrigerate for 8 hours or overnight, turning bag serveral times to distribute marinade. Drain meat; reserve marinade. Pat meat dry with paper toweling. Place meat on unheated rack of broiler pan. Broil 4 inches from heat till meat is desired doneness (14 to 16 minutes for medium rare), brushing occasionally with reserved marinade and turning once. Meanwhile, in medium saucepan cook cauliflower in the ½ cup water, covered, for 5 minutes or till just crisp-tender. Do not drain. Drain pineapple, reserving liquid. Set aside 2 teaspoons pimiento. In blender container puree the remaining pimiento; set aside. Blend cornstarch and pineapple juice; add to cauliflower in saucepan along with green pepper squares. Cook and stir till thickened and bubbly; cook and stir 2 minutes more. Stir in pineapple, the pureed pimiento, vinegar, paprika, bouillon granules, and the 2 teaspoons reserved pimiento; heat through. Slice meat across grain into thin slices. Top with vegetable mixture. Makes 6 servings.

Per serving: 180 calories, 22 g protein, 9 g carbohydrate, 4 g fat, 319 mg sodium.

CHEESE 'N ONION POPOVERS

  1½ teaspoons shortening
    3 egg whites
    1 cup skim milk
    1 tablespoon cooking oil
    1 cup all-purpose flour
    ¼ cup chopped green onion
    2 tablespoons grated Parmesan
        cheese
    ¼ teaspooon salt

Grease six 6-ounce custard cups with ¼ teaspoon of the shortening for each cup. Place custard cups in a 15x10x1-inch baking pan and place in oven; preheat oven to 450°. Meanwhile, in a 4-cup liquid measure or mixing bowl combine egg whites, milk, and oil. Add flour, green onion, cheese, and salt. Beat with electric mixer or rotary beater till mixture is blended. Remove pan from oven. Fill the hot custard cups half full with batter. Return to oven. Bake in 450° oven for 20 minutes. Reduce oven to 350° and bake 15 to 20 minutes more or till popovers are very firm. (If popovers brown too quickly, turn off oven and let them finish baking in the cooling oven till they're very firm.) A few minutes before removing popovers from oven, prick each with a fork to let steam escape. Serve hot. Makes 6 popovers.

Per popover: 136 calories, 6 g protein, 18 g carbohydrate, 4 g fat, 148 mg sodium.

TOFU DRESSING

    8 ounces fresh bean curd (tofu),
        cubed
    1 8-ounce carton plain yogurt
    ½ cup chopped fresh spinach
    1 tablespoon snipped fresh basil
        or 1 teaspoon dried basil,
        crushed
    ¼ teaspoon salt

In blender container of food processor bowl place the tofu, yogurt, spinach, basil, and salt; cover and blend just till smooth. Turn into storage container; cover. Chill dressing thoroughly before serving. Serve dressing with vegetable or main-dish salads. Makes about 1¾ cups.

Per tablespoon: 10 calories, 1 g protein, 1 g carbohydrate, 24 mg sodium.

BULGUR SALAD POCKETS

½ cup bulgur wheat
¼ cup raisins
1 cup cold water
1 cup shredded carrot
⅔ cup plain yogurt
¼ cup slivered almonds, toasted
3 whole wheat pita bread rounds,
  halved crosswise
  Lettuce leaves

In bowl mix bulgur wheat and raisins. Pour cold water over; let stand 1 hour or till bulgur is soft. Drain. Stir in carrot. Cover, chill. Before serving, stir in yogurt and almonds. Line pita halves with lettuce; spoon ⅓ cup bulgur mixture into each. Serves 6.

Per serving: 176 calories, 6 g protein, 32 g carbohydrate, 4 g fat, 146 mg sodium.

HEARTY VEGETABLE STEW

2 16-ounce cans tomatoes, cut up
1 15½-ounce can red kidney
  beans
1 15-ounce can northern beans
1 15-ounce can garbanzo beans
3 medium onions, chopped
  (1½ cups)
2 medium green peppers,
  chopped (1½ cups)
2 stalks celery, sliced (1 cup)
1 medium yellow summer squash
  or zucchini, halved lengthwise
  and sliced (1 cup)
½ cup water
2 cloves garlic, minced
2 teaspoons chili powder
1½ teaspoons dried basil, crushed
¼ teaspoon pepper
1 bay leaf
1 cup cashews or peanuts

In 4-quart Dutch oven combine *undrained* tomatoes, *undrained* beans, onions, green pepper, celery, squash, water, garlic, chili powder, basil, pepper, and bay leaf. Bring to boiling. Reduce heat; cover and simmer about 1 hour or till vegetables are tender. Add nuts; heat through. Serves 10.

Per serving: 273 calories, 13 g protein, 40 g carbohydrate, 8 g fat, 297 mg sodium.

BANANA SURPRISE MUFFINS

½ cup all-purpose flour
½ cup whole wheat flour
2 tablespoons sugar
1 teaspoon baking powder
⅛ teaspoon baking soda
⅛ teaspoon salt
1 beaten egg yolk
½ cup milk
2 tablespoons butter, melted
1 small banana, finely chopped
  (½ cup)
2 tablespoons chopped pecans
1 egg white
3 tablespoons sugar

In small bowl stir together flours, the 2 tablespoons sugar, the baking powder, soda, and salt; make a well in center. Combine egg yolk, milk, and butter; add all at once to dry ingredients. Stir just till moistened (batter will be lumpy). Fold in banana and pecans. Spoon into greased and floured 2¾-inch muffin cups, filling each about ¾ full. Bake in 400° oven about 10 minutes or till almost done. Remove from oven. Meanwhile, in small mixing bowl beat egg white with rotary beater till soft peaks form (tips curl over). Gradually add the 3 tablespoons sugar, beating till stiff peaks form (tips stand straight). Spread meringue evenly over each muffin; top with about ½ *teaspoon* desired jelly or jam, if desired. Return to 400° oven for 10 to 15 minutes more or till meringue is golden and muffin is done. Makes 6.

Per muffin: 209 calories, 5 g protein, 32 g carbohydrate, 8 g fat, 192 mg sodium.

ORANGE-SAUCED CHICKEN

3 whole medium chicken breasts
  (1½ pounds), skinned, halved
  lengthwise, and boned
  Several dashes ground red
  pepper
1 small orange
2 tablespoons all-purpose flour
1 tablespoon sugar
1¼ cups orange juice
2 teaspoons aromatic bitters
1 cup brown rice
½ teaspoon dried basil, crushed
¼ cup snipped parsley

Arrange chicken breasts in a 12x7½x2-inch baking dish; sprinkle with the red pepper. Bake, covered, in a 350° oven for 25 minutes. Remove peel from the orange. Slice *half* the peel into julienne strips; discard remaining peel. Simmer julienne strips in enough water to cover about 15 minutes; drain well and set aside. Section oranges; set aside. Meanwhile, cook the brown rice according to package directions, omitting salt and adding basil and snipped parsley; toss to mix.

For sauce: In small saucepan stir together flour and sugar. Stir in the 1¼ cups orange juice. Cook and stir till thickened and bubbly. Add orange peel and bitters. Remove chicken from oven; place on a cutting board. Hold a sharp knife so the blade is at a 45° diagonal angle to the edge of meat. Slice each chicken breast against the grain of the meat, making slices that are 1½ inches to 2 inches wide. Reassemble each chicken breast and return to baking dish. Spoon sauce over chicken. Return to oven; bake, uncovered, for 5 to 10 minutes longer. Arrange chicken slices on cooked brown rice; spoon orange sauce atop. Garnish with reserved orange sections. Serves 6.

Microwave method: Arrange chicken in a 12x7½x2-inch baking dish; sprinkle with the red pepper. Micro-cook, covered, on HIGH for 8 to 10 minutes. Remove chicken from oven; drain. Meanwhile, remove peel from the orange. Slice *half* the peel into julienne strips; discard remaining peel. Place orange peel in small bowl with enough water to cover. Cook on HIGH for 2 minutes; drain well. Section orange.

For sauce: In a 4-cup measure combine flour and sugar. Stir in 1¼ cups orange juice. Micro-cook, uncovered, on HIGH 3 to 5 minutes or till thickened and bubbly, stirring after each minute. Add orange peel and bitters. Cover and set aside. Place chicken on a cutting board. Slice each chicken breast as directed. Reassemble and return to baking dish. Spoon sauce atop. Return chicken to microwave oven and cook, uncovered, on HIGH for 1 to 2 minutes longer or till heated through. Cook brown rice atop range as directed above. Serve as above.

Per serving: 262 calories, 22 g protein, 36 g carbohydrate, 3 g fat, 5 mg sodium.

ITALIAN PUFFY OMELET

4 egg whites
2 tablespoons water
⅛ teaspoon cream of tartar
2 egg yolks
2 tablespoons butter *or*
    margarine
1 medium tomato, peeled,
    seeded, and chopped (½ cup)
1 cup chopped peeled eggplant
2 tablespoons finely chopped
    onion
½ teaspoon dried oregano,
    crushed
    Dash pepper
½ cup shredded mozzarella
    cheese (2 ounces)
    Snipped parsley

In large mixer bowl beat egg whites till frothy. Add water and cream of tartar; continue beating about 1½ minutes or till stiff peaks form (tips stand straight). Beat egg yolks at high speed of electric mixer about 5 minutes or till thick and lemon-colored. Fold egg yolks into egg whites.

In 10-inch skillet with an oven-proof handle heat *1 tablespoon* of the butter or margarine till a drop of water sizzles. Pour in egg mixture, mounding it slightly higher at the sides. Cook over low heat for 6 minutes or till eggs are puffed and set, and the bottom is golden brown. Meanwhile, in small skillet melt the remaining 1 tablespoon butter or margarine; add chopped tomato, eggplant, onion, oregano, and pepper. Cover and simmer about 3 minutes or till vegetables are tender. Uncover and cook for 3 minutes more. Set aside; keep warm.

Place skillet in a 325° oven; bake for 8 to 10 minutes or till a knife inserted near center comes out clean. Loosen sides of omelet with a metal spatula. Make a shallow cut across the omelet, cutting slightly off center. Fill omelet with tomato mixture and cheese. Fold the smaller portion of omelet over the larger portion. Slip omelet onto a warm platter. Garnish with snipped parsley. Serves 2.

Per serving: 312 calories, 20 g protein, 10 g carbohydrate, 22 g fat, 413 mg sodium.

FRUITY POACHED APPLES

4 medium red cooking apples
⅔ cup apple juice
¼ cup raisins
¼ cup dry sherry
1 teaspoon finely shredded
    lemon peel
3 inches stick cinnamon

Core apples. Peel strip from top of each apple. In a medium skillet combine apple juice, raisins, sherry, lemon peel, and cinnamon. Bring to boiling. Add apples to skillet. Reduce heat; simmer, covered, for 8 to 10 minutes. Turn apples over; simmer for 3 to 5 minutes more or till tender. Remove cinnamon. Serve apples warm in dessert dishes with cooking liquid spooned over. Makes 4 servings.

Per serving: 182 calories, 1 g protein, 38 g carbohydrate, 1 g fat, 6 mg sodium.

ZESTY VEGETABLE DIP

1 10-ounce package frozen peas
½ cup chopped onion
1 8¾-ounce can whole kernel
    corn, drained
½ teaspoon dried oregano,
    crushed
¼ teaspoon garlic salt
    Dash bottled hot pepper sauce
½ cup dairy sour cream
½ cup plain yogurt
1 4-ounce can green chili
    peppers, rinsed, seeded, and
    chopped
    Vegetable dippers *or* melba
    toast rounds

In a saucepan combine peas, onion, and ½ cup *water*. Bring to boiling. Reduce heat; cook, covered, about 5 minutes. Drain, reserving ⅓ cup cooking liquid. In blender container or food processor bowl combine cooked vegetables, reserved liquid, the corn, oregano, garlic salt, and hot pepper sauce. Cover; process till smooth, scraping sides as necessary. Stir in sour cream, yogurt, and chili peppers. Cover and chill. Garnish with pimiento, if desired. Serve with assorted vegetable dippers or melba toast. Makes 3½ cups.

Per tablespoon: 12 calories, 1 g protein, 2 g carbohydrate, 1 g fat, 25 mg sodium.

BROILED ORANGE-GRAPE BOATS

2 large oranges
1 cup green grapes, halved and
    seeds removed
2 tablespoons butter *or*
    margarine, melted
2 teaspoons sugar
¼ teaspoon ground cinnamon
    Flaked coconut

Halve orange, using a sawtooth cut. Remove fruit from each orange half, leaving shells intact. Section orange pulp, discarding membrane. Combine orange sections, grapes, butter or margarine, sugar, and cinnamon; spoon into orange shells. Place in shallow baking pan. Sprinkle coconut atop each. Broil 5 to 6 inches from heat for 3 to 4 minutes or till coconut is golden. Makes 4 servings.

Per serving: 133 calories, 1 g protein, 20 g carbohydrate, 7 g fat, 72 mg sodium.

WINE-POACHED HALIBUT

4 fresh *or* frozen halibut steaks
    (about 1⅓ pounds total)
¾ cup dry white wine *or* water
½ cup water
½ cup sliced fresh mushrooms
¼ cup thinly sliced celery
1 clove garlic, minced
½ teaspoon dried mint, crushed
¼ teaspoon salt
⅛ teaspoon pepper
    Chopped pimiento
    Lemon wedges

Thaw fish, if frozen. In a large skillet combine wine, water, mushrooms, celery, garlic, mint, salt, and pepper. Bring to boiling; reduce heat. Simmer, covered, for 5 minutes. Add fish; spoon poaching liquid over fish. Simmer, covered, for 6 to 8 minutes or till fish flakes easily when tested with a fork. Remove fish to platter; keep warm. Boil vegetable mixture gently, uncovered, for 3 to 6 minutes or till reduced to ½ to ⅔ cup. Spoon atop steaks. Sprinkle with chopped pimiento. Garnish with lemon wedges. Serve with steamed broccoli, if desired. Serves 4.

Per serving: 279 calories, 32 g protein, 3 g carbohydrate, 13 g fat, 229 mg sodium.

September

ALL-PURPOSE SEASONING

- 2 teaspoons dried marjoram, crushed
- 2 teaspoons ground coriander seed
- 2 teaspoons paprika
- ½ teaspoon dry mustard
- ⅛ teaspoon garlic powder

Mix all ingredients. Store in tightly covered container in a cool dry place.

For salad dressing: In a screw-top jar combine 3 parts *salad oil*, 1 part *vinegar*, and 1 part *water*. Add All-Purpose Seasoning to taste. Cover; shake well. Chill. Shake before using.

SEASONED FRENCH LOAF

Combine ½ cup *butter* and 1½ teaspoons *All-Purpose Seasoning*. Cut one 16-ounce unsliced *French bread loaf* into ½-inch-thick slices, cutting to but not through bottom crust. Spread cut surfaces with seasoned butter. Wrap in foil. Bake in a 350° oven 15 minutes. Makes ½ cup spread.

Per serving: 266 calories, 5 g protein, 32 g carbohydrate, 13 g fat, 469 mg sodium.

MARINATED POTATO SALAD

- 1 pound red potatoes
- 1 cup chopped cucumber
- ½ cup thinly sliced radishes
- ¼ cup white wine vinegar
- 1 tablespoon sugar
- ½ cup low-sodium mayonnaise
- ½ teaspoon poppy seed
- 2 hard-cooked eggs, chopped

Cook potatoes in boiling water for 12 to 15 minutes. Drain. Cut into thick slices. In large bowl combine cooked potatoes, cucumber, and radishes. Stir together vinegar, ¼ cup *water,* and sugar; pour over vegetables. Chill at least 2 hours. Drain vegetable mixture thoroughly, reserving 1 tablespoon marinade. Combine mayonnaise, reserved marinade, and poppy seed; pour over potato mixture. Toss to coat. Fold in egg. Serves 8.

Per serving: 91 calories, 3 g protein, 12 g carbohydrate, 4 g fat, 37 mg sodium.

FRUITED BARLEY PUDDING

- 2 slightly beaten egg yolks
- 1¼ cups cooked barley
- ¾ cup chopped mixed dried fruits
- ½ cup skim milk
- 2 tablespoons sugar
- 2 tablespoons butter *or* margarine, melted
- ½ teaspoon vanilla
- 2 egg whites
- ¼ cup bite-size shredded bran squares, crumbled
- 2 tablespoons finely chopped pecans
- 1 tablespoon butter *or* margarine, melted
- ⅛ teaspoon ground cloves

In bowl stir together egg yolks, cooked barley, dried fruits, skim milk, sugar, the 2 tablespoons butter or margarine, and the vanilla. Beat egg whites to stiff peaks (tips stand straight). Fold egg whites into barley mixture. Turn mixture into six 6-ounce custard cups. Place custard cups in a 13x9x2-inch baking pan.

In small bowl combine bran squares, pecans, the 1 tablespoon butter, and the cloves. Sprinkle evenly atop barley mixture in cups. Pour boiling water into pan around cups to a depth of 1 inch. Bake in a 325° oven for 20 to 25 minutes. Serve warm or chilled. Makes 6 servings.

Note: To cook regular barley, bring 1¼ cups water to boiling. Add ¼ cup barley; reduce heat. Cover and simmer 1 hour; cool. For quick barley proceed as above *except* cover and simmer 10 to 12 minutes. Makes about 1¼ cups.

Per serving: 310 calories, 8 g protein, 51 g carbohydrate, 10 g fat, 126 mg sodium.

CURRIED CHEESE SPREAD

- 1 8-ounce package Neufchâtel cheese, softened
- 2 slices skim milk American cheese product (1½ ounces), finely chopped
- ½ teaspoon finely shredded lemon peel
- ½ teaspoon curry powder
- ⅛ teaspoon ground allspice
- 2 tablespoons snipped parsley
- ½ cup alfalfa sprouts, snipped

Assorted crackers
Assorted fresh fruit slices

In small mixer bowl combine cheeses, lemon peel, curry powder, and allspice. Beat with electric mixer till smooth. Stir in parsley. (Add 1 to 2 tablespoons skim milk, if necessary, for a smoother consistency.) Line a 2-cup mold or bowl with clear plastic wrap. Turn mixture into lined bowl. Cover and chill. Unmold onto serving plate. Remove plastic wrap. Press alfalfa sprouts onto top of cheese. Serve with crackers or sliced fruit. Make 1¼ cups.

Per tablespoon: 35 calories, 2 g protein, 3 g fat, 78 mg sodium.

4-GRAIN COOKIES

- ½ cup whole bran cereal
- ½ cup milk
- ½ cup whole wheat flour
- ½ cup all-purpose flour
- ½ cup quick-cooking rolled oats
- ½ cup Grape Nuts cereal
- 1 teaspoon baking powder
- ¼ teaspoon baking soda
- ¼ teaspoon salt
- ½ cup packed brown sugar
- ½ cup cooking oil
- 2 tablespoons molasses
- ½ teaspoon vanilla
- 1 egg
- ¼ cup peanut butter
- ½ cup raisins

In bowl combine bran cereal and milk; let stand for 5 minutes. Stir together flours, oats, Grape Nuts cereal, baking powder, baking soda, and salt. In large mixer bowl combine sugar, oil, molasses, and vanilla; beat well to mix. Add egg, peanut butter, and bran mixture; beat till smooth. Stir in dry ingredients and raisins. Drop by level tablespoons onto ungreased cookie sheet. Bake in 350° oven about 10 minutes or till done. Remove to wire rack to cool. Makes 42 cookies.

Per 2 cookies: 148 calories, 3 g protein, 19 g carbohydrate, 8 g fat, 113 mg sodium.

OCTOBER

TEAR-OUT BONUS BOOKLET ›

October 1982 ● $1.50

Better Homes
and Gardens

CLASSIC
AMERICAN RECIPES
FROM OUR NEWEST COOKBOOK

Is preschool education right for your child?

Affordable solar homes—factory-made

Stylish scrap-yarn sweaters to knit

Survey: What's happening to American families?

Five fabulous family dinners for under $40

Autumn bulb-planting ideas for spring color

**Uptown Country:
The New Look
of PINE**

Photographs: Maselli-Sanders. Food stylist: Fran Paulson

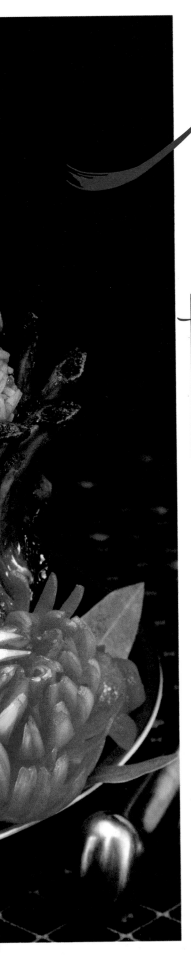

Meal Planning

5 CREATIVE DINNERS FOR UNDER $40

By Nancy Byal

Wait a minute! Before giving up on your family food budget because of rising food prices, consider this. By looking beyond tonight's dinner to next week's or even next month's meals, you can hold down food spending considerably. To get you started, we've put together a five-dinner plan that incorporates all of the tried-and-true money-saving strategies—from using economical ingredients to making the most of leftovers. The delicious and satisfying results will serve a family of four for less than $40! And besides saving you money, this meal-planning method saves you time and effort—four of the five meals can be ready in less than an hour!

MEAL 1

Even when your budget is Spartan, you can splurge on this impressive dinner. That's because it features foods that are short-term investments—recipe portions are saved for later so the cost is spread over five meals.

To fit a magnificent crown roast into your budget, serve **Rice-Stuffed Rib Crown.** It gets its royal shape from pork spareribs in place of costlier loin chops. Launch the save-it-for-later strategy by reserving some stuffing and ribs for upcoming meals. A cranberry dressing tops apples and pears for **Harvest Fruit Salad.** You also use the dressing as a dessert in Meal 3. The easy-to-fix vegetable is **Crumb-Topped Beans.** And the meal's finale is **Peach-Walnut Torte.** Part of the walnut mixture is used in the torte; the remainder is saved for a later dessert.

MEAL 2

Thanks to the rice stuffing you saved from Meal 1, you have a bargain-hunter's start on the next dinner. The seasoned rice takes on its own personality in **Cottage Cheese-Rice Bake,** a crustless quiche highlighted with pork sausage links and peas. Plenty of crunchy-good, sesame-seed-topped

Toasted Pita Chips are oven-baked alongside the egg-based casserole. The surplus chips are served as a soup accompaniment in Meal 5.

Shredded zucchini, shredded carrot, and fresh alfalfa sprouts are arranged atop lettuce leaves for wholesome **Carrot-Zucchini Salad;** serve with your favorite oil-vinegar dressing. Hold out some of the shredded vege-

tables for the easy cream-cheese-based cake prepared for Meal 5.

Fudge-Mint Sundaes are as easy to make as they are fun to eat. Alternately layer slices of vanilla and mint chocolate chip ice cream, cut the stack into serving-size pieces, then refreeze them while you prepare the rest of the meal. Top each serving with purchased fudge topping and peanuts.

MEAL 3

This dinner introduces economical chicken into your planned-over cooking. Budget-wise chicken legs and thighs are glazed with a full-flavored mixture of honey, prepared mustard, and Worcestershire sauce. Then the cooked poultry is served Oriental-style atop shredded lettuce. Serve some of the **Honey-Glazed Chicken** at this dinner but be sure to save a portion for the hearty main-dish stew in Meal 4.

Do you usually cook too many vegetables for your family to eat, and end up discarding the leftovers? Well, **Occidental Stir-Fry** lets you capitalize on that tendency. To make it, you purposely cook more broccoli, celery, and onion than you'll need, then use what's left for the creamed vegetable soup that's featured in Meal 5.

Turn the reserved cranberry-orange salad dressing from Meal 1 into fluffy and puddinglike **Fruit Whip** with the addition of whipped cream. To accent each individual serving of dessert, add half-slices of pineapple.

MEAL 4

Two out of three recipes prepared for tonight's dinner piggyback on foods from previous meals. **Germantown Stew** is a hearty, quick main dish that's ready to eat in about a fourth the time of most stews because you start with cooked meats. To the leftover pork spareribs from Meal 1 and chicken pieces from Meal 3, you simply add fresh cabbage wedges, onion slices, and turnip strips.

That leaves you time to make the **Caraway Wheat Biscuits** from scratch. To save a step, the whole wheat dough is shaped into one large round instead of individual biscuits. Just break the warm bread into wedges along the scoring and serve with your favorite savory spread.

Surprise! The tasty crust for **Caramel Apple Crisp** is the crumb mixture you saved from the peach torte in Meal 1 and embellished with rolled oats, ground cinnamon, and butter or margarine. Caramel topping keeps the apple slices moist as they bake, and light cream adds extra lusciousness to each serving.

MEAL 5

For this finale meal, you use the same carry-over planning strategy you've followed for the other four dinners. Two of tonight's dishes are made with the foods you've kept on call. As a result, the meal is extra economical and timesaving. The reserved vegetables from the Meal 3 stir-fry are pureed with milk and Monterey Jack cheese to make **Creamed Vegetable-Cheese Soup.** And the extra **Toasted Pita Chips** make the perfect crisp crackers to serve with the wholesome soup.

The accompanying salads, **Berry-Orange Aspic Molds,** are a snap to put together, thanks to the quick-gel method for molded salads. To shorten the chilling time, you put the individual molds in the freezer while you assemble the rest of the meal.

Remember the carrot-zucchini salad from Meal 2? No one will guess you slipped some of the shredded vegetables into this evening's delicious three-layered dessert, **Cheesy Carrot-Zucchini Cake.**

FOOD NOTES

Meal Planning

TASTY ENTRÉES FROM LEFTOVERS

You can produce a world of great eating from an assortment of leftover foods. For starters, combine whatever cooked meats, vegetables, and cheeses you've stashed away to create these two popular main dishes—lasagna and enchiladas. Recycled leftovers never tasted so good!

EASY LASAGNA
2 cups sauce*
1½ cups chopped cooked meat**
1 cup cooked vegetables***
½ teaspoon dried oregano *or* dried basil, crushed
⅛ teaspoon pepper
1 cup cream-style cottage cheese *or* ricotta cheese
1 beaten egg
4 lasagna noodles *or* 4 ounces wide noodles, cooked and drained
4 ounces mozzarella cheese, Monterey Jack cheese *or* mild cheddar cheese, thinly sliced
2 to 3 tablespoons grated Parmesan cheese

In saucepan combine desired sauce, meat, vegetables, herb, and pepper. Simmer, covered, about 10 minutes, stirring occasionally. Combine the cottage cheese or ricotta cheese and egg. Place *half* of the cooked noodles in a 10x6x2-inch baking dish. Spread with

half the cheese-egg mixture. Top with *half* the mozzarella, then *half* the meat-vegetable mixture. Repeat layers. Sprinkle with Parmesan cheese. Bake, covered, in a 375° oven about 40 minutes or till bubbly. Let stand 10 minutes before serving. Makes 6 servings.
Sauce suggestions: one 15½-ounce can or jar spaghetti sauce *or* one 7½-ounce can tomatoes, cut up *plus* one 8-ounce can pizza sauce.
**Meat suggestions:* cooked beef, pork, ham, lamb, chicken, *or* turkey.
***Vegetable suggestions:* cooked peas, green beans, diced carrots, sliced zucchini, chopped broccoli, *or* spinach.

SKILLET ENCHILADAS
1½ cups chopped cooked meat*
½ cup chopped onion
2 tablespoons butter *or* margarine
1 4-ounce can green chili peppers, drained, seeded, and chopped
½ teaspoon ground cumin *or* coriander seed
1 10¾-ounce can condensed soup**
1 cup milk

½ cup dairy sour cream
1 tablespoon all-purpose flour
1 cup cooked vegetables***
6 7-inch flour tortillas
½ cup shredded cheese****

In skillet heat meat and onion in butter or margarine till onion is tender but not brown. In a bowl combine meat mixture, chili peppers, and cumin or coriander; set aside. In same skillet combine soup and milk. Combine sour cream and flour. Stir into sauce mixture. Cook and stir till bubbly. Stir ⅓ *cup* of the sauce into the meat mixture. Stir vegetables into remaining sauce in skillet. Fill each tortilla with about ¼ *cup* of the meat mixture. Roll up and place in sauce in skillet. Spoon some sauce over tortillas. Cover; simmer about 8 minutes or till bubbly. Sprinkle with cheese and serve. Makes 4 servings.
Meat suggestions: cooked beef, pork, ham, chicken, *or* turkey.
**Soup suggestions:* cream of chicken, cream of celery, *or* cream of mushroom.
***Vegetable suggestions:* cooked corn, diced carrots, peas, green beans, lima beans, *or* mixed vegetables.
****Cheese suggestions:* Monterey Jack, cheddar, *or* American cheese.

October

RICE-STUFFED RIB CROWN

The "flower" garnishes add an extra-festive touch to this special entrée—

- **4 pounds meaty pork loin back ribs (should have 16 to 20 ribs)**
- **½ cup chopped onion**
- **¼ cup chopped green pepper (½ medium pepper)**
- **2 cloves garlic, minced**
- **2 tablespoons butter *or* margarine**
- **1 16-ounce can tomatoes, cut up**
- **1 cup water**
- **2 bay leaves**
- **½ teaspoon dried thyme, crushed**
- **½ teaspoon dried basil, crushed**
- **¼ teaspoon salt**
- **⅛ teaspoon ground red pepper**
- **1 cup long grain rice**
- **¼ cup light corn syrup**
- **1 teaspoon soy sauce**
- **Onion Mums and Cherry Tomato Roses (optional)**
- **Whole bay leaves (optional)**

Tie the 2 or 3 slabs of ribs together, rib side outward, forming a circle and leaving a center 5 inches in diameter (center will be filled with a stuffing). If possible, have butcher tie ribs together for you. Place rib crown in a shallow roasting pan. Roast, uncovered, in a 450° oven for 20 minutes.

Meanwhile, in saucepan cook onion, green pepper, and garlic in butter or margarine till tender but not brown. Stir in *undrained* tomatoes, water, the 2 bay leaves, the thyme, basil, salt, and red pepper. Stir in uncooked rice. Bring to boiling; reduce heat. Cover and simmer 15 to 20 minutes or till rice is done and liquid is absorbed. Remove from heat. Remove bay leaves. Remove meat from oven and drain off excess fat. Reduce oven temperature to 350°. Spoon rice mixture into center of crown. Cover rice loosely with foil to prevent drying out. Brush meat with a mixture of the corn syrup and soy sauce. Bake in a 350° oven about 1¼ hours more or till meat is done. Brush again with corn syrup mixture before serving. Serve roast garnished with Onion Mums, Cherry Tomato Roses, and whole bay leaves.

(Reserve one-fourth of the ribs and 1 cup of the rice mixture to use for later meals. Cover and refrigerate the ribs and rice mixture separately. Or, seal, label, and freeze the ribs and rice mixture in separate moisture-vaporproof containers.) Makes 4 servings.

Onion Mums: For each "flower," cut off top of a small onion and peel off the outer skin; leave root end intact. Using a sharp, thin-bladed knife, cut onion into quarters from top to about ¼ inch from the root end. Cut each quarter in half again to about ¼ inch from the root end. Repeat the cutting, making many small wedge-shaped pieces. Be sure you don't cut through the root end. To tint onion flowers orange, use 4 parts yellow food coloring to 1 part red food coloring; add food coloring to ice water. Add the cut onion to ice water; cover and refrigerate. After soaking onion for a few hours, gently pull back some of the sections, forming flower petals. Let onion soak in water till it is the desired color.

Cherry Tomato Roses: To make each "rose," score an "X" on the blossom end of each cherry tomato. Using a sharp knife carefully peel back the skin part way down the side of the tomato, making 4 petals.

HARVEST FRUIT SALAD

The dressing goes well with all kinds of fresh fruits—

- **1 10-ounce package frozen cranberry-orange relish**
- **1 8-ounce carton orange yogurt**
- **1 large red apple, cored and sliced into wedges**
- **1 large pear, cored and sliced into wedges**
- **Lettuce**

Thaw package of relish in very warm water. In a bowl gently stir the thawed relish into the orange yogurt. Reserve 1¼ cups of the yogurt mixture to use for Fruit Whip Meal 3. Cover and store in refrigerator; or seal, label, and freeze. Arrange the apple and pear wedges on lettuce-lined plates. Spoon the remaining yogurt mixture over each serving of fruit. Serve immediately. Makes 4 servings.

PEACH-WALNUT TORTE

- **1 cup finely crushed vanilla wafers**
- **¾ cup ground walnuts (about 3 ounces)**
- **3 tablespoons butter *or* margarine, softened**
- **½ cup packed brown sugar**
- **1 egg**
- **¾ cup all-purpose flour**
- **¼ teaspoon baking soda**
- **¼ teaspoon salt**
- **½ cup milk**
- **1 cup whipping cream**
- **1 cup frozen unsweetened peach slices, thawed; *or* use one 8¾-ounce can unpeeled apricot halves *or* peach slices (juice-pack), drained thoroughly**
- **Mint leaves**

Combine crushed vanilla wafers and ground nuts. Reserve *1 cup* of the crumb mixture to use for Caramel Apple Crisp. Place in a covered container; refrigerate. Grease and lightly flour one 8x1½-inch baking pan. In small mixer bowl beat butter or margarine, brown sugar, and egg with electric mixer till mixture is creamy. Stir together flour, baking soda, and salt. Add to beaten mixture alternately with milk, beating on low speed after each addition just till combined. Stir in crumb mixture. Turn batter into prepared pan. Bake in a 325° oven 30 minutes or till cake tests done. Cool in pan 10 minutes. Remove from pan and cool on wire rack. (If desired, prepare cake the day ahead and store it tightly covered.)

Split cake layer in half horizontally. (Center wooden picks on side of cake. Use picks as a guide to evenly slice cake in half.) Cut each split layer in half vertically, making four thin semicircles. To assemble, beat whipping cream with rotary beater to soft peaks. Place one semicircle on a plate. Spread with one-fourth of the whipped cream; top with second cake layer. Spread with another one-fourth of the whipped cream; arrange half the fruit atop. Repeat with remaining cake layers, whipped cream, and fruit. Chill till serving time. Cut into wedges to serve. Trim with mint sprigs, if desired. Makes 4 to 6 servings.

CRUMB-TOPPED BEANS

For quicker preparation, make this easy crumb mixture ahead—

1 10-ounce package frozen Italian green beans *or* cut green beans
2 tablespoons butter *or* margarine
3 tablespoons fine dry bread crumbs
1 tablespoon snipped parsley

Cook green beans according to package directions. Meanwhile, in small saucepan heat butter or margarine till lightly browned. Stir in the crumbs and parsley. Drain beans and sprinkle with the crumb mixture. Makes 4 servings.

COTTAGE CHEESE-RICE BAKE

If you don't have leftover rice stuffing from the Rice-Stuffed Rib Crown, substitute this mixture: in saucepan bring ½ cup water to boiling. Stir in ½ cup quick-cooking rice; 2 teaspoons minced dried onion; ⅛ teaspoon dried rosemary or thyme, crushed; ⅛ teaspoon dried basil, crushed; and dash ground red pepper. Cover. Remove from heat and let stand, covered, 5 minutes—

2 beaten eggs
1 cup cream-style cottage cheese
1 cup frozen peas
½ cup milk
¼ teaspoon seasoned salt
1 cup reserved rice mixture from Rice-Stuffed Rib Crown
4 brown-and-serve sausage links, halved lengthwise
Rosemary sprig (optional)

In a bowl combine the beaten eggs, cottage cheese, peas, milk, and seasoned salt. Stir in the rice mixture. Turn into an ungreased 8-inch quiche dish or baking dish. Arrange sausage halves in spoke fashion atop. Bake, uncovered, in a 325° oven about 45 minutes or till knife inserted near center comes out clean. Let stand 5 minutes before serving. Garnish with a sprig of rosemary, if desired. Makes 4 servings.

TOASTED PITA CHIPS

Your family will love these for snacking, too—

4 large pita bread rounds (6½-inch diameter)
2 tablespoons cooking oil
Sesame seed *or* caraway seed

Split each pita round in half; cut each half in quarters. Brush the outside with cooking oil; sprinkle with sesame or caraway seed. Place on 15x10x1-inch baking pan. Bake in 325° oven for 25 to 30 minutes or till crisp and golden, rearranging once. Reserve half of the chips to use for Meal 5. Freeze in a plastic bag. Serve remaining chips while warm. Makes 32 chips total.

HONEY-GLAZED CHICKEN

Remember this honey mixture for basting barbecued poultry—

¼ cup honey
3 tablespoons prepared mustard
2 tablespoons butter *or* margarine
1 tablespoon Worcestershire sauce
3 pounds (12) chicken thighs *or* legs
Shredded lettuce (optional)
Spiced crab apples (optional)

In small saucepan combine the honey, mustard, butter or margarine, and Worcestershire sauce. Heat and stir till butter melts. Brush chicken pieces with some of the honey mixture. Arrange chicken pieces, skin side up, in a large shallow baking pan. Bake, uncovered, in a 375° oven for 45 to 50 minutes or till chicken is tender; baste with sauce once during baking. Reserve four pieces of chicken for Germantown Stew in Meal 4. Cool. Cover and refrigerate; or freeze in moisture-vaporproof freezer material. To serve remaining chicken, arrange pieces on a bed of shredded lettuce, if desired. Brush remaining honey mixture over the chicken pieces. Garnish with crab apples, if desired. Makes 4 servings.

OCCIDENTAL STIR-FRY

Broccoli, celery, and onion make a tasty trio in this easy side dish—

1 20-ounce package *or* two 10-ounce packages frozen cut broccoli, thawed
3 tablespoons cold water
1½ teaspoons cornstarch
3 tablespoons soy sauce
1 teaspoon sugar
2 tablespoons cooking oil
1 cup celery bias-sliced into ½-inch pieces
1 large onion, cut into thin wedges

Thoroughly drain thawed broccoli cuts. In small bowl combine cold water and cornstarch. Stir in soy sauce and sugar; set aside. Heat large skillet over high heat; add cooking oil. Add celery, onion, and drained broccoli. Stir-fry about 5 minutes or till vegetables are crisp-tender. Stir soy mixture; stir into vegetables. Cook and stir about 1 minute more or till vegetables are well coated. Reserve 2 cups of the vegetables to use for Creamed Vegetable-Cheese Soup in Meal 5. Cover and refrigerate; or seal, label, and freeze in moisture-vaporproof container. Serve remaining vegetables at once. Makes 4 servings.

FUDGE MINT SUNDAES

Cut the slices from ½-gallon blocks of ice cream; mix and match flavors to your liking—

2 slices mint chocolate chip ice cream (4½x3¼x½-inch each)
2 slices vanilla ice cream (4½x3¼x½-inch each)
¼ cup fudge topping
2 tablespoons peanuts

On a chilled plate stack the ice cream slices, alternating the flavors. Cut the ice cream stack into eight pieces; place two pieces in each of four dessert dishes. Freeze till serving time. To serve, spoon about 1 tablespoon fudge topping over each serving and sprinkle with a few peanuts. Makes 4 servings.

CARROT-ZUCCHINI SALAD

Use purchased or homemade dressing for this fluffy salad—

1¾ cups shredded unpeeled
zucchini
1¾ cups shredded carrots
4 lettuce leaves
¼ cup alfalfa sprouts
2 to 3 tablespoons vinegar and oil
dressing
Carrot flowers (optional)

Reserve ½ cup of the shredded carrots and ½ cup of the shredded zucchini to use for Carrot-Zucchini Cake in Meal 5. Refrigerate or freeze the reserved vegetables in a tightly covered container. Line salad plates with letture. Layer remaining zucchini and carrot on each plate. Place some alfalfa sprouts atop each serving. Pass dressing to serve with salad. If desired, garnish salads with "carrot flowers" made with paper-thin slices of carrot. Makes 4 servings.

FRUIT WHIP

If you don't have leftover yogurt dressing from Meal 1, substitute one 8-ounce can whole cranberry sauce and ½ cup orange yogurt. Stir cranberry sauce to break up before folding into the whipped cream—

1 8- or 8¼-ounce can pineapple
slices, chilled
½ cup whipping cream
1¼ cups reserved yogurt dressing
from Harvest Fruit Salad
⅛ teaspoon ground nutmeg

Drain pineapple; halve each slice. Set aside. Beat whipping cream till soft peaks form. Fold in the reserved dressing and the nutmeg. Spoon the whipping cream mixture into sherbet dishes. Arrange two half-slices pineapple along edges of each dish. Chill 20 minutes in freezer or 1 hour in refrigerator. Makes 4 servings.

GERMANTOWN STEW

You also can start with uncooked meats for this delicious main dish. See the directions below—

2 cups water
1 6-ounce can tomato paste
2 tablespoons brown sugar
2 tablespoons vinegar
½ teaspoon salt
¼ teaspoon pepper
Reserved cooked ribs from
Rice-Stuffed Rib Crown (4 to 5
ribs or 13 ounces)
4 reserved cooked chicken thighs
***or* legs from Honey Glazed**
Chicken
2 small turnips, peeled and cut
into strips (8 ounces)
1 onion, sliced and separated into
rings
1 small head green cabbage, cut
into 4 wedges

In a 4-quart Dutch oven combine the water, the tomato paste, the brown sugar, the vinegar, the salt, and the pepper. Cut the reserved ribs into one-rib portions. Add to the Dutch oven with the chicken thighs, the turnip strips, and the onion rings. Bring stew mixture to boiling. Reduce heat. Cover stew mixture and simmer for 10 minutes. Stir

Arrange the cabbage wedges atop the vegetable-meat mixture and continue to simmer, covered, for 25 to 30 minutes more or till vegetables are done. Serve stew in bowls. Makes 4 servings.

To use uncooked ribs and chicken: Use 1 pound meaty *pork loin back ribs,* cut into one-rib potions, and 4 *chicken thighs* or *legs.* In a Dutch oven brown the ribs and the chicken thighs or legs in 1 tablespoon *cooking oil.* Remove the chicken. Drain off fat from Dutch oven.

Add the water, the tomato paste, the brown sugar, the vinegar, the salt, and the pepper to the ribs. Bring mixture to boiling; reduce heat and simmer, covered, for 45 minutes. Add the chicken thighs or legs, the turnip strips, and the onion rings. Cover the stew and simmer for 15 minutes more. Stir. Add the cabbage wedges; simmer, covered, for 30 minutes or till vegetables are done. Serve stew in bowls.

Microwave directions: In a 3-quart casserole combine the water, the tomato paste, the brown sugar, the vinegar, the salt, and the pepper.

Cut the cooked ribs into one-rib portions. Add to the casserole with the cooked chicken thighs or legs. Microcook, covered, on MEDIUM-HIGH for 10 minutes, stirring once. Stir in the turnip strips and the onion rings.

Arrange the cabbage wedges atop. Cook, covered, on HIGH for 22 to 25 minutes or till the vegetables are done. Serve stew in bowls.

CARAWAY WHEAT BISCUITS

Scoring the wedges of dough makes it easy to break off individual pieces—

¾ cup all-purpose flour
¾ cup whole wheat flour
2 teaspoons baking powder
½ teaspoon salt
½ teaspoon caraway seed
⅓ cup shortening
½ cup milk
Milk
½ teaspoon caraway seed

In a large mixing bowl stir together the all-purpose flour, the whole wheat flour, the baking powder, the salt, and the ½ teaspoon caraway seed. Cut in shortening till mixture resembles coarse crumbs. Make a well in the center. Add the milk all at once. Stir just till dough clings together. Knead gently on lightly floured surface for 10 to 12 strokes.

On greased baking sheet roll or pat dough to an 8-inch round. Prick surface with tines of a fork, scoring into 8 wedges. Brush with a little additional milk. Sprinkle with remaining caraway seed. Bake in a 400° oven for 20 to 25 minutes or till golden. Serve warm. Makes 8 biscuits.

CHEESY CARROT-ZUCCHINI CAKE

If you aren't making the Carrot-Zucchini Salad in Meal 2, you can easily use 1 cup shredded carrot or zucchini in this recipe—

- 2 3-ounce packages cream cheese softened
- ⅓ cup sugar
- 1 egg
- 1⅓ cups packaged biscuit mix
- ⅓ cup sugar
- 2 teaspoons pumpkin pie spice
- ½ cup *each* reserved shredded carrot and zucchini from Carrot-Zucchini Salad
- ¼ cup cooking oil
- 2 eggs
- 1 teaspoon vanilla
  Powdered sugar (optional)

In small mixer bowl beat cream cheese and the first ⅓ cup sugar on medium speed of electric mixer till fluffy; beat in the 1 egg. Set aside. In large mixer bowl stir together biscuit mix, the remaining sugar, and the spice. Add reserved vegetables, cooking oil, the 2 eggs, and the vanilla. Beat on low speed 30 seconds. Beat on medium speed 2 minutes. Pour *half* of the batter into a greased 8x8x2-inch baking pan. Spoon cream cheese mixture atop. Spoon remaining batter over cream cheese layer. Bake in a 350° oven for 35 to 40 minutes or till done. To serve, dust top with powdered sugar, if desired.

BERRY-ORANGE ASPIC MOLDS

If you make this salad ahead, chill the molds in the refrigerator instead of the freezer—

- 1½ teaspoons unflavored gelatin
- ½ cup cold water
- ¼ cup frozen orange juice concentrate
- 2 tablespoons honey
- ½ cup frozen whole unsweetened strawberries
- ½ of an 11-ounce can mandarin orange sections, drained
  Curly endive

In a small saucepan soften gelatin in cold water. Heat and stir till gelatin dissolves. Remove from heat. Pour into a blender container. Add frozen juice concentrate and honey. Cover and blend just till mixed. Add the frozen berries, one at a time, blending till pureed. Divide the mandarin orange sections among 4 individual molds. Add the blended mixture to each mold, stirring gently to mix in the oranges. Place in the freezer about 2 minutes or till firm. Place in a refrigerator until serving time. Unmold onto endive leaves. Garnish each salad with a mandarin orange section, if desired. Makes 4 servings.

CREAMED VEGETABLE-CHEESE SOUP

If you don't have leftover Vegetable Stir-Fry, substitute 2 cups cooked vegetables, such as broccoli or carrots—

- 2 cups reserved Vegetable Stir-Fry
- 1 cup chicken broth
- 3 cups milk
- 3 tablespoons all-purpose flour
- 1½ cups shredded Monterey Jack cheese (6 ounces)
- 1 cup diced fully cooked ham
  Several dashes bottled hot pepper sauce
  Pepper
  Celery leaves (optional)
- ½ recipe reserved Toasted Pita Chips

Place vegetable mixture in blender container or food processor bowl with chicken broth. Cover and process till mixture is pureed. Turn into a saucepan. In screw-top jar shake together *1 cup* of the milk and the flour. Stir milk mixture, remaining milk, cheese, ham, and hot pepper sauce into pureed vegetables. Heat and stir till bubbly and cheese is melted. Season to taste with pepper. Garnish each serving with celery leaves, if desired. Serve with Toasted Pita Chips. Makes 4 servings.

CARAMEL APPLE CRISP

If you're not making the Peach-Walnut Torte in Meal 1, you can use ½ cup finely crushed vanilla wafers and ½ cup finely chopped walnuts in place of the reserved nut-crumb mixture—

- 1 cup reserved nut-crumb mixture from Peach Walnut Torte
- ¼ cup quick-cooking rolled oats
- ½ teaspoon ground cinnamon
- ¼ teaspoon salt
- 3 tablespoons butter *or* margarine
- 3 cups thinly sliced, peeled apples (3 large apples)
- 1 tablespoon lemon juice
- ½ cup caramel topping
  Light cream *or* whipped dessert topping (optional)
  Gouda *or* cheddar cheese (optional)

In a bowl stir together the nut-crumb mixture, oats, cinnamon, and salt. Cut in butter or margarine till mixture resembles coarse crumbs. Pat about *half* of the mixture into a 6½x6½x1½-inch ceramic baking dish, patting mixture about 1 inch up the sides. Bake in a 400° oven for 5 to 8 minutes. Toss apples with lemon juice to coat; arrange apples atop warm crust. Drizzle caramel topping over apples. Sprinkle with remaining crumb mixture. Bake about 45 minutes more or till apples are tender. Serve warm with light cream or whipped dessert topping and a wedge of cheese, if desired. Makes 4 servings.

Microwave directions: In a bowl stir together the nut-crumb mixture, the oats, cinnamon, and salt. Cut in butter till mixture resembles coarse crumbs. Pat about *half* of the mixture into a 6½x6½x1½-inch ceramic baking dish, patting mixture about 1 inch up the sides. Micro-cook, uncovered, on HIGH for 1 to 1½ minutes. Toss apples with lemon juice to coat; arrange apples atop crust. Drizzle caramel topping over apples. Sprinkle with remaining crumb mixture. Cook, uncovered, for 4 to 5 minutes more or till apples are tender, giving dish a half-turn after 2½ minutes. Serve warm with cream or dessert topping.

NOVEMBER

November 1982 • $1.50

Better Homes and Gardens

Bedazzling Recipes
· for Special Occasions ·

Decorating: Great-looking
ways to cut energy costs

The discipline problem
in our schools:
What's happening?

A century-old home
made new again

Make-aheads
for Christmas

Family skiing
vacation guide

How to make
the most of a
pint-size kitchen

Solar greenhouses
for food and heat

Caramel-Filigree Hazelnut Pie
Recipe inside

Bedazzling recipes

FOR SPECIAL OCCASIONS

BY DIANA McMILLEN

Whether you're celebrating a landmark anniversary, entertaining hard-to-impress guests, or just brightening the day for the special people in your life, you want to serve something extraordinary. Any one of the spectacular foods on these pages will help you do just that. Granted, our four-star recipes do call for a little extra effort, time, and expense—but why hold back? This is your chance to strut your culinary skills. And when you present one of these show-stopping foods, the ohs and ahs from your audience will pronounce you a star.

The natural beauty of a sliced carrot petal pattern gives **Carrot Mousse Tart** *(below)* a look of classic elegance. You'll be amazed how everyday ingredients can yield this extra-special side dish—a fitting accompaniment to a meat entrée. Start by overlapping thinly sliced carrots on the bottom and sides of a baking pan. Then fill this "crust" with a mixture of pureed carrots, potato, eggs, sour cream, and seasonings.

Squab Calvados With Rice Sticks *(right)* is an amalgamation of intriguing ingredients. Dried figs, apple, and apple brandy combined with lemon juice and nutmeg fill each petite apple-glazed bird. Oriental rice sticks provide the crowning touch for this spectacular entrée. These wire-thin noodles puff instantly when they're deep-fat fried.

Bedazzling recipes
FOR SPECIAL OCCASIONS

End a meal on a festive note by serving this colorful **Pastel Ribbon Bavarian** (below) topped with dollops of whipped cream and purchased crisp rolled cookies. Like the recipe for a rich classic Bavarian, this one features a billowy egg mixture made with gelatin and whipped cream. Three distinct fresh-flavored fruit layers—raspberry, peach, and lime—delight the eye and the taste buds. To show off this easy and elegant make-ahead dessert, spoon the pastel layers into a glass serving bowl before chilling.

A caramelized sugar dome makes **Caramel-Filigree Hazelnut Pie** (right) a culinary *tour de force*. Under the lacy brittlelike sphere is a hazelnut crust, fresh hazelnut-coconut filling, and fruit topping. The filigree is surprisingly easy to make: just caramelize some sugar, drizzle the hot syrup over a round-bottomed dish creating a pattern, then let the filigree harden.

After carefully removing the brittle sphere from the dish, place it atop the chilled pie. For the crowning touch, pipe a swirl of whipped cream around the inside of the crust. To serve this exquisite pie with a flourish (and surprise your guests), shatter the caramel filigree dome with a knife before cutting out each mouth-watering serving.

Bedazzling recipes
FOR SPECIAL OCCASIONS

You're the sculptor as you form **Harvest Grape Bread** *(left),* placing balls of the dough in the shape of a grape cluster and crowning it with leaves and a stem formed from the same dough. But the interesting shape isn't the only thing that's special about this bread. It also has a tender texture and a unique orange liqueur flavor with just a hint of cardamom and nutmeg. Serve this show-off golden bread as an appetizer with wine and a variety of cheeses. Or, present it on an attractive cutting board or a napkin-lined flat basket as a unique accompaniment to a gala evening meal.

Spinach Ravioli With Squash Filling

(below) is proof that the classic Italian ravioli can be a lot more than meat-filled pasta with tomato sauce. These ravioli tidbits are fit for a king because the "envelopes" are homemade spinach pasta, and the filling is a golden mixture of squash, nutmeg, and Parmesan cheese. You can shape these filled envelopes by hand or simplify the job with a ravioli mold, ravioli pin, or ravioli maker.

Serve these savories topped with rich **Nutmeg Cheese Sauce** as a lavish side dish or a first-course appetizer. Include fresh grated Parmesan cheese on the side to sprinkle atop the sauced ravioli. A light salad of mixed greens drizzled with an Italian dressing makes the perfect complement.

Bedazzling recipes
FOR SPECIAL OCCASIONS

Genoise (jen-WAHZ), a special European-style cake with a fine texture similar to rich sponge cake, is a celebration in itself. And our version, **Chocolate Genoise Cake With Espresso Buttercream,** is exquisite proof. It does require some special preparation techniques, but the results are well worth the effort. To give the sides and top of this *pièce de résistance* a geometric pattern, brush a cake decorator's comb over the buttercream-frosted cake. And for a professional looking finish, pipe the cake with contrasting buttercream.

When you serve French-style **Salmon Quenelles** (ka-NELL) with **Chive Crème Fraîche** (krem FRESH) *(below),* do as the French would do—serve it *nouvelle cuisine* style. Arrange steamed leeks, beets, and carrots on the plate to frame each serving. This delicate-flavored and light-textured dumpling is typically made with fish, veal, or poultry, then shaped and gently poached in a fish broth. Although quenelles are usually served as an entrée, they also make a first-rate appetizer course.

In keeping with the French theme, top the mousse-like salmon with chive-studded crème fraîche, a classic topping that's as fresh-tasting as its name promises. This sauce is a combination of whipping cream, cultured buttermilk, and fresh snipped chives that thickens upon standing.

155

November

SQUAB CALVADOS WITH FRIED RICE STICKS

3 large apples, peeled, cored, and
  chopped (about 3 cups)
2 tablespoons butter *or*
  margarine
½ cup snipped dried figs
2 tablespoons Calvados, apple
  brandy, *or* brandy
1 teaspoon lemon juice
⅛ teaspoon ground nutmeg
⅓ cup apple jelly
1 tablespoon Calvados, apple
  brandy, *or* brandy
4 12- to 16-ounce ready-to-cook
  squab *or* four 1¼-pound
  Cornish game hens
  Butter *or* margarine, melted
4 ounces rice sticks
  Shortening *or* cooking oil for
  deep-fat frying
  Curly endive (optional)
  Dried figs (optional)
  Kumquats (optional)

In a skillet cook chopped apple in the 2 tablespoons butter or margarine for 2 minutes. Remove from heat. Stir in the snipped figs, the 2 tablespoons Calvados, the lemon juice, and nutmeg. For glaze, in a small saucepan melt apple jelly; remove from heat and stir in the 1 tablespoon Calvados.

Season cavities of squab or Cornish hens with salt and pepper. Lightly stuff birds with fruit mixture. Tie legs together with string. Place birds, breast side up, on a rack in a shallow roasting pan. Brush skin with a little melted butter or margarine; cover loosely with foil. Roast squab in a 375° oven for 30 minutes. Uncover and roast about 30 minutes more or till birds are tender. (Roast Cornish game hens, covered, in a 375° oven for 30 minutes. Uncover and roast about 1 hour more.) Brush birds with glaze the last 15 minutes of roasting.

For rice sticks: fry unsoaked rice sticks, a few at a time, in deep hot fat (360°) about 5 seconds or just till sticks puff and rise to top. Remove; drain on paper toweling. Keep warm in oven.

Arrange cooked birds on serving platter. Brush birds with remaining glaze. Top with rice sticks. Garnish platter with endive, figs, and kumquats, if desired. Makes 4 servings.

CHOCOLATE GENOISE CAKE WITH ESPRESSO BUTTERCREAM

½ cup unsalted butter
2 squares (2 ounces) semisweet
  chocolate
6 slightly beaten eggs
1 cup sugar
1 teaspoon vanilla
1 cup all-purpose flour
4 egg yolks
1 cup unsalted butter, softened
⅔ cup sugar
¼ cup water
1 tablespoon instant espresso
  coffee powder

Grease and lightly flour two 9x1½-inch round cake pans. In a saucepan melt together the ½ cup unsalted butter and chocolate; set aside. In a large mixer bowl combine 6 eggs, 1 cup sugar, and vanilla; stir till just combined. Set bowl over large saucepan containing 1 to 2 inches of hot (not boiling) water. Heat over low heat, stirring occasionally, about 10 minutes or till mixture is lukewarm (105° to 110°). Remove saucepan from heat; remove bowl from saucepan. Beat mixture at high speed of electric mixer about 15 minutes or till nearly tripled in volume. By hand, lightly fold in flour, *one-third* at a time. Gradually fold in chocolate mixture. Spread batter evenly into pans. Bake in a 350° oven for 25 to 30 minutes or till done. Cool 10 minutes on wire racks. Remove from pans; cool.

For Espresso Buttercream, beat egg yolks till thick and lemon colored; set aside. In mixer bowl, beat remaining 1 cup butter till light and fluffy; set aside. In a saucepan stir together the ⅔ cup sugar, water, and instant espresso coffee powder; bring to boiling, stirring till dissolved. Cook over medium-high heat, stirring constantly, till mixture reaches the soft-ball stage (236°). Quickly pour hot mixture in a steady stream over beaten egg yolks, beating constantly at high speed. Continue beating till mixture is thick and smooth; cool 15 minutes. Beat in butter, one tablespoon at a time. Cover and chill about 30 minutes or just till stiff enough to spread. Fill and frost cooled cake layers with buttercream. Makes 12 to 16 servings.

HARVEST GRAPE LOAF

Let your guests serve themselves by pulling off pieces of bread—

2½ to 3 cups all-purpose flour
1 package active dry yeast
¼ teaspoon ground cardamom
¼ teaspoon ground nutmeg
¾ cup milk
¼ cup sugar
3 tablespoons butter *or*
  margarine
1 teaspoon salt
2 tablespoons orange liqueur *or*
  orange juice
1 egg white
  Poppy seed

In a small mixer bowl combine 1¼ cups of the flour, the yeast, cardamom, and nutmeg. In a saucepan heat together the milk, sugar, butter or margarine, and salt till warm (115° to 120°) and butter is almost melted. Add the warm liquid, liqueur or orange juice, and egg white to dry ingredients. Beat at low speed of electric mixer for ½ minute, scraping sides of bowl. Beat 3 minutes at high speed. By hand, stir in as much of the remaining flour as possible. Turn out onto a lightly floured surface. Knead in enough remaining flour to make a moderately stiff dough that is smooth and elastic (5 to 8 minutes). Place dough in greased bowl; turn once to grease surface. Cover; let rise in warm place till double (about 1 hour). Punch down; let rest 10 minutes.

Remove one-fourth of the dough; cover and set aside. Using remaining dough, shape into thirty 1-inch balls. Arrange on greased baking sheet in the shape of a bunch of grapes. Brush with mixture of egg white and water; sprinkle with poppy seed. On lightly floured surface, roll the reserved dough to an 8x4-inch rectangle; cut in half crosswise. Cut each square in half diagonally to form "grape leaves." Position leaves atop the widest end of the bunch of "grapes." Brush the "leaves" with egg white mixture; sprinkle with additional sugar. Cover loosely; let rise in a warm place till nearly double (30 to 40 minutes). With a very sharp knife, slash ribs in the "leaves." Bake the bread in a 375° oven for 20 to 25 minutes or till bread tests done. Remove from baking sheet; cool on wire rack. Serve warm or cool. Makes 1 loaf.

SALMON QUENELLES WITH CHIVE CRÈME FRAÎCHE

8 ounces fresh *or* frozen salmon,
   pike, *or* cod fillets
¼ cup fish stock *or* water
2 tablespoons butter *or*
   margarine
¼ cup all-purpose flour
¼ teaspoon salt
¼ teaspoon dried tarragon,
   crushed
   Dash pepper
1 egg
1 egg white
1 tablespoon light cream *or* milk
2 cups hot water
½ teaspoon salt
   Cooked leeks (optional)
   Julienne beets, cooked
   (optional)
   Julienne carrots, cooked
   (optional)
1 recipe Chive Crème Fraîche
   Snipped fresh chives (optional)

Thaw fish, if frozen. In saucepan bring the ¼ cup fish stock or water and the butter or margarine to boiling, stirring till butter melts. Add flour, the ¼ teaspoon salt, the tarragon, and pepper all at once, stirring vigorously till well blended. Cook and stir over low heat till mixture forms a ball that doesn't separate. Remove from heat. Cool for 10 minutes. Beat in the whole egg, then the egg white. Set mixture aside. Pat fish dry with paper toweling; remove skin, if necessary. Chop fish. Blend fish, *half* at a time, in blender container or food processor bowl, stopping frequently to scrape sides of container. Beat fish and light cream or milk into flour mixture. Cover and chill mixture thoroughly.

Grease a 12-inch skillet. Using two large spoons, mold *one-fourth* of the fish mixture (about ⅓ cup) into an oval shape; gently place in skillet. (Or, for small quenelles mold a scant *2 tablespoons* fish mixture into an oval shape.) Repeat with remaining fish mixture. Combine the 2 cups hot water and the ½ teaspoon salt; gently pour down side of skillet. Bring mixture just to simmering. Cover and simmer gently 25 minutes for the large quenelles or 10 minutes for the small quenelles or till mixture is set. Remove quenelles from skillet with slotted spoon; drain on paper toweling. Serve immediately on individual serving plates with leeks,

beets, and carrots, if desired. Spoon Chive Crème Fraîche atop; sprinkle with snipped chives, if desired. Makes 4 large or 15 small quenelles.

Chive Crème Fraîche: In a small saucepan heat 1 cup *whipping cream* over low heat till temperature measures 90° to 100°. Pour into a small bowl. Stir in 2 tablespoons *cultured buttermilk*. Cover; let stand at room temperature for 24 to 30 hours or till thickened. Do not stir. Stir in 1 teaspoon snipped *chives* just before serving. (Mixture may be stored in a covered container in the refrigerator for up to one week.) Makes 1 cup.

CARAMEL-FILIGREE HAZELNUT PIE

Instead of creating a dome, drizzle the caramel filigree right atop the pie no more than one hour before serving to form a delicate webbed design—

1 cup all-purpose flour
½ cup ground hazelnuts *or* pecans
½ teaspoon salt
⅓ cup shortening
3 tablespoons cold water
1 fresh medium coconut
¼ cup sugar
1 envelope unflavored gelatin
¼ cup hazelnut liqueur, praline
   liqueur, *or* brandy
3 egg whites
2 tablespoons sugar
¾ cup whipping cream
   Sliced fresh fruit (optional)
   Whipped cream
1 recipe Caramel Filigree

For crust, in medium mixing bowl stir together the flour, the ½ cup ground nuts, and the salt. Cut in shortening till pieces are the size of small peas. Sprinkle 1 tablespoon of the water over part of the mixture; gently toss with a fork. Push to side of bowl. Repeat with remaining cold water till all is moistened. Form dough into a ball. On lightly floured surface flatten dough with hands; roll out to a 12-inch circle. Transfer to a 9-inch pie plate; trim pastry to ½ inch beyond pan edge. Flute edge. Prick bottom and sides well. Bake pastry shell in a 450° oven for 10 to 12

minutes or till golden brown. Cool on wire rack.

For filling, open coconut, reserving milk. Measure coconut milk, adding enough water, if necessary, to measure ¾ cup liquid. Finely shred the coconut, reserving 1 cup for the pie. (Store any remaining coconut, covered, in the refrigerator for another use). In a small saucepan stir together the ¼ cup sugar and the gelatin. Stir in the reserved ¾ cup coconut milk; heat and stir till the sugar and gelatin dissolve. Cool 10 minutes. Stir the shredded coconut and liqueur into the cooled gelatin mixture. Chill till mixture is the consistency of corn syrup, stirring occasionally. Remove from refrigerator (gelatin mixture will continue to set up.) Beat egg whites till soft peaks form (tips curl over). Gradually add the remaining 2 tablespoons sugar, beating till stiff peaks form (tips stand straight). When gelatin mixture is partially set (consistency of unbeaten egg whites), fold in some of the stiff-beaten egg whites to lighten the mixture. Fold the lightened mixture into the egg whites. Beat whipping cream till soft peaks form. Fold the whipped cream into the coconut mixture. Chill till mixture mounds when spooned. Pile mixture into the baked pastry shell. Chill pie about 8 hours or till firm. Before serving, arrange desired fruit in center of pie. Top pie with Caramel Filigree. Pipe whipped cream around edge. Garnish with additional fresh fruit. Using a knife, tap firmly atop pie to shatter the filigree "dome" before cutting into the filling. Makes 8 to 12 servings.

Caramel Filigree: Prepare the filigree topping up to 1 hour before serving. Lightly oil the bottom of a 7½-inch round bowl. In a heavy 1-quart saucepan heat ½ cup *sugar* over medium-low heat without stirring. When sugar begins to melt, heat and stir constantly till the mixture is almost a medium caramel color. (Syrup will darken after removing from heat.) Stir in a few drops of *hot water*. Let stand 1 minute. Using a spoon, quickly drizzle caramelized sugar over the bottom of the oiled bowl till a delicate web of caramel is built up. Let stand 10 minutes to harden. Carefully loosen caramel from bowl. If necessary, chip off caramel around bottom of bowl to fit atop pie. Gently lift hardened caramel off bowl to place atop pie.

CARROT MOUSSE TART

Although this is not a true mousse, its light texture is reminiscent of the dish—

- **4 large carrots, very thinly sliced**
- **1 tablespoon butter *or* margarine, melted**
- **3 cups shredded carrots (about 8 medium)**
- **1 potato, peeled and cubed**
- **2 eggs**
- **¼ cup dairy sour cream**
- **1 teaspoon finely shredded orange peel**
- **¼ teaspoon salt**
- **⅛ teaspoon ground turmeric (optional)**
- **⅛ teaspoon ground white pepper**

In saucepan cook sliced carrots in a small amount of boiling salted water for 3 to 4 minutes or till crisp-tender; drain. Brush an 8-inch round flan pan or cake pan with the melted butter or margarine. Beginning in the center of the pan and working toward the outer edges, arrange the drained carrot slices in circles, petal fashion, slightly overlapping slices to cover the bottom and overlapping and pressing onto the sides of pan. Set aside while preparing the filling.

For filling, cook shredded carrots and cubed potato in a small amount of boiling salted water about 15 minutes or just till tender; drain well. In blender container or food processor bowl place the eggs, sour cream, orange peel, salt, turmeric (if desired) and pepper. Add half of the cooked carrots and potato. Cover and blend till smooth. Add remaining cooked vegetables; cover and blend till smooth. Turn into the carrot-lined pan; smooth top with a spatula. Bake in a 350° oven for 30 to 35 minutes or till mixture is set; let stand 5 minutes. With a knife, carefully loosen carrot slices from sides of pan. Place a serving plate atop pan; invert mousse, carefully lifting pan off. (If necessary, replace any carrot slices remaining in pan.) To serve, cut into wedges. Serve hot. Serves 8.

SPINACH RAVIOLI WITH SQUASH FILLING

- **½ pound spinach, cooked and drained, *or* one 10-ounce package frozen chopped spinach, thawed and well drained**
- **1 egg yolk**
- **1 teaspoon cooking oil**
- **¼ teaspoon salt**
- **1½ to 2 cups all-purpose flour**
- **1 cup unseasoned mashed cooked winter squash *or* one 12-ounce package frozen mashed cooked winter squash, thawed and drained**
- **½ cup grated Parmesan cheese**
- **1 tablespoon butter *or* margarine, melted**
- **½ teaspoon ground nutmeg**
- **Dash pepper**
- **1 recipe Nutmeg Cheese Sauce**

In a blender container or food processor bowl blend spinach till smooth (should have ¾ cup pureed spinach). In mixing bowl beat together the spinach puree, egg yolk, cooking oil, and salt. Stir in as much of the flour as you can mix in with a spoon. Turn out onto lightly floured surface; knead in enough of the remaining flour to make a dough that is smooth and elastic (8 to 10 minutes). Cover; let rest 10 minutes. Divide dough into two portions.

For filling, combine squash, Parmesan cheese, butter or margarine, nutmeg, and pepper. To shape ravioli by hand, roll each portion of dough to an 18x11-inch rectangle. Cut each rectangle into 1¾-inch squares (about 60 squares total). Spoon *1 teaspoon* of the filling onto *half* of the squares. Moisten edges of dough with water. Top with remaining squares. Seal edges of squares with tines of fork. (To use ravioli molds, flour tray of molds well. Roll out dough; cut to fit top of tray with dough overlapping edge. Place dough atop tray. With finger, press dough lightly making indentations for each mold. Fill each mold with *1 teaspoon* squash filling. Cut another rectangle of dough to fit tray; place over filled molds. Using a rolling pin, roll over dough pressing to cut and seal squares. Turn out of molds and cut into separate squares, if necessary.)

Cook ravioli in boiling salted water for 6 to 8 minutes or till tender.

Serve with Nutmeg Cheese Sauce. Makes 8 side-dish servings.

Nutmeg Cheese Sauce: In a medium saucepan melt 2 tablespoons butter or margarine. Stir in 2 tablespoons all-purpose flour, ¼ teaspoon ground nutmeg, and ⅛ teaspoon salt. Add 1 cup milk all at once; cook and stir till thickened and bubbly. Cook and stir 1 minute more. Stir in ½ cup shredded Monterey Jack cheese (2 ounces) till cheese is melted. Add ½ cup cream-style cottage cheese, drained; heat through. Pour sauce mixture into a blender container or food processor bowl; cover and blend till smooth. Serve immediately with ravioli.

PASTEL RIBBON BAVARIAN

- **1 envelope unflavored gelatin**
- **¾ cup sugar**
- **4 slightly beaten egg yolks**
- **4 egg whites**
- **1½ cups whipping cream**
- **1½ cups frozen loose-pack unsweetened red raspberries, thawed and pureed (about ¾ cup puree)**
- **1 cup frozen loose-pack unsweetened peaches, thawed and pureed (about ½ cup puree)**
- **2 tablespoons lime juice**
- **Few drops green food coloring**
- **Whipping cream**
- **Rolled cookies**

In saucepan combine gelatin and sugar; stir in ¾ cup *water* then egg yolks. Cook and stir till gelatin is dissolved and mixture is thickened. Cool to room temperature. Beat egg whites till stiff peaks form; fold into gelatin mixture. Beat the 1½ cups whipping cream just till soft peaks form; fold into gelatin mixture. Divide into three equal portions. Lightly fold pureed raspberries into one portion, fold pureed peaches into another, and fold lime juice and green food coloring, if desired, into remaining portion. Pour lime mixture into 6½- or 7-cup glass bowl. Carefully spoon peach layer atop. Then, carefully spoon berry layer atop. Cover; chill 4 to 6 hours or till firm. Before serving, pipe whipped cream atop; garnish with rolled wafers. Makes 12 servings.

DECEMBER

SHARING *the Spirit* OF CHRISTMAS

BY JOY TAYLOR

 Sharing—that's the heart of Christmas! To celebrate, people share traditions—from gift giving to party going—with family, friends, and acquaintances, too. And food plays a special part in these yuletide activities. Christmas just wouldn't be Christmas without the aroma of the festive bird and baked goods wafting from the kitchen!

 On these pages you'll find over 50 recipes to help you make the most of favorite holiday

activities. Everything you'll need for the festivities is here—from international foods to make-ahead nibbles. Once the sharing begins, and you've sampled our treats, you'll realize that fellowship and food go hand in hand in making your holidays memorable.

For Christmas dinner this year, why not invite distant relatives and new neighbors in addition to your immediate family? It needn't be extra work for you—if you plan a potluck-style holiday feast. You provide the extraordinary entrée and have each guest bring a family specialty to the Christmas dinner table. Then all the diners can enjoy their favorite foods, and everyone can sample a holiday smorgasbord of food traditions.

The main attraction at the dinner, of course, is the stuffed poultry. Whether you choose a turkey, goose, or capon, make it a real standout by preparing **Roast Poultry With Rockefeller Dressing** *(left)*. The stuffing is a delicious mixture of oysters, spinach, and bread cubes. And the **Rich Sour Cream Gravy** *(back)* puts the poultry drippings to toothsome use. Serve **Rosé Jelly** *(far left)* and **Spiced Parsnip Relish** *(below)* as the poultry accompaniments.

The Swedish side of the family might bring the **Scandinavian Appetizer Tray** *(above left)*. Its centerpiece is **Swedish Meatballs**, surrounded by an assortment of traditional foods—pickled herring, cucumber slices, potato sausage, and dill pickles.

The secret of Canada's fluffy mashed potatoes is the addition of turnips. **Potatoes With Turnips** *(above right)* are ideal for serving with the gravy.

Photographs: William Sladcik. Food stylist: Fran Paulson

With a houseful of families—each contributing a food
specialty—you're bound to end up with an intriguing
assortment of dishes to complement the entrée. Here's a United
Nations sampling that guests can easily transport to your home.

Appropriately, the finale for this international feast is a worldwide favorite—steamed pudding. Our version, **Hingham Pudding** *(left)*, is sure to please all, no matter what their food heritage. And best of all, this tempting finale can be steamed a day ahead, carried to the dinner, then resteamed just before dessert-time and served warm. No one can resist this light dessert, spiced with molasses and cloves and served with **Poached Pears and Apples**. Slices of the delightful pudding are accented by **Sherried Custard Sauce** *(far left)* and a **Molded Hard Sauce** that's piped into candy cups *(below right)*. You also might offer whipped cream to dollop atop. And for those who dare eat another bite, offer **Buttermilk Pralines** *(below right)*.

SQUASH-STUFFED BAKED APPLES

(far left) To make this favorite German dish, flavor winter squash with brown sugar, orange juice, and nutmeg; spoon the squash into hollowed apples, then bake.

ENDIVE WITH DIJON SAUCE

(top middle left) This French-style recipe tastes world class whether you use Belgian endive or more familiar celery. Dijon mustard is the zesty seasoning in the sauce.

MEXICAN CHRISTMAS SALAD

(top left) Lucky you, if someone brings this crisp and colorful salad to the dinner. It features bananas, beets, jicama, pineapple, and oranges, all flavored with aniseed and pomegranate seeds.

BROWN-AND-SERVE PANETTONE ROLLS

(above left) This updated version of a classic Italian bread lets you do some of the work ahead yet still serve the bread warm. The rolls are partially baked and frozen; baking is completed at serving time.

BOHEMIAN CROWN CAKE

(left) Although this yeast-based delight is called a cake, it's reminiscent of a coffee bread and makes a delightful accompaniment to the dinner.

LIGHT WASSAIL BOWL and IRISH COFFEE

(left) Start and end the meal with two internationally renowned beverages. The punch will whet appetites, and the coffee will be savored after dinner.

ROAST POULTRY WITH ROCKEFELLER DRESSING

2 cups sliced fresh mushrooms
1 large onion, chopped (1 cup)
½ cup shredded carrot
½ cup chopped celery
1 clove garlic, minced
¼ cup butter or margarine
1 pint shucked oysters or two 8-ounce cans whole oysters
8 cups dry bread cubes (about 11 slices bread)
2 tablespoons snipped parsley
1 teaspoon dried basil, crushed
½ teaspoon salt
½ teaspoon poultry seasoning
¼ teaspoon pepper
1 10-ounce package frozen chopped spinach, cooked and well-drained
¼ to ½ cup milk
1 12-pound turkey or two 5- to 6-pound capons or domestic geese
Melted butter or margarine or cooking oil
1 recipe Rich Sour Cream Gravy
1 recipe Rosé Jelly
1 recipe Spiced Parsnip Relish
1 recipe Candied Cranberries (see recipe, page 166)
Orange slices (optional)
Parsley sprigs (optional)
Celery leaves (optional)

For dressing: In a skillet cook the mushrooms, onion, carrot, celery, and garlic in the ¼ cup butter or margarine till tender. Drain the oysters, reserving liquid. Coarsely chop oysters, if large. In large bowl combine the bread cubes, snipped parsley, basil, salt, poultry seasoning, and pepper. Stir in the cooked vegetable mixture, oysters, and spinach. Add oyster liquid to moisten. If necessary, add milk to moisten further.

Spoon dressing loosely into neck cavity of desired poultry. Pull the neck skin to the back of the bird and fasten securely with a small skewer.

Lightly spoon some of the remaining stuffing into the body cavity. If bird opening has a band of skin across the tail, tuck drumsticks under band; if not present, tie legs securely to tail with string. Twist wing tips under back. Cover and chill remaining stuffing.

Place poultry, breast side up, on rack in shallow roasting pan. Brush skin of bird (except geese) with melted butter or margarine or oil. (Prick skin of geese.) Insert meat thermometer. Cover turkey loosely with foil. Roast turkey in a 325° oven for a total of 4½ to 5½ hours. About 45 minutes before turkey is done, remove foil. Roast capons or geese, uncovered, in a 375° oven. Roast capons for 2 to 3 hours. Roast geese 1½ to 2 hours. Brush dry areas of poultry skin occasionally with pan drippings or melted butter or margarine. Poultry is done when thermometer registers 180° to 185° and drumstick moves easily in socket.

Remove bird from oven; cover loosely with foil. Let stand 15 minutes before carving. Meanwhile, prepare Rich Sour Cream Gravy. Serve roast poultry with the gravy, Rosé Jelly, and Spiced Parsnip Relish. If desired, garnish with Candied Cranberries, orange slices, parsley sprigs, and celery leaves. Makes about 12 servings.

Note: To cook remaining stuffing, place stuffing in a casserole; cover and refrigerate. About 30 minutes before serving, heat the casserole, covered, in oven with poultry. Or, prepare Stuffing Balls: Add additional milk to stuffing to moisten and hold mixture together. Form mixture into balls, using ½ cup of the stuffing mixture for each. Bake in greased muffin pans in a 325° oven for 25 to 30 minutes (20 minutes in a 375° oven). Let stand 5 to 10 minutes before removing from muffin pans. If desired, arrange Stuffing Balls around roasted poultry on platter.

RICH SOUR CREAM GRAVY

Hot poultry drippings
¼ cup all-purpose flour
1 teaspoon Worcestershire sauce
½ teaspoon dried basil, crushed
¼ teaspoon minced dried onion
¼ teaspoon salt
Dash pepper
Water
¾ cup dairy sour cream

Pour the drippings from the roast poultry into a 2-cup glass measure. Skim off fat. Return ¼ cup fat to roasting pan. Blend 2 tablespoons of the flour into fat in pan. Cook and stir 1 to 2 minutes, loosening crusty bits in pan. Add Worcestershire, basil, onion, salt, and pepper to juices in glass measure. Add enough water to juices to make 2 cups; stir into mixture in roasting pan. Cook and stir till thickened and bubbly. Stir the remaining 2 tablespoons of flour into sour cream. Gradually blend about ½ cup hot mixture into sour cream. Stir sour cream mixture into gravy. Cook and stir till bubbly; cook 1 minute more. Makes 2½ cups.

SPICED PARSNIP RELISH

2 pounds parsnips
2 medium onions
12 ounces carrots
2 cups white vinegar
2 cups water
1½ cups sugar
1 tablespoon whole allspice
2 teaspoons salt
2 teaspoons mustard seed
½ teaspoon whole cloves

Peel parsnips; coarsely grind (should have 6 cups). Finely chop onions and carrots. In a 5-quart Dutch oven combine all ingredients. Cover; bring to boiling. Simmer, covered, for 18 to 20 minutes or till all vegetables are just tender. Pack relish into hot, clean pint jars, leaving ½-inch headspace. Wipe rims; adjust lids. Process in boiling water bath for 15 minutes (start timing when water boils). Serve at room temperature or chilled. Makes 5 pints.

ROSÉ JELLY

3 cups sugar
1½ cups rosé wine
1 teaspoon finely shredded
    orange peel
½ cup orange juice
½ of a 6-ounce package liquid fruit
    pectin
Paraffin

Combine sugar, wine, orange peel, and orange juice in 5-quart Dutch oven. Bring to full rolling boil. Boil hard for 1 minute, stirring constantly. Remove from heat. Immediately stir in pectin; mix well. Skim off foam, if necessary. Place a metal spoon in a large hot, clean, heat-proof wineglass; quickly pour jelly into glass to within ⅛ inch of top. Remove the spoon. Repeat with five more wineglasses. Immediately cover the wineglasses with hot paraffin. Makes 6 glasses.

WHIPPED POTATOES WITH TURNIPS

4 large potatoes, peeled and
    quartered
2 large turnips, peeled and cut
    into chunks
½ cup finely chopped onion
¼ cup butter or margarine
2 tablespoons snipped parsley
½ teaspoon salt
½ cup shredded cheddar cheese

In large saucepan cook potatoes, covered, in lightly salted boiling water for 10 minutes. Add turnips and onion. Cook 15 minutes more or till vegetables are tender. Drain well. Using electric mixer or potato masher, mash the vegetables with the butter, parsley, salt, and ⅛ teaspoon *pepper* till smooth. Remove 1 cup mixture. Transfer remaining mixture to a 1½-quart casserole; spread evenly in casserole. Spoon reserved vegetable mixture into pastry bag fitted with decorative tip. Pipe a border atop casserole. Cover and chill several hours or overnight. To serve, bake casserole, uncovered, in a 350° oven for 35 to 40 minutes. Sprinkle cheese in center of casserole. Return to oven 5 minutes more or till cheese is melted and casserole is heated through. Makes 8 to 10 servings.

SCANDINAVIAN APPETIZER TRAY

1 recipe Swedish Meatballs
½ pound potato sausage or Polish
    sausage
1 tablespoon cooking oil
1 pint pickled herring, chilled
1 medium cucumber, sliced
    Dill pickle slices

Prepare the Swedish Meatballs; keep warm. Pierce sausage with fork in several places. Place sausage links in skillet; add ¼ cup *water*. Bring to boiling. Cover and simmer for 5 minutes; drain well. Add the oil to skillet. Cook slowly, uncovered, for 12 to 14 minutes more or till liquid from sausage has evaporated and sausage is thoroughly cooked. Slice sausage into ½-inch-thick slices. If desired, line serving tray with leaf lettuce; arrange the sausage, herring, cucumber, pickles, and bowl of meatballs on tray. Garnish with fresh dill, if desired. Makes 8 to 10 appetizer servings.

SWEDISH MEATBALLS

1 beaten egg
⅓ cup light cream
1 cup soft bread crumbs
⅓ cup finely chopped onion
2 tablespoons snipped parsley
¼ teaspoon ground nutmeg
½ pound ground veal
½ pound lean ground pork
1 tablespoon butter
1 tablespoon all-purpose flour
1 teaspoon instant chicken
    bouillon granules
1¼ cups light cream

In mixing bowl combine the egg and the ⅓ cup cream. Stir in the bread crumbs, onion, parsley, ⅛ teaspoon nutmeg, and ¾ teaspoon *salt*. Add ground meats; mix well. Shape into forty-eight 1-inch meatballs. Place meatballs in a 15x10x1-inch baking pan. Bake in a 350° oven about 20 minutes or till done. Meanwhile, in saucepan melt butter. Blend in flour, bouillon granules, and remaining nutmeg. Add remaining light cream. Cook and stir till thickened and bubbly. Cook and stir 2 minutes more. Drain the meatballs; combine with sauce and transfer to heatproof serving bowl. Makes 48.

HINGHAM PUDDING

This light dessert has a coarser texture than most other steamed puddings—

2½ cups all-purpose flour
¼ cup granulated sugar
1 teaspoon baking powder
1 teaspoon ground cinnamon
½ teaspoon baking soda
¼ teaspoon salt
¼ teaspoon ground cloves
2 beaten eggs
¾ cup molasses
¾ cup milk
½ cup butter or margarine, melted
½ cup chopped pecans
1 recipe Poached Pears and
    Apples (see recipe, page 166)
    Powdered sugar
1 recipe Sherried Custard Sauce
    (see recipe, page 166)
1 recipe Molded Hard Sauce (see
    recipe, page 166)
    Sweetened whipped cream

In large bowl stir together flour, granulated sugar, baking powder, cinnamon, soda, salt, and cloves. In bowl combine eggs, molasses, milk, and butter or margarine; stir into dry ingredients. Fold in pecans. Pour batter into a greased and floured 8-cup fluted tube pan. Cover mold with foil; if necessary, tie securely with string. Place mold on rack in deep kettle; add boiling water to kettle to a depth of 1 inch. Cover kettle; steam pudding 1¼ hours or till wooden pick inserted near center comes out clean, adding more water to kettle as necessary. Let mold stand 10 minutes. Carefully unmold; let stand 30 to 40 minutes on wire rack to slightly cool. Cover and chill.

At serving time, return steamed pudding to the same mold. Cover and resteam for 30 minutes or till warm. Unmold; let pudding stand till slightly cool for easier slicing. Meanwhile, prepare the Poached Pears and Apples. To serve, place steamed pudding on a shallow plate. Sift powdered sugar atop. Arrange the poached fruits and syrup around pudding. Serve pudding and fruits with Sherried Custard Sauce, Molded Hard Sauce, and whipped cream. Makes 12 servings.

SQUASH-STUFFED BAKED APPLES

    8 medium baking apples
    ½ cup packed brown sugar
    ½ cup orange juice
    ½ cup water
    2 tablespoons butter *or*
      margarine
    1 12-ounce package frozen
      mashed cooked winter
      squash
    1 tablespoon brown sugar
    ¼ teaspoon salt
    ¼ teaspoon ground nutmeg

Core apples and peel ¼ of the way down; trim bottoms to stand upright. Scoop out the apple centers, leaving a ½-inch-thick shell. Chop removed apple; set aside. Place apple shells in a 13x9x2-inch baking dish. Combine the ½ cup brown sugar, the orange juice, and water. Pour over apples. Bake, uncovered, in a 325° oven about 50 minutes or till nearly tender.

Meanwhile, in saucepan cook the chopped apple in butter or margarine for 2 to 3 minutes. Add squash. Cover and cook over low heat 15 minutes, stirring frequently. Stir in the 1 tablespoon brown sugar, salt, and nutmeg. Remove apples from oven. Spoon squash mixture into apple shells. Sprinkle with additional nutmeg, if desired. Return to the 325° oven and bake 30 minutes or till heated through. Transfer to serving platter; drizzle pan juices over apples. Serves 8.

LIGHT WASSAIL BOWL

    1 large orange, halved
   15 whole cloves
    9 inches stick cinnamon, broken
      up
    ¾ teaspoon whole allspice,
      crushed
    3 750-ml bottles (about 9 cups)
      light Burgundy *or* Burgundy
    ¾ cup brandy
    ½ cup packed brown sugar

Stud the orange halves with cloves. Wrap and tie cinnamon and allspice in cheesecloth bag. In a Dutch oven combine the orange, spice bag, Burgundy, brandy, and brown sugar. Cover; simmer 15 minutes. Transfer to a heat-proof punch bowl. Discard spice bag. Float orange halves atop. Makes 9 cups.

BOHEMIAN CROWN CAKE

    4¼ cups all-purpose flour
    2 packages active dry yeast
    1½ teaspoons salt
    ¾ cup butter *or* margarine
    1 cup granulated sugar
    4 egg yolks
    2 eggs
    1½ cups warm milk (115° to 120°)
    1 cup dried currants
      Powdered sugar

Combine 2½ cups of the flour, the yeast, and salt. In mixer bowl beat the butter or margarine and sugar on medium speed of electric mixer till fluffy. Add yolks and whole eggs, one at a time, beating after each addition till blended. Stir the yeast mixture into egg mixture; beat on high speed 2 minutes. Add the remaining flour alternately with milk, beating well after each addition. Stir in currants. Cover; let rise in warm place till double (1½ hours). Stir dough down; transfer to a greased 10-inch tube pan. Let rise till almost double (1 hour). Bake in a 325° oven 55 to 60 minutes, covering with foil after 30 minutes to prevent overbrowning. Cool 30 minutes in pan. Remove cake from pan; cool on wire rack. Sift powdered sugar atop to serve. Makes 1.

CANDIED CRANBERRIES

In a saucepan combine 2½ cups *sugar* and 1½ cups *water;* bring to boiling, stirring occasionally. Place 4 cups *cranberries* in 10x6x2-inch baking pan. Pour boiling syrup over cranberries. Bake in a 300° oven, uncovered, for 40 minutes, stirring occasionally. Cover loosely and store overnight.

The next day, drain off syrup into a medium saucepan; bring syrup to boiling. Boil 2 minutes. Pour syrup over cranberries and cool without stirring. Cover loosely and store overnight. Repeat twice. Transfer berries to baking sheet and cover loosely; let stand for 3 days to dry. Turn several times for even drying. Roll dried cranberries in sugar and store in tightly covered container. Use berries as a garnish for roast poultry. Makes about 3½ cups.

POACHED PEARS AND APPLES

In 12-inch skillet combine 1 cup *water,* ½ cup *sugar,* and 2 teaspoons *lemon juice.* Bring to boiling. Meanwhile, core 3 large *apples* and 2 large *pears;* cut each into six wedges. Add fruit wedges to syrup in skillet. Reduce heat; simmer, covered, for 10 to 12 minutes or till fruit is just tender, gently turning occasionally. Remove fruit from skillet with a slotted spoon. Boil syrup about 4 minutes or till reduced to ⅓ cup. Stir in 3 tablespoons *orange liqueur;* remove skillet from heat. Arrange fruits around base of Hingham Pudding (see recipe, page 165). Pour syrup over fruits.

SHERRIED CUSTARD SAUCE

In a small heavy saucepan combine 2 beaten *egg yolks,* 2 tablespoons *sugar,* and dash *salt.* Add ¾ cup *milk.* Cook and stir over medium-low heat till mixture starts to thicken and coats a metal spoon. Remove from heat. Pour mixture into a bowl and set in a larger bowl of ice water to cool. Stir sauce for 1 to 2 minutes. Stir in 1 tablespoon *cream sherry* and ½ teaspoon *vanilla.* Cover; chill. Makes 1 cup.

MOLDED HARD SAUCE

    ½ cup butter *or* margarine
    2 cups sifted powdered sugar
    2 tablespoons whipping cream
    ½ teaspoon finely shredded lemon
      peel
    ½ teaspoon vanilla
      Ground cinnamon (optional)

In medium mixer bowl thoroughly beat together the butter or margarine, 1 cup of the powdered sugar, whipping cream, lemon peel, and vanilla on medium speed of electric mixer. Add the remaining powdered sugar. Beat till smooth. Spoon or pipe the mixture into paper or foil bonbon cups, using about 1 tablespoon for each. (Or, spoon mixture into a covered container.) Chill sauce till serving time. If desired, sprinkle ground cinnamon atop sauce before serving. Makes about 1½ cups.

ENDIVE WITH DIJON SAUCE

    4 Belgian endive, halved, or 8
       large ribs celery, halved
 ⅓ cup water
 ¼ teaspoon salt
    1 small onion, sliced and
       separated into rings
    1 cup dairy sour cream
    3 tablespoons Dijon-style
       mustard
    2 tablespoons all-purpose flour
    2 teaspoons sugar
    1 teaspoon instant chicken
       bouillon granules
 ⅛ teaspoon pepper
 ¼ cup fine dry bread crumbs
    2 tablespoons snipped chives
    1 tablespoon butter or margarine

With a small knife trim the ends of each
endive bunch. In 10-inch skillet combine the water and salt. Add endive or
celery and onion. Bring to boiling. Reduce heat; cover and simmer for 10
minutes. Using a slotted spoon, transfer the vegetables to a 12x7½x2-inch
baking dish. Add enough water to
cooking liquid to measure ½ cup liquid; set aside. Stir together the sour
cream, Dijon-style mustard, flour,
sugar, bouillon granules, and pepper.
Stir in the reserved liquid. Spoon sauce
over vegetables in baking dish. Chill
till ready to bake.

    At serving time, stir together the
dry bread crumbs, snipped chives, and
the butter or margarine; sprinkle over
the casserole. Bake, covered, in 325°
oven for 30 minutes or till hot. Makes
8 servings.

IRISH COFFEE

    6 cups hot strong coffee
    1 cup Irish whiskey or bourbon
 ¼ cup packed brown sugar
 ½ cup whipping cream, whipped

In coffeepot or heat-proof decanter
combine coffee, liquor, and sugar. Stir
to dissolve sugar. To serve, pour into
heat-proof mugs; top with whipped
cream. Makes 8 to 10 servings.

MEXICAN CHRISTMAS SALAD

    2 cups peeled, sliced jicama
    1 20-ounce can pineapple chunks
    1 8-ounce can julienne beets
    1 tablespoon lemon juice
    1 to 2 teaspoons aniseed
       Shredded lettuce
    2 bananas
    2 large oranges, peeled and
       sectioned
 ¼ cup peanuts
    2 tablespoons pomegranate
       seeds
 ½ cup mayonnaise

In large bowl combine the jicama, undrained pineapple, and undrained beets.
Stir in lemon juice, aniseed, and ¼ teaspoon salt. Cover; chill for several hours,
gently stirring once or twice.

    Drain beet mixture; reserve 2 ta-
blespoons of the liquid. Line serving
platter with lettuce. Arrange beets,
pineapple, and jicama atop lettuce.
Slice the bananas; arrange banana
slices and orange sections on platter.
Sprinkle peanuts and pomegranate
seeds over salad. For dressing in bowl
stir together mayonnaise and the 2 tablespoons reserved beet liquid; pass
dressing to spoon atop fruits and vegetables. Makes 10 servings.

BUTTERMILK PRALINES

    2 cups packed dark brown sugar
    1 cup buttermilk
 ¼ cup butter or margarine
    1 teaspoon vanilla
    2 cups pecan halves or pieces

In a heavy 3-quart saucepan stir together the brown sugar, buttermilk,
and ¼ teaspoon salt. Bring to boiling,
stirring constantly. Cook and stir over
medium heat till candy thermometer
registers 234° (soft-ball stage), about
10 minutes; stir as necessary to prevent mixture from sticking to pan. Remove from heat. Add butter and vanilla. Do not stir. Cool about 30
minutes, without stirring, to 150°.
Quickly stir in pecans. Beat candy for
3 minutes or till slightly thickened and
glossy. Drop candy by tablespoonfuls
onto a baking sheet lined with waxed
paper. If candy becomes too stiff to drop,
add a little hot water to make it of the
right consistency. Makes 30.

BROWN AND SERVE PANETTONE ROLLS

 5¼ to 5¾ cups all-purpose flour
    2 packages active dry yeast
    1 cup milk
 ½ cup honey
 ½ cup butter or margarine
    1 teaspoon salt
    3 eggs
 ¾ cup dried currants
 ¼ cup chopped candied citron
 ½ teaspoon finely shredded lemon
       peel
    1 slightly beaten egg
    1 tablespoon water

In large mixer bowl combine 2 cups of
the flour and the yeast. In saucepan
heat milk, honey, butter or margarine, and salt just till warm (115° to
120°) and butter is almost melted; stir
constantly. Add to flour mixture; add
eggs. Beat at low speed of electric mixer
for ½ minute, scraping sides of bowl
constantly. Beat 3 minutes at high
speed. Stir in currants, citron, and
lemon peel. Stir in as much of the remaining flour as you can mix in with
a spoon. Turn out onto lightly floured
surface. Knead in enough of the remaining flour to make a moderately
stiff dough that is smooth and elastic
(6 to 8 minutes total). Shape into a ball.
Place in lightly greased bowl; turn once
to grease surface. Cover; let rise in
warm place till double (1½ to 2 hours).

    Punch dough down. Divide dough
into thirds. Cover; let rest 10 minutes.
Turn out onto floured surface. Divide
each portion of dough into 12 pieces;
shape into balls. Place on greased
baking sheets or in greased muffin
pans. Cover; let rise till double (about
45 minutes). Cut a cross in the top of
each roll. Bake in 325° oven for 10 to
12 minutes; do not brown. Remove from
pan; cool. Wrap in moisture-vaporproof wrap. Seal, label and freeze.

    To serve, let wrapped rolls stand
at room temperature 10 to 15 minutes.
Unwrap; place on baking sheet. Brush
rolls with a mixture of slightly beaten
egg and water. Bake in 400° oven 8 to
10 minutes or till golden. Makes 36.

SHARING
Holiday Festivity

Go ahead! Make this the Christmas you throw the gala party you've been putting off for years. Having a holiday bash needn't mean a lot of pre-party work or last-minute headaches, and we'll prove it. Our recipes can be adjusted to fit the affair, no matter how many names appear on your guest list—10, 25, or even 50. And all of our nibbles require little party-day effort. With just a few last-minute preparations, you can relax and visit with your guests, not fuss in the kitchen.

From left to right: Melt-in-the-mouth *Pork Pastries* are formed by wrapping phyllo dough around a meat and apple filling. Chill the pastries, then bake and serve.

Slip *Romano Shrimp-Stuffed Mushrooms* in the oven alongside the pastries. Canned shrimp and Romano cheese are the flavor boosters in these fix-ahead morsels.

Prepare *Whole Wheat Nut Bread* ahead, too, then serve it with creamy *Pumpkin Butter*.

Being the host and hostess needn't mean you do all the work. Let guests create their own mini-wiches with *Quince-Glazed Ham*, our chutney spread, and bakery buns.

Holiday Fruit Diamonds will impress even fruitcake connoisseurs. Why tell them you short-cut the work with a cake mix?

If you're tired of that party staple, the cheese ball, serve slices of *Sherry-Cheese Log*.

Add extra cheer to the evening by serving *Spiced Spritzers*.

PORK PASTRIES

½ pound ground pork
¼ cup finely chopped onion
1½ cups finely shredded cabbage
2 medium apples, cored and
  finely chopped
3 tablespoons cold water
1 tablespoon Dijon-style mustard
2 teaspoons all-purpose flour
½ teaspoon salt
½ teaspoon ground cinnamon
  Dash bottled hot pepper sauce
3 tablespoons fine dry bread
  crumbs
10 sheets frozen phyllo dough
  (17x13-inch rectangles),
  thawed
½ cup butter, melted

In skillet cook pork and onion till meat is brown; drain. Place cabbage and apples over meat. Cover; cook over low heat for 10 minutes or till cabbage is tender. Combine the water, mustard, flour, salt, cinnamon, and hot pepper sauce. Add to meat mixture, stirring till all is coated. Stir in bread crumbs. Cool slightly.

Unfold the phyllo dough; spread one sheet flat. (Keep remaining sheets covered with a damp towel.) Brush the one sheet with some of the melted butter. Top with second sheet; brush with butter. Cut stack crosswise into eight 2-inch strips. Spoon 2 teaspoons filling near one end of each strip. Fold end over filling at 45-degree angle. Continue folding to form a triangle that encloses the filling, using entire strip of phyllo. Repeat with remaining dough and filling. Cover; chill. To serve, place pastries on a baking sheet. Bake in 400° oven about 20 minutes or till golden. Makes 40.

For 25 servings: Prepare filling for Pork Pastries as directed *except* use 1 pound *ground pork,* ½ cup *chopped onion,* 3 cups *shredded cabbage,* 4 *apples,* ⅓ cup *cold water,* 2 tablespoons *Dijon-style mustard,* 4 teaspoons all-purpose *flour,* 1 teaspoon *salt,* 1 teaspoon ground *cinnamon,* several dashes *bottled hot pepper sauce,* and ⅓ cup *fine dry bread crumbs.* Use 10 sheets *frozen phyllo dough.* For each Pork Pastry Roll, layer 5 phyllo dough sheets on a pastry cloth, using ¼ cup melted *butter* to brush lightly between each sheet. Place half of the filling along the long side of the dough near the edge. Roll up starting on long side near

the filling; fold in ends. Brush with any remaining butter. Repeat with remaining 5 sheets phyllo and filling. Cover; chill. To serve, place rolls, seam side down, on a rack in a 15x10x1-inch baking pan. Bake in 400° oven 25 to 30 minutes or till golden brown. Serve warm; slice.

For 50 servings: Double the recipe for 25 servings.

ROMANO SHRIMP-STUFFED MUSHROOMS

This easy appetizer can go in the oven along with the Pork Pastries since they both are heated at 400°—

20 large fresh mushrooms (2- to
  2½-inch diameter)
1 4½-ounce can shrimp, drained,
  rinsed, and broken up
1 4-ounce container whipped
  cream cheese with chives
½ teaspoon Worcestershire sauce
  Dash garlic powder
  Dash bottled hot pepper sauce
  Grated Romano cheese

Remove the stems from mushrooms. Simmer mushroom caps in boiling water for 2 minutes. Drain; invert caps on paper toweling. Cool.

Meanwhile, combine shrimp, cream cheese, Worcestershire sauce, garlic powder, and hot pepper sauce. Spoon shrimp mixture into mushroom caps; place in shallow baking pan or dish. Sprinkle with Romano cheese. Cover; chill 3 to 24 hours.

Before serving, uncover and bake in a 400° oven 15 minutes. Makes 20.

For 25 servings: Prepare *filling* for the Romano Shrimp-Stuffed Mushrooms as directed above *except* use two 4-ounce containers *whipped cream cheese with chives,* 1 teaspoon *Worcestershire sauce,* ⅛ teaspoon *garlic powder,* and several dashes bottled *hot pepper sauce.* Beat ¼ cup grated *Romano cheese* and ¼ cup *milk* into the mixture. Cover; refrigerate 3 to 24 hours. Serve as a dip with *sliced mushrooms* and additional *vegetable dippers.*

For 50 Servings: Double the recipe for 25 servings.

WHOLE WHEAT NUT BREAD

You can prepare this bread several days or weeks before the party. Just wrap the cooled, baked loaves in moisture-vaporproof material and store in the freezer. Thaw before serving—

1 cup all-purpose flour
¾ cup whole wheat flour
¾ cup sugar
2 teaspoons baking powder
½ teaspoon salt
1 egg
¾ cup milk
¼ cup cooking oil
1 tablespoon lemon juice
1 teaspoon vanilla
½ cup chopped walnuts
1 recipe Pumpkin Butter

In mixing bowl stir together flours, sugar, baking powder, and salt; set aside. In another mixing bowl beat together egg, milk, oil, lemon juice, and vanilla. Add dry ingredients to beaten mixture, stirring just till moistened. Fold in the walnuts.

Turn batter into four greased and floured 10-ounce soup cans. Bake in a 350° oven for 30 to 35 minutes or till done. Cool 10 minutes. Remove from cans; cool on wire racks. Wrap in clear plastic wrap and store overnight.

To serve, slice the bread and spread Pumpkin Butter over one side of each slice. Halve each slice and form half-moon sandwiches. Makes 4 loaves.

Pumpkin Butter: In mixer bowl beat ½ cup *butter or margarine* on medium speed of electric mixer 30 seconds. Gradually beat in ½ cup canned *pumpkin,* ¼ cup sifted *powdered sugar,* and ¼ teaspoon *pumpkin pie spice.* Cover; chill 3 to 24 hours. Let stand at room temperature 30 to 45 minutes to soften for spreading. Makes 1 cup.

For 25 servings: Prepare the Whole Wheat Nut Bread as directed *except* double all ingredients and bake in two 8x4x2-inch loaf pans for 50 minutes. Double the recipe for Pumpkin Butter.

For 50 servings: Prepare the Whole Wheat Nut Bread as directed *except* double the recipe two times (do not mix all the batter at one time; instead mix two separate batches). Serve with four recipes Pumpkin Butter.

SHERRY-CHEESE LOG

1 8-ounce package Neufchâtel cheese
1½ cups shredded Swiss cheese
1 tablespoon snipped parsley
2 tablespoons cream sherry
⅓ cup chopped almonds, toasted
Snipped parsley
Toasted sesame seed
Assorted crackers

Let cheeses stand at room temperature 1 hour. In small mixer bowl beat cheeses and the 1 tablespoon parsley till blended. Add sherry, beating till nearly smooth. Stir in nuts. Cover; chill 1 hour. Mold into a 10-inch log. Press snipped parsley and sesame seed into log, forming rows. Wrap log in moisture-vaporproof wrap. Chill. Serve with crackers; garnish with grapes, if desired. Serves 10.

For 25 servings: Prepare log as directed *except* double ingredients; make 2 logs.

For 50 servings: Prepare log as directed *except* use four times ingredients; make 2 large logs.

SPICED SPRITZERS

8 inches stick cinnamon, broken
3 whole cloves
5 cups rosé wine
2½ cups ginger ale, chilled

Tie spices in cheesecloth. Heat wine and spice bag just to simmering. Cool. Pour into pitcher; chill. To serve, pour 4 ounces chilled wine and 2 ounces ginger ale into each wineglass. Garnish with lemon peel strips and Fruited Ice Cubes, if desired. Makes 10 (6-ounce) servings.

Fruited Ice Cubes: Place 1 *frozen raspberry or tart red cherry* in each compartment of ice cube tray. Add water and freeze into cubes.

For 25 servings: Prepare spritzer as directed *except* heat together 13 cups *rosé wine* and the spice bag. Stir in 6 cups *cranberry-apple juice cocktail* and ⅓ cup *sugar*. Heat through. Serve punch warm or chilled. Omit ginger ale. If served chilled, prepare a 3- or 4-cup ice ring using raspberries or cherries as decorations.

For 50 servings: Prepare a double recipe as directed for 25 servings.

QUINCE-GLAZED HAM

1 recipe Chutney Spread
1 1½-pound canned ham
¼ cup quince *or* apple jelly
2 tablespoons honey
1 tablespoon dry white wine
Miniature hamburger buns

Prepare Chutney Spread. Place ham on rack in shallow baking pan. Bake, uncovered, in a 325° oven 45 minutes. Meanwhile, combine jelly, honey, and wine; heat and stir till jelly melts. Spoon jelly glaze over ham. Continue baking 20 minutes more or till meat thermometer registers 140°, basting occasionally. To serve, slice ham; arrange on platter with kumquats and curly endive, if desired. Serve with miniature buns and Chutney Spread. Makes 10 servings.

Chutney Spread: In mixer bowl combine 6 ounces (1½ cups) shredded process *Gruyere or Swiss cheese,* one 3-ounce package *cream cheese,* softened, ¼ cup *chutney,* and ¼ cup *quince or apple jelly;* beat till smooth. Cover; chill.

For 25 servings: Prepare *two* recipes Chutney Spread. Cover and chill. Bake one 3-pound *canned ham* as above for 1½ to 2 hours or till meat thermometer registers 140°. Prepare the glaze as directed using ½ cup *jelly,* ¼ cup *honey,* and 2 tablespoons *wine.* Spoon the glaze on ham during last 20 minutes of baking. Serve as directed.

For 50 servings: Prepare *four* recipes Chutney Spread. Cover and chill. Bake one 5-pound canned *ham* as above 1½ to 2 hours or till meat thermometer registers 140°. Prepare glaze as directed using ¾ cup *jelly,* ½ cup *honey,* and ¼ cup *wine.* Spoon glaze on ham during last 20 minutes of baking. Serve as directed.

HOLIDAY FRUIT DIAMONDS

1 package 1-layer-size yellow cake mix
½ teaspoon shredded orange peel
⅓ cup orange juice
2 eggs
1 6-ounce package dried fruit bits, finely chopped
¾ cup chopped walnuts
Brandy
1 recipe Icing

Line bottom and sides of an 8x8x2-inch baking pan with foil. In large mixer bowl combine cake mix, orange peel, orange juice, and eggs. Beat on medium speed of electric mixer about 2 minutes till smooth. Fold in the fruit and nuts. Spoon batter into prepared pan. Bake cake in a 300° oven for 45 minutes or till done. Place on wire rack; cool. Carefully remove cake from pan; remove foil. Wrap cake in brandy-soaked cheesecloth. Overwrap in foil. Store in refrigerator up to 4 days.

To serve, cut cake with a serrated knife into 10 diamonds. Place on a wire rack over waxed paper. Drizzle Icing over diamonds. If desired, drizzle a crisscross pattern with tinted Icing. Let dry. Garnish with halved candied cherries, if desired. Makes 10.

Icing: In saucepan stir together 2¼ cups *granulated sugar,* 1 cup *hot water,* and ¼ teaspoon *cream of tartar.* Cover and cook till boiling. Uncover; attach candy thermometer to saucepan. Cook till mixture reaches 226°. Remove from heat. Cool at room temperature to 110°. Stir in ½ teaspoon *vanilla.* Stir in enough sifted *powdered sugar* (about 1 cup) to make pourable consistency. Add 2 tablespoons *hot water* if mixture is too thick. If desired, remove a small portion of the icing and tint with *red or green food coloring.*

For 25 servings: Prepare Holiday Fruit Diamonds as directed. In addition to an 8x8x2-inch cake, prepare a second cake as directed above using 1 package 2-layer-size *yellow cake mix,* 1 teaspoon shredded *orange peel,* 1 cup *orange juice,* 4 eggs, two 6-ounce packages *dried fruit bits,* finely chopped and 1½ cups chopped *walnuts;* mix as directed. Turn batter into a 13x9x2-inch baking pan lined with foil. Bake in a 300° oven for 50 to 55 minutes. Place on a wire rack; cool thoroughly. Carefully remove cake from pan (cut cake in half, if necessary, to remove). Wrap, soak, and store cake as directed. To serve, cut the two cakes into 25 diamonds total. Prepare three recipes of the *Icing* to drizzle over the 25 diamonds. (Prepare Icing in three separate batches.)

For 50 servings: Prepare Holiday Fruit Diamonds as directed. In addition to the 8x8x2-inch cake, prepare two 13x9x2-inch cakes as directed for 25 servings, mixing the batter for each 13x9x2-inch cake separately. Prepare four recipes Icing.

SHARING
Goodies and Goodwill

This year, why not spread Christmas cheer beyond your circle of close family and friends? With a few fellow merrymakers and plenty of homemade goodies, you can play Santa Claus at a retirement home, a children's home, or a hospital. Who could resist your glad tidings when they come in the form of old-fashioned yuletide treats?

All of our tasty take-along foods can be prepared at home, then carried to the party spot without mishap in sturdy carrying containers. When you and your co-Santas arrive, arrange the foods attractively and watch all of your guests' eyes open wide. Whether young or old or both participate in the celebration, everyone will savor the fellowship, not to mention the fruitcake, candies, cookies, punch, and more!

Transport **Citrus Cider** *(top left)* in insulated jugs; then when you arrive at the party location, transfer the drink to a heat-proof punch bowl set on a warmer. Garnish the warm beverage with sliced apple.

Delight all of your guests of honor with delicate bites of **Chicken-Stuffed Cream Puffs** *(top right)*. These mini cheese puffs can be filled with the creamy mixture, then wrapped and carried to the social.

Both **No-Cook Peanutty Fudge** and **Pinwheel Divinity** *(right)* will remind anyone over 60 of old-fashioned treats—and show the youngsters the goodies they've been missing!

You can treat the crowd to **Shrimp Mousse** *(bottom right)* for a pittance if you call on canned seafood and shrimp soup. To keep the mousse shapely, unmold it at the party.

Cherry Butter Horns *(bottom left)* get their spicy flavor from cardamom and nutmeg, and their colorful centers from cherry cake and pastry filling.

The **Whole Wheat Sour Cream Fruitcake** *(middle left)* is our quick version of fruitcake. For easy slicing, make the cake at least a day before and wrap the loaf in brandy-soaked cheesecloth.

Photographs: William Sladcik; Mike Dieter

173

December

CITRUS CIDER

2 quarts apple cider *or* juice
3 cups water
1 6-ounce can frozen orange-
    pineapple juice concentate,
    thawed
½ cup light molasses
4 inches stick cinnamon
1 teaspoon whole cloves
    Apple slices (optional)

In a 4-quart Dutch oven combine cider or juice, water, orange-pineapple juice concentrate, molasses, cinnamon, and cloves. Simmer 10 minutes. Transfer to insulated jugs to keep warm. To serve, transfer warm cider to a heat-proof punch bowl placed on a warming tray; or pour into an electric slow crockery cooker turned to low-heat setting. If desired, float apple slices atop cider. Makes 24 (4-ounce) servings.

NO-COOK PEANUT FUDGE

¾ cup peanut butter
½ cup butter *or* margarine
½ cup light corn syrup
1 teaspoon vanilla
3½ cups sifted powdered sugar
½ cup unsweetened cocoa powder
½ cup finely chopped peanuts

In large mixer bowl beat together peanut butter, butter or margarine, corn syrup, and vanilla. Gradually beat in *half* the sugar and all of the cocoa powder. Stir in remaining sugar; knead mixture on wooden board till well blended and smooth. Add peanuts by pressing and kneading into candy. Press fudge into individual candy molds. Unmold, using wooden picks to loosen corners. Allow candies to set on waxed paper. Or, pat candy into an 8x8x2-inch pan; cut into squares. Transfer candy to sturdy container to transport. Makes 2 pounds candy.

CHICKEN-STUFFED CREAM PUFFS

½ cup water
¼ cup butter *or* margarine
½ cup all-purpose flour
2 eggs
½ cup shredded muenster *or*
    Swiss cheese
1 5-ounce can boned white
    chicken, drained and flaked
½ cup finely chopped water
    chestnuts
¼ cup buttermilk salad dressing
    with chives, mayonnaise, *or*
    salad dressing
1 2-ounce can mushroom stems
    and pieces, drained and
    chopped
1 tablespoon chopped pimiento
¼ teaspoon dry mustard
    Parsley sprigs (optional)

In 2-quart saucepan bring the ½ cup water and butter or margarine to boiling. Add flour, stir vigorously. Cook and stir till mixture forms a ball that doesn't separate. Remove from heat; cool 10 minutes. Add eggs, one at a time, beating 1 minute after each addition or till smooth. Stir in cheese. Spoon mixture into a pastry bag fitted with a decorative tip. Pipe batter into spirals, 1 inch in diameter, onto greased baking sheet. Or, using 1 rounded teaspoon dough for each puff, drop dough onto greased baking sheet. Bake in a 400° oven 20 minutes or till puffed. Remove from oven; cut off tops. Remove any soft dough. Cool puffs on wire rack. If desired, store, tightly covered, up to 1 day at room temperature. Or cover tightly with moisture-vapor-proof wrap; freeze. To thaw, let stand for one hour at room temperature.

For filling, combine chicken, water chestnuts, salad dressing, mushrooms, pimiento, and mustard. Cover; chill. To serve, fill puff bottoms with chicken filling; replace tops. Transfer to sturdy containers to carry to party. To serve, garnish with parsley sprigs, if desired. Makes 28 puffs.

ALMOND PINWHEEL DIVINITY

Like any other divinity, this one should not be made on a humid day—

2½ cups sugar
½ cup light corn syrup
½ cup water
¼ teaspoon salt
2 egg whites
½ teaspoon almond extract
    Powdered sugar
⅔ cup finely chopped toasted
    almonds
⅔ cup finely chopped red and
    green candied cherries

In a heavy 2-quart saucepan combine sugar, corn syrup, water, and salt. Cook and stir till sugar dissolves and mixture boils. Cook over medium heat, without stirring, to 260° (hard-ball stage). (Mixture should boil gently over entire surface.)

As temperature nears 250°, in large mixer bowl beat egg whites with electric mixer to stiff peaks (tips stand straight). Gradually pour hot syrup in a thin stream over egg whites, beating at high speed of electric mixer. Add almond extract; beat 4 to 5 minutes more or till mixture holds its shape.

Turn candy onto a towel dusted generously with powdered sugar. Roll candy with a rolling pin dusted with additional powdered sugar to a 14-inch square, ¼ inch thick. Cut in half to form two 14x7-inch rectangles.

Combine chopped almonds and the candied cherries. Sprinkle each candy rectangle with half the nut mixture to within 1 inch of the long edges; press in lightly. Roll up each piece from the long edge, jelly-roll fashion, sealing at ends. Wrap tightly in foil to store and transport.

To serve, slice candy crosswise into ⅜-inch-thick pieces. Place individual pieces in *petit four* cups. Store any remaining candy in foil. Makes 60 pieces.

174

HONEY-CHERRY BUTTER HORNS

If you don't have ground cardamom on your spice rack, you can substitute ground cinnamon—

¾ cup butter *or* margarine
1 cup packed light brown sugar
¼ cup honey
1 egg
3¼ cups all-purpose flour
¾ teaspoon baking soda
½ teaspoon ground cardamom
½ teaspoon ground nutmeg
¼ teaspoon salt
¾ cup canned cherry *or* apricot cake and pastry filling
Powdered sugar (optional)

In large mixer bowl beat the butter or margarine for 30 seconds. Add the light brown sugar and honey; beat till fluffy. Beat in the egg.

In a bowl stir together the all-purpose flour, baking soda, ground cardamom, ground nutmeg, and salt. Add dry ingredients to creamed mixture, stirring to make a soft dough.

Divide the dough into thirds; wrap each third in waxed paper or clear plastic wrap. Chill in refrigerator at least 3 hours.

On well-floured surface roll one portion of dough to a 12-inch circle with a rolling pin. (Refrigerate the remaining dough while working with one portion at a time.) Spread ⅓ of the cherry or apricot pastry filling over dough to within ¾ inch of edge.

With a fluted pastry wheel or sharp knife, cut dough into 16 wedges. Roll each wedge into crescent. Place cookies on an ungreased cookie sheet.

Bake in a 350° oven for 11 minutes or till golden. Cool on wire rack. Repeat with remaining dough and filling. If desired, sprinkle cooled cookies with powdered sugar. Makes 4 dozen.

SHRIMP MOUSSE

If you like, make this mousse in two 3-cup molds and arrange two platters—

1 10¾-ounce can condensed cream of shrimp soup
½ cup cold water
2 envelopes unflavored gelatin
¼ teaspoon pepper
1 cup cream-style cottage cheese
1 cup mayonnaise *or* salad dressing
½ cup plain yogurt
1 tablespoon lemon juice
1 7-ounce package frozen cooked shrimp, thawed
4 hard-cooked eggs, finely chopped
2 tablespoons sliced green onion
Sieved hard-cooked egg yolk (optional)
Chopped hard-cooked egg white (optional)
Fresh dill (optional)
Party rye bread slices *or* crackers

In a medium saucepan stir together the cream of shrimp soup, cold water, unflavored gelatin, and pepper. Let stand 10 minutes.

Stir soup mixture over low heat till gelatin is dissolved. With rotary beater beat in cream-style cottage cheese, mayonnaise or salad dressing, plain yogurt, and lemon juice.

Set aside a few whole shrimp for garnish. Finely chop remaining shrimp. Fold in the chopped shrimp, chopped hard-cooked eggs, and sliced green onion. Turn mixture into 6-cup mold. Chill till firm.

Transport shrimp mousse to party in the mold. Unmold just before serving. Garnish with reserved shrimp, sieved hard-cooked egg yolk, chopped hard-cooked egg white, and fresh dill. Serve with party rye bread slices or crackers. Makes about 5 cups.

WHOLE WHEAT-SOUR CREAM FRUITCAKE

3 cups diced mixed candied fruits and peels
2 cups raisins
1 cup chopped walnuts
1½ cups whole wheat flour
⅔ cup packed brown sugar
½ cup toasted wheat germ
2 teaspoons baking powder
1 teaspoon ground cinnamon
1 teaspoon ground nutmeg
½ teaspoon salt
½ teaspoon ground cloves
4 eggs
1½ cups dairy sour cream
⅓ cup butter *or* margarine, melted
1 teaspoon vanilla
Red and green candied cherries (optional)
Corn syrup (optional)

In a bowl combine the mixed candied fruits and peels, raisins, and chopped walnuts; set aside.

In large mixing bowl stir together the whole wheat flour, packed brown sugar, toasted wheat germ, baking powder, ground cinnamon, ground nutmeg, salt, and ground cloves.

In small mixing bowl beat together the eggs, dairy sour cream, melted butter or margarine, and vanilla. Add to flour mixture. Add fruit-nut mixture; mix well. Turn batter into two greased 8x4x2-inch loaf pans. Bake in 325° oven 60 to 65 minutes or till done. Remove loaves from pans; cool on wire rack.

Wrap cooled loaves in foil and refrigerate at least 24 hours. If desired before leaving for the party, garnish with candied cherries using corn syrup to attach them to loaves.

Transport, covered, to party. Slice to serve. Makes 2 loaves.

SHARING
Homemade Specialties

What better way to say you care than to bestow gifts that you made in your own kitchen? You'll find all the inspiration you need in our lineup of handmade holiday presents—from sweet nibbles to a soothing liqueur. And you don't have to be a culinary wizard to make them—each gift is surprisingly easy. Plus, these presents will be remembered long after the holidays because they're packaged in reusable containers.

EDIBLE CHRISTMAS CARDS

(top) These holiday greetings will certainly be savored! Inscribe your messages on giant spice cookies—then keep them fresh for giving in show-off envelopes.

HOMEMADE ITALIAN LIQUEUR

(above left) Aniseed, banana, and vanilla season this sophisicated libation. To blend the flavors, stir the liqueur together several weeks before you present it.

BANANA-BERRY JAM

(opposite page, right) Cranberry fanciers can relish their favorite fruit year round with this spread. Transport the jam in an easy-to-craft wood crate.

PLUM PUDDING CANDY

(top) Enchant Christmas traditionalists with these morsels, reminiscent of the English dessert, packed in a homemade box.

JAVA WALNUT SAUCE

(above left) Indulge your favorite coffee lovers with this rich sauce. It's best served over ice cream, but some may sample it straight from the jar! Nestle the sauce in a nut-filled basket.

WILD RICE PILAF MIX

(above right) Your gourmet cousins will welcome this shelf-stable mix. Just by adding water, they can have an elegant pilaf in minutes.

EDIBLE CHRISTMAS COOKIES

    4 cups all-purpose flour
    1 teaspoon ground cinnamon
    ½ teaspoon ground nutmeg
    ¼ teaspoon baking soda
    ⅛ teaspoon salt
 1½ cups butter *or* margarine
    1 cup granulated sugar
    1 cup packed brown sugar
    2 eggs
    1 teaspoon vanilla
      Green food coloring
      Red food coloring
      Colored sugar (optional)
      Plastic Christmas Card
      Envelopes (optional)

In a bowl stir together all-purpose flour, ground cinnamon, ground nutmeg, baking soda, and salt; set aside.

In large mixer bowl beat butter or margarine on high speed of electric mixer for 30 seconds. Add the granulated sugar and brown sugar; beat till the mixture is fluffy.

Separate eggs. Place each egg yolk in a separate small bowl. Cover and chill egg yolks. Add egg whites and vanilla to batter; beat till smooth. Stir flour mixture into beaten mixture. Mix well. Chill dough, covered, 2 hours or till firm.

On lightly floured surface roll ¾ cup of the dough to ⅛-inch thickness. Using several cookie cutters, cut dough into small desired shapes (Christmas tree, bell, star, angel, or other decorations). Place the decorative cutouts on an ungreased cookie sheet; cover with clear plastic wrap and chill.

For each Christmas card, roll ¾ cup chilled dough about ¼ inch thick directly on an ungreased cookie sheet. Shape or cut into a 6-inch square. Trim, if necessary, with a knife or a pastry wheel. Crimp edge of each Christmas card cookie with fork. If desired, reroll trimmings to ⅛-inch thickness and cut into additional decorative cutouts.

To one beaten egg yolk, add a few drops of green food coloring; to the second egg yolk add a few drops of red food coloring.

Using paintbrushes, paint a colored egg yolk wash over all or part of each Christmas card and decorative cutouts. (You can paint an entire cookie one color or paint a design on the dough with two colors. Or, write a holiday greeting.)

Arrange one or two decorative dough cutouts atop each card. Sprinkle colored sugar atop decorative cutout, if desired.

Bake Christmas card in 350° oven 12 minutes or till light brown. Cool on cookie sheet for 5 to 10 minutes. Remove to wire rack; cool. Repeat with remaining dough, coloring, and sugar to make 4 more cookies.

To present as a gift, place each cookie in a Plastic Christmas Card Envelope. Or, place cookie in a sturdy box and wrap. Makes 5 cards.

PLASTIC CHRISTMAS CARD ENVELOPES

Materials: Tablecloth plastic (available in fabric stores); purchased appliqués; nylon fastening tape; tissue paper; cardboard; decorative wrapping paper; tape.

Instructions: Using butcher paper or newsprint, enlarge pattern so the inner box measure 9¼x8¾ inches.

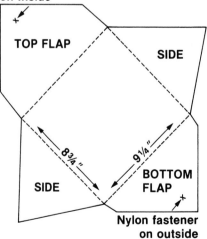

Nylon fastener on inside

TOP FLAP
SIDE
8¾"
9¼"
SIDE
BOTTOM FLAP

Nylon fastener on outside

For each envelope, cut one pattern from the plastic. Fold in sides of envelope and attach points at center with a few machine stitches. (Slip tissue paper under plastic and over the machine's feed dogs for smooth, nonstick sewing.)

Fold up bottom of envelope. With a few stitches, sew one side of a ½-inch piece of nylon fastening tape over previous stitches on outside of envelope, sewing through all 3 layers of plastic. On inside of top flap, attach the other side of the nylon tape (see pattern for X's).

On outside of flap, sew an appliqué to hide nylon tape.

To prevent cookie from breaking in the envelope, cover a 9¼x8¾-inch piece of thin cardboard with wrapping paper. Slip cardboard and cookie inside envelope; fasten closed.

ITALIAN-STYLE LIQUEUR

    2 cups sugar
 1½ cups water
    1 vanilla bean, split
    1 to 1½ teaspoons aniseed
    2 ounces candied pineapple,
      chopped (optional)
    ½ teaspoon banana extract
    1 750-milliliter bottle gin
    2 drops yellow food coloring
      (optional)

In small saucepan combine sugar, water, vanilla bean, and aniseed. Bring to boiling. Boil hard for 5 minutes. Remove from heat. Stir in candied pineapple and banana extract. Cool to room temperature.

In a large glass container combine sugar mixture and gin; mix well. If desired, stir in a few drops yellow food coloring. Cover tightly. Store at least two weeks before serving.

Present as a gift in a decorative decanter. Makes 5 cups.

Gift instructions: Strain liqueur. Pour strained liqueur into glasses.

BANANA BERRY JAM

12 ounces fresh cranberries, chopped
1½ cups water
7 cups sugar
2 cups mashed banana
½ of a 6-ounce package liquid fruit pectin

Combine cranberries and water in a 5-quart Dutch oven or large kettle. Simmer, covered, 10 minutes. Add sugar and banana; stir to combine. Bring to boiling. Boil hard 1 minute. Remove from heat. Stir in pectin. Skim off foam. Spoon at once into clean, hot half-pint jars, leaving ¼-inch headspace. Wipe jar rims; adjust lids. Process in boiling water bath for 15 minutes (start timing when water boils). To present as a gift, place jars in napkin-lined wooden carrier, if desired. Makes 8 half-pints.

COFFEE WALNUT SAUCE

2 cups sugar
3 tablespoons instant coffee crystals
3 cups hot water
½ cup cold water
¼ cup cornstarch
¼ cup butter *or* margarine
1 cup broken walnuts

In heavy 10-inch skillet melt sugar slowly over low heat till golden brown, stirring constantly. Remove from heat. Dissolve coffee crystals in hot water; carefully stir into melted sugar. Heat and stir over low heat till sugar redissolves. Combine cold water and cornstarch; stir into sugar mixture. Cook and stir till mixture is thickened and bubbly. Cook and stir 2 minutes more. Stir in butter and walnuts. Pour into three 1-cup heat-proof glass jars. Store, covered, in refrigerator. Makes 3 cups.

Gift instructions: Store sauce in refrigerator for up to 2 weeks. To serve, slowly reheat in saucepan or serve chilled. Serve over ice cream or cake.

WILD RICE PILAF MIX

3 cups wild rice
2 cups dry lentils
2 cups light raisins
1½ cups dried mushrooms, chopped
1 cup barley
½ cup shelled sunflower nuts
3 tablespoons instant beef bouillon granules
3 tablespoons dried parsley flakes
2 tablespoons minced dried onion
1 tablespoon dried basil, crushed
2 teaspoons minced dried garlic
½ teaspoon ground cinnamon
¼ teaspoon pepper

Rinse wild rice and lentils thoroughly in cold water; drain. Spread wild rice and lentils in a thin layer in a 15x10x1-inch baking pan. Heat in 300° oven 10 to 15 minutes or till wild rice is dry, stirring frequently. Remove from oven. Cool. In large bowl combine wild rice, lentils, raisins, dried mushrooms, barley, sunflower nuts, beef bouillon granules, dried parsley flakes, minced dried onion, basil, minced dried garlic, cinnamon, and pepper; mix well. Store in airtight container. To present pilaf mix as a gift, stir to distribute seasonings. Spoon ⅓- or 1-cup portions into plastic bags; secure with decorative ribbons. Place several portions in a decorative container. Makes 10 cups pilaf mix.

Gift instructions: Stir dry mix to distribute seasonings. In saucepan combine ⅓ cup pilaf mix with 1 cup *water*. Bring to boiling; reduce heat. Cover and simmer 50 minutes or till rice and barley are tender. (If desired, add 1 cup sliced carrots or chopped broccoli to rice mixture after 30 minutes of cooking.) Makes 2 servings.

PLUM PUDDING CANDY

1¼ cups chopped peanuts
1 8-ounce package pitted dates, finely snipped
1 cup finely chopped dried figs
¾ cup coarsely chopped dried apricots
½ cup flaked coconut, toasted
3 cups sugar
1 cup milk
1 tablespoon light corn syrup
1 tablespoon butter *or* margarine
1 teaspoon vanilla
Homemade Candy Box (optional)

Combine nuts and fruits; mix well. Set aside. In 3-quart buttered saucepan combine sugar, milk, and corn syrup. Heat and stir over medium heat till sugar is dissolved. Boil gently till mixture reaches 234°. Remove from heat. Stir in butter and vanilla. Cool without stirring to 110°.

Beat for 3 to 4 minutes or till mixture starts to lose its gloss and is satiny in appearance. Quickly stir in fruit mixture. Immediately turn mixture out onto a buttered baking sheet. Knead with buttered hands till gloss is gone. Halve mixture. Roll each half to a 12-inch-long log. Wrap each roll in clear plastic wrap. To present as a gift, cut each roll into ¼-inch slices. Place candy in a Homemade Candy Box. Securely cover to keep fresh. Makes 3 pounds.

HOMEMADE CANDY BOX

Materials: Rubber stamps; colored ink pad; white shelf-lining paper; tape; empty boxes, cardboard.

Instructions: Using desired rubber stamps and colored ink, randomly stamp decorations over paper. Let dry. Using tape, cover desired candy boxes and lids with the decorated paper. Arrange candy in boxes, placing a piece of cardboard between layers of candy.

Florentines are irresistible, no matter how you look at them! Semisweet chocolate is spread on one side of these fruit-filled cookies to make them extra rich.

Cocoa Kisses are sure to be warmly received by anyone who fancies crisp meringue. Each cocoa-flavored meringue is formed into a delicate kiss with the help of a pastry bag and a fluted tip. Cherry pie filling adorns the top of each cookie.

Almond Pinecones will be a sophisicated addition to your cookie assortment. Each rich oval is adorned with crunchy almonds.

SHARING
the Fun of
BAKING

Round up the troops, head for the kitchen, and turn your holiday baking into a group affair. Your children and the kids next door will have great fun learning to make an old (or new) favorite. The sweets featured here are ideal for an all-hands effort—while someone mixes, others shape or decorate. And whether the working hands are big or little, the collective effort and the results are sure to be enjoyed.

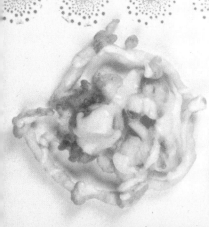

Sweet Fried Pretzels are fun both to make and to eat. The batter slips through a funnel into hot fat to form the lacy, crisp pretzels. Then a lemon glaze is brushed on for a glistening final touch.

No special cookie cutters are necessary to form these adorable **Teddy Bears, Funny Faces, Elves, and Angels**. Instead, creative fingers shape the three tasty doughs into an assortment of edible creatures.

Honey Fruitcake Cookies are sure to please all of your cookie jar customers. But be sure to save a few for Santa's visit! The fruit-filled treats are perfectly spiced with a special blend of cinnamon, ginger, and nutmeg.

COCOA KISSES

1 cup sugar
¼ cup unsweetened cocoa powder
2 tablespoons all-purpose flour
4 egg whites
¼ teaspoon cream of tartar
1 21-ounce can cherry pie filling

Combine ¼ *cup* of the sugar, cocoa powder, and flour. In small mixer bowl beat egg whites and cream of tartar on high speed of electric mixer till soft peaks form. Gradually beat in remaining sugar, beating till stiff peaks form. Fold in cocoa mixture. Spoon meringue into pastry bag fitted with large star tip. Pipe 1½-inch rosettes onto greased cookie sheet. With a small spoon, make an indentation in top of each meringue. Bake in a 325° oven for 15 to 20 minutes. Cool. To serve, place one cherry from pie filling in indentation of each cookie. Makes 48.

ALMOND PINECONES

1 cup butter *or* margarine
2 3-ounce packages cream
    cheese, softened
½ cup sugar
1 egg
1 teaspoon finely shredded lemon
    peel
½ teaspoon almond extract
2 cups all-purpose flour
    Sliced almonds *or* whole
        blanched almonds, halved
    Light corn syrup
    Sugar

In large mixer bowl beat butter and cheese for 30 seconds. Add the ½ cup sugar; beat till fluffy. Add egg, lemon peel, and extract; beat well. Add flour; mix well. Divide dough in half; cover and chill about 3 hours. Working with half the dough at a time, roll out on well-floured surface to ⅛-inch thickness. Cut with a 2½- to 3½-inch oval or round cookie cutter with fluted edge; place cookies on ungreased cookie sheet. Arrange almonds atop cookies, overlapping to resemble pinecones and lightly brushing with corn syrup. Brush with additional corn syrup. Sprinkle lightly with additional sugar. Bake in 325° oven 13 to 15 minutes. Cool on rack. Makes 48.

FLORENTINES

1 cup blanched almonds, finely
    chopped
½ cup mixed candied fruits and
    peels, finely chopped
6 tablespoons butter
⅓ cup milk
¼ cup sugar
2 tablespoons honey
¼ cup all-purpose flour
¾ cup semisweet chocolate
    pieces
2 tablespoons shortening

Combine almonds and fruits and peels; set aside. In saucepan combine butter, milk, sugar, and honey. Bring to full rolling boil, stirring occasionally. Remove from heat. Stir in almond mixture and flour. Drop by level tablespoonfuls, at least 3 inches apart, onto greased and floured baking sheet. (Prepare only six cookies at a time.) Using back of spoon, spread dough to 3-inch circles. Bake in 350° oven 8 to 10 minutes. Let stand 1 minute. Carefully remove with spatula to waxed paper. Cool completely.

Melt chocolate and shortening over low heat. Evenly spread bottom of each cookie with about 1 teaspoon chocolate mixture. When chocolate is almost set, draw wavy lines through it with tines of a fork. Store cookies, covered, in refrigerator. Makes 28.

HONEY-WHEAT FRUITCAKE COOKIES

1½ cups whole wheat flour
1 cup all-purpose flour
1½ teaspoons ground cinnamon
1 teaspoon baking powder
½ teaspoon ground ginger
½ teaspoon ground nutmeg
¼ teaspoon baking soda
¼ teaspoon salt
½ cup butter *or* margarine
½ cup sugar
½ cup honey
2 eggs
1 teaspoon vanilla
¼ cup milk
1 8-ounce package pitted dates,
    quartered
1 cup candied cherries, halved
1 cup broken pecans
    Pecan halves (optional)
    Red candied cherries (optional)

Stir together flours, cinnamon, baking powder, ginger, nutmeg, soda, and salt. In large mixer bowl beat butter or margarine for 30 seconds. Add sugar and honey; beat till well blended. Add eggs and vanilla; beat well. Stir in milk. Add flour mixture, beating till well blended. Fold in dates, cherries, and pecans. Drop the dough from a teaspoon 2 inches apart onto ungreased cookie sheets. Top each with a pecan half or a candied cherry, if desired. Bake in 375° oven 8 to 10 minutes. Cool on rack. Makes 48.

SWEET FRIED PRETZELS

Plan on serving these treats the same day you prepare them, since they will soften upon standing—

¼ cup sugar
¼ cup water
¼ teaspoon finely shredded lemon
    peel
2 teaspoons lemon juice
1 beaten egg
¾ cup milk
1 cup all-purpose flour
½ teaspoon baking powder
¼ teaspoon salt
    Cooking oil for shallow-fat
        frying

In a small saucepan cook and stir sugar and water till mixture comes to boiling; boil, uncovered, 2 minutes. Remove from heat; stir in lemon peel and juice. Set aside.

In mixing bowl combine egg and milk. Stir together flour, baking powder, and salt. Add to egg mixture; beat with rotary beater till smooth.

In a 10-inch skillet heat ½ inch of cooking oil to 360°. Using a funnel with small spout (about ⅛- to ¼-inch inside diameter), cover spout opening with finger. Fill funnel with batter. Remove finger and release batter into hot oil moving the funnel to make lacy cookie that is about 2 inches wide. Fry cookie about 1 minute, turning once with tongs. Lift cookie from oil; drain on paper toweling. Place on wire rack; set over waxed paper. Continue with remaining batter. Brush cookies with reserved lemon syrup. Makes 50.

GINGERBREAD DOUGH

1 cup butter *or* margarine
⅔ cup packed brown sugar
⅔ cup dark corn syrup *or* molasses
1½ teaspoons vanilla
1 beaten egg
4 cups all-purpose flour
¾ teaspoon baking soda
1½ teaspoons ground cinnamon
1 teaspoon ground ginger
½ teaspoon ground cloves

In saucepan combine the butter or margarine, sugar, and corn syrup or molasses. Cook and stir over medium heat till butter is melted and sugar dissolves. Pour into mixing bowl. Stir in vanilla. Cool 5 minutes.

Add the egg; mix well. In a bowl stir together flour, baking soda, cinnamon, ginger, and cloves. Add dry ingredients to egg mixture; mix well. Divide dough in half. Cover and chill at least 2 hours or overnight.

Continue as directed in Teddy Bears, Funny Faces, Angels, and Elves.

Vanilla Dough: Prepare Gingerbread Dough as directed *except* substitute ⅔ cup *granulated sugar* for the brown sugar and use *light corn syrup* in place of the dark corn syrup or molasses. Omit the cinnamon, ginger, and cloves. Continue as directed.

Chocolate Dough: Prepare Gingerbread Dough as directed *except* substitute ⅔ cup *granulated* sugar for the brown sugar, reduce *butter* to ⅔ cup, and melt 2 squares (2 ounces) *unsweetened chocolate* with the butter mixture in saucepan. Omit the cinnamon, the ginger, and the cloves. Continue as directed.

TEDDY BEARS, FUNNY FACES, ELVES, AND ANGELS

1 recipe Gingerbread Dough, Vanilla Dough, *and/or* Chocolate Dough
1 beaten egg yolk
1 tablespoon water
Several drops red food coloring
Sifted powdered sugar
Milk *or* light cream
Several drops blue food coloring

Prepare Gingerbread Dough, Vanilla Dough, and/or Chocolate Dough. Chill 2 hours or overnight.

Working with half of the dough at a time, roll out on lightly floured surface to ⅛-inch thickness. For each type of cookie, cut and trim as directed below and at right.

Place on ungreased cookie sheets. (Make a small hole at top of cookies if they are to be used as tree ornaments.) Brush facial or body features of cookies with a mixture of egg yolk mixed with the water and red food coloring, using a fine paintbrush.

Bake cookies in a 350° oven 8 to 10 minutes or till set and light brown. (Thick cookies such as Teddy Bears may require longer baking time.) Transfer to wire racks; cool cookies completely.

For decorating icing, mix sifted powdered sugar with enough milk or light cream to make of piping consistency. Tint half the icing with blue food coloring. Use blue and white icing in a pastry bag fitted with decorative tip to decorate cookies.

To shape Teddy Bears: For each cookie, shape dough into one large ball (body), five medium-size balls (head, arms, and legs), three small balls (nose and ears), and four tiny balls (paws). On an ungreased cookie sheet flatten the large ball slightly for body. Attach medium-size balls for head, arms, and legs. Place small balls on head for nose and ears. With a wooden pick, draw eyes and mouth. Arrange tiny balls of dough atop ends of legs and arms for paws, tracing a circular indentation around each.

To shape Funny Faces: Cut dough with 2½- to 3-inch round cookie cutter. For nose, eyes, cheeks, mouth, and hair, use scraps of dough. For nose, shape a narrow strip of dough into a ½-inch-long nose; place dough in cen-

ter of cookies. For eyes, with tip of finger make indentations on both sides of nose. For cheeks, roll small pieces of dough into balls and place below eyes. For mouth, roll a thin strip of dough; arrange dough under nose to form a smile or frown. For hair, fill a garlic press with dough. Gently squeeze out dough. Cut off strands with a sharp knife; starting at top of cookies, press dough strands onto outer edge. Repeat pressing and cutting till desired amount of hair is obtained.

To shape Elves: For each cookie, shape dough into one 1½-inch ball (body), one 1-inch ball (head), five ½-inch balls (feet, arms, and hat), and two tiny balls for cheeks. (Combine pieces of the different doughs for a layered effect.) On ungreased cookie sheet flatten large ball for body into an oval shape. Use a knife to make an impression of legs within body. Attach ½-inch balls for feet and arms. Place 1-inch ball on top for head. Arrange remaining ½-inch ball atop head and shape into a triangle. Pull tip of triangle down to imitate a hat. For hair, fill a garlic press with dough. Gently squeeze out dough. Cut off strands with sharp knife. Attach strands of dough to head to create a hairline. Place tiny balls on face for cheeks. For eyes and nose, make indentations with finger.

To shape Angels: Roll dough to ⅛-inch thickness. For each cookie cut a 2½-inch rectangle; place on an ungreased cookie sheet. For wings, cut out a 2-inch circle; halve circle and attach to body as wings. For head attach a ¾-inch ball. For hair, fill a garlic press with dough. Gently squeeze out dough. Cut off strands with sharp knife. For hair, starting at the top of the cookie attach strands of dough to head. Place two small balls of dough at bottom of body for feet. Place one small ball of dough in center of body for button. For eyes and nose, make an indentation with finger. Place tiny balls of dough on face for cheeks.

SHARING
Christmas Eve Supper

Don't let the hustle and bustle of December festivities rob your family of time together. Plan an intimate family supper and select a menu that doesn't interfere with the merriment. This meal is ideal for your gathering because the foods can be prepared beforehand. After an evening of gift giving or tree decorating, everyone can relax and savor this self-serve meal.

Concocting **Creamy Oyster Broccoli Stew** *(front left)* is a snap when you start with cheese soup, frozen potatoes, and broccoli. Chill the stew till serving time, then just heat it through.

An ideal accompaniment to this robust soup is **Christmas Wreath** *(back center)*—a rich bread baked in a classic holiday shape and trimmed with pecans.

Round out this easy meal with **Dill Relish Tray** *(front right)*. It features cauliflower, carrots, and onion marinated in salad dressing for extra zestiness. Radish chrysanthemums and slices of jellied cranberry sauce make the vegetables look festive.

Fluffy Cranberry Cheese Pie *(back right)* is the grand ending for this family meal. Cranberry juice cocktail and ground berries give the layered pie its brilliant coloring, and a cheese mixture contributes the richness. Whipped cream is the trimming.

CHRISTMAS WREATH

2¼ to 2¾ cups all-purpose flour
1 package active dry yeast
¾ cup milk
3 tablespoons sugar
3 tablespoons butter *or*
    margarine
¼ teaspoon salt
1 egg
  Milk
  Pecan halves

In large mixer bowl combine *1 cup* of the flour and the yeast. Heat milk, sugar, butter or margarine, and salt just till warm (115° to 120°) and butter starts to melt, stirring constantly. Add to flour mixture; add egg. Beat at low speed of electric mixer for ½ minute, scraping sides of bowl constantly. Beat 3 minutes at high speed.

Stir in as much remaining flour as you can mix in with a spoon. Turn out onto lightly floured surface. Knead in enough remaining flour to make a moderately soft dough that is smooth and elastic (3 to 5 minutes total). Place in lightly greased bowl; turn once to grease surface. Cover; let rise till double (about 1 hour).

Punch dough down; divide into 3 portions and shape into balls. Cover; let rest 10 minutes. Roll each ball to a 20-inch rope. Grease the outside of a 6-ounce custard cup and invert the dish in the center of a greased baking sheet. Starting at center, braid ropes loosely to the ends. Wrap braid around custard cup, stretching as necessary to join ends; pinch to seal. Cover; let rise till nearly double (30 minutes).

Brush carefully with milk; tuck pecan halves in braid. Bake in 375° oven 20 minutes. Cool bread on wire rack. Loosen braid from custard cup with narrow spatula; remove cup. If desired, wrap, seal, label, and freeze bread till needed. To thaw, let stand at room temperature.

DILLED RELISH TRAY

2 cups cauliflower flowerets *or*
    one 10-ounce package frozen
    cauliflower
1 pound carrots, cut into 1-inch
    pieces, *or* one 16-ounce can
    whole carrots, drained
1 small onion, sliced and
    separated into rings
½ cup Italian salad dressing
½ teaspoon dried dillweed
1 bunch radishes
1 8-ounce can jellied cranberry
    sauce, chilled
  Celery leaves (optional)
  Parsley sprigs (optional)

Cook fresh cauliflower and fresh carrots separately in boiling unsalted water for 10 minutes; drain. (Or, cook frozen cauliflower according to package directions; drain. Cut large pieces in half. Drain canned carrots.) Place cauliflower, carrots, and onion in shallow dish.

In a screw-top jar shake together the Italian dressing and dillweed. Pour over vegetables in dish. Cover; marinate several hours or overnight, spooning marinade over vegetables several times. Meanwhile, cut radishes to resemble chrysanthemums; chill in ice water several hours.

At serving time, arrange marinated vegetables, radishes, and slices of jellied cranberry sauce on serving tray. Garnish with celery leaves and parsley, if desired. Serves 4 to 6.

CREAMY OYSTER BROCCOLI STEW

3 cups milk
2 11-ounce cans condensed
    cheddar cheese soup
1 10-ounce package frozen
    chopped broccoli
1 cup frozen loose-pack hash
    brown potatoes
1 small onion, chopped
1 pint shucked oysters *or* two 8-
    ounce cans whole oysters

In 3-quart saucepan combine milk and soup. Stir in broccoli, potatoes, and onion. Cook, stirring occasionally, over medium heat till bubbly, breaking up broccoli with fork till thawed. Simmer, covered, for 10 minutes. Remove from heat; cool. Cover and chill. At serving time, in a 3-quart saucepan reheat soup. In saucepan place the fresh undrained oysters; cook over medium heat till edges curl. Add to broccoli mixture; heat through. (If using canned oysters, just add undrained oysters directly to soup; heat through.) Serves 4 to 6.

FLUFFY CRANBERRY-CHEESE PIE

1 3-ounce package raspberry *or*
    cranberry-orange-flavored
    gelatin
⅓ cup sugar
1¼ cups cranberry juice cocktail
1 cup fresh cranberries, ground
1 3-ounce package cream cheese,
    softened
¼ cup sugar
1 tablespoon milk
1 teaspoon vanilla
½ cup whipping cream
1 9-inch baked and cooled pastry
    shell
  Whipped cream (optional)
  Whole fresh cranberries
    (optional)

In bowl combine gelatin and the ⅓ cup sugar. Bring cranberry juice to boiling; pour over gelatin mixture, stirring to dissolve. Stir in ground cranberries. Chill till mixture is consistency of unbeaten egg whites.

Meanwhile, in small mixer bowl beat cream cheese, the ¼ cup sugar, the milk, and vanilla till fluffy. Beat the ½ cup whipping cream just to soft peaks; fold into cheese mixture.

Place cranberry mixture in bowl of ice water; beat with electric mixer till fluffy. If necessary, let stand till mixture mounds.

Spread cream cheese mixture over bottom of piecrust. Top with cranberry mixture. Chill several hours or overnight. Store, covered, in refrigerator till needed.

To serve, pipe additional whipped cream atop pie; garnish with whole fresh cranberries.

Cover Recipes for April and August

SUMMER FRUIT PUFF

This delectable dessert featuring fresh fruits is shown on page 107—

- ⅔ cup water
- ⅓ cup butter *or* margarine
- 1⅓ cups all-purpose flour
- 1 tablespoon sugar
- ¼ cup butter *or* margarine
- 3 eggs
- 1 4-serving-size package *instant* vanilla pudding mix
- 1½ cups milk
- ½ cup whipping cream
- 2 cups fresh fruit such as sliced peaches, halved strawberries, halved grapes, blueberries, *or* raspberries
- ¼ cup apple jelly *or* orange marmalade

To make cream puff dough: In medium saucepan bring water and the ⅓ cup butter or margarine to boiling, stirring to melt butter. Add ⅔ cup of the flour all at once. Cook and stir till mixture forms a ball that doesn't separate. Set aside to cool 15 minutes.

Meanwhile, *to make crust:* Combine the remaining flour and the sugar. Cut in the ¼ cup butter or margarine till mixture is crumbly. Firmly press crumbs into an 8-inch circle on an ungreased baking sheet (mixture will be slightly dry and crumbly); set aside.

To mixture in saucepan add eggs, one at a time, beating well after each addition. Gently spread about *one-fourth* of the dough over crust, forming a 5-inch circle (a 1½-inch border of crust will remain exposed). Using a large fluted tip, pipe the remaining dough atop the outside edge of the 5-inch circle, leaving a 2- to 2½-inch circle in the center. *Angle the dough toward the center as you pipe and do not allow the dough to lap over onto the exposed crust* (see how-to photo). Dough will puff and spread as it bakes. (Or, instead of piping the remaining dough, drop spoonfuls of dough atop the outside edge of the 5-inch circle.) Bake in a 400° oven for 15 minutes. Reduce oven temperature to 350°. Bake 35 to 40 minutes more. Place baking sheet on wire rack. Cool pastry on baking sheet. Gently slide pastry to plate with wide spatulas.

To serve: Prepare pudding mix according to package directions *except* use the 1½ cups milk. Beat cream to soft peaks; fold into pudding. Spoon mixture into center of puff. Arrange fruit atop. In small saucepan melt jelly; brush atop fruit. Chill 1 to 2 hours. Makes 10 servings.

SPANISH-STYLE CHICKEN PAELLA

This tasty and colorful one-pot meal is pictured on page 45—

- 4 ounces chorizo *or* Italian sausage, sliced
- 8 chicken legs and wings (4 each)
- 1 medium onion, chopped (½ cup)
- 1 small sweet red *or* green pepper, cut into chunks
- 1 clove garlic, minced
- ¾ cup long grain rice
- 1½ teaspoons instant chicken bouillon granules
- ¼ teaspoon ground turmeric
- 3 cups hot water
- 8 baby carrots *or* 3-inch carrot chunks
- 1 10-ounce package frozen peas
- 1 10-ounce package frozen artichoke hearts (optional)
- ¼ cup pitted ripe olives
- 6 cherry tomatoes, halved *or* ½ cup tomato wedges

Range-top method: In a 12-inch skillet or 4-quart Dutch oven brown sausage over medium heat about 10 minutes. Drain, reserving drippings in skillet; set sausage aside. Season chicken with salt and pepper. Brown chicken in reserved drippings; remove chicken, reserving *1 tablespoon* drippings in skillet. Add onion, red or green pepper, and garlic to pan; cook till onion is tender. Stir in uncooked rice, bouillon granules, turmeric, and water; bring to boiling. Add sausage and carrots. Arrange chicken atop. Reduce heat; cover and simmer 20 minutes.

Meanwhile, rinse peas and artichokes under hot tap water to separate. Arrange peas, artichokes, and olives atop chicken. Cover and cook 15 to 20 minutes more or till rice and chicken are tender. Just before serving, add tomatoes; heat through. To serve, toss mixture gently together. Makes 4 servings.

Oven method: Using an oven-going skillet or Dutch oven, follow the steps for the range-top method through placing chicken pieces atop rice mixture. Cover and bake in a 375° oven for 20 minutes. Rinse peas and artichokes as directed; place atop chicken along with tomatoes and olives. Bake, covered, for 15 to 20 minutes longer or till chicken and rice are tender. Serve as directed for range-top method.

Microwave method: In a 2-quart nonmetal casserole micro-cook sausage, onion, pepper, and garlic, covered, on HIGH for 4 to 5 minutes, stirring once. Drain sausage mixture, reserving *1 tablespoon* drippings in dish. Set mixture aside. Place chicken in casserole; cook, covered, for 5 minutes. Drain off fat; set chicken aside. In same dish combine the uncooked rice, bouillon granules, turmeric, and *2½ cups* hot water. Cook, covered, for 5 minutes or till boiling. Stir in the sausage mixture and carrots. Arrange chicken pieces atop. Cook, covered, on MEDIUM for 10 minutes. Rinse peas and artichokes under hot tap water. Arrange peas, artichokes, and olives atop chicken; cover and cook on MEDIUM for 8 to 10 minutes or till chicken and rice are tender. Top with tomatoes; cook 2 minutes more. Serve as directed for range-top method.

INDEX

A-B

Aebleskivers, 42
All-Purpose Seasoning, 134
Almond Pinecones, 182
Almond Pinwheel Divinity, 174
Animal Breads, 52
Antipasto Tuna Tray, 105
Appetizers
  Antipasto Tuna Tray, 105
  Chicken-Stuffed Cream Puffs, 174
  Crab-Artichoke Appetizers, 70
  Curried Cheese Spread, 134
  Curried Shrimp and Cucumber
    Cocktail, 102
  Dilled Relish Tray, 186
  Easy Guacamole, 91
  Fish in Sour Cream, 92
  Fried Won Ton Strips with Soy-
    Lemon Sauce, 92
  Fromajadas, 41
  Glacéed Sandwiches, 32
  Pork Pastries, 170
  Romano Shrimp-Stuffed
    Mushrooms, 170
  Scandinavian Appetizer Tray, 165
  Sherry-Cheese Log, 171
  Shrimp Mousse, 175
  Smoked Mussels Rockefeller, 72
  Sunflower Cheese Balls, 53
  Toasted Pita Chips, 144
  Tomato Pesto Tart, 92
  Tri-Level Salmon-Tomato
    Appetizer, 73
  Vegetable Basket with Very Cheesy
    Dip, 53
  Zesty Vegetable Dip, 133
Applesauce Beef Pie, 16
Applesauce, Brandied, 121
Apples, Poached Pears and, 166
Apricot Sauce, 94
Artichoke-Mushroom Salad
  Remoulade, 92
Baklava Tarts, 94
Banana Berry Jam, 179
Banana Surprise Muffins, 132
Béarnaise Dip, 91
Beef
  Applesauce-Beef Pie, 16
  Beef and Potato Bake, 18
  Beef Paprikash, 16
  Frozen Meat Base, 16
  Great Caesar Burgers, 102
  Horseradish-Beef Sandwiches, 18
  Indonesian Sâté with Peanut
    Sauce, 93
  Meatball Soup with Spinach
    Pistou, 62
  Steak Pinwheel Pitas, 89

Beef (continued)
  Teriyaki Marinated Steak with
    Sweet-Sour Vegetables, 131
  Tortilla-Beef Casserole, 16
  Vegetable Rutabaga Soup, 121
Beet-Spinach Salad, 18
Berry-Orange Aspic Molds, 146
Beverages
  Citrus Cider, 174
  Easter Punch, 41
  Flaming Tea Punch, 29
  Irish Coffee, 167
  Italian-Style Liqueur, 178
  Light Wassail Bowl, 166
  Melon Daiquiri Slush, 102
  Peach Daiquiris, 119
  Raspberry-Apple Cider, 117
  Snack-in-a-Glass, 55
  Sonoma Sangria, 117
  Spiced Spritzers, 171
Blueberry Corn Muffins, 118
Blueberry Pie, 119
Bohemian Crown Cake, 166
Bouquet Garni, 30
Bouquet Garni Jelly, 30
Brandied Applesauce, 121
Bratwurst 'n Rye, 103
Breads, Quick
  Aebleskivers, 42
  Banana Surprise Muffins, 132
  Blueberry Corn Muffins, 118
  Caraway Wheat Biscuits, 145
  Cheese 'n Onion Popovers, 131
  Dried Cherry Bread, 121
  Peach and Brown Sugar
    Muffins, 117
  Peach Jam Bread, 118
  Peach Kuchen, 120
  Rhubarb Bread, 118
  Sfinghi, 44
  Whole Wheat Nut Bread, 170
  Zucchini Bread, 117
Breads, Yeast
  Animal Breads, 52
  Bohemian Crown Cake, 166
  Brown and Serve Panettone
    Rolls, 167
  Cheesy Chili Roll, 54
  Christmas Wreath, 186
  Gugelhupf, 94
  Harvest Grape Loaf, 156
  Kulich, 42
  Mini-Bagels, 55
  St. Joseph's Bread, 42
  Tabouleh Bread, 93
  Thumbprint Sweet Rolls, 53
  Whole Wheat Caramel Rolls, 30
Broiled Orange-Grape Boats, 133
Brown and Serve Panettone
  Rolls, 167
Bulgur Salad Pockets, 132
Buttercream Frosting, 76
Buttermilk Pralines, 167

C

Caesar Toast, 102
Cakes
  Cheese 'n Chocolate
    Mini-Cakes, 90
  Cheesy Carrot-Zucchini Cake, 146
  Chocolate Genoise Cake with
    Espresso Buttercream, 156
  Coloring Book Cake, 76
  Holiday Fruit Diamonds, 171
  Live Wire Cake, 77
  Nut and Seed Cake, 77
  Passover Carrot-Nut Cake, 40
  Peach-Walnut Torte, 143
  Rainbow Cake, 78
  Stained-Glass Window Cake, 78
  Surprise Cake Roll, 130
  Whole Wheat-Sour Cream
    Fruitcake, 175
Candied Cranberries, 166
Candies
  Almond Pinwheel Divinity, 174
  Buttermilk Pralines, 167
  No-Cook Peanut Fudge, 174
  Plum Pudding Candy, 179
Cannoli, 44
Caramel Apple Crisp, 146
Caramel Filigree, 157
Caramel-Filigree Hazelnut Pie, 157
Caramelized Onions in Squash, 30
Caraway Wheat Biscuits, 145
Carrots
  Carrot Mousse Tart, 158
  Carrot-Zucchini Salad, 145
  Cheesy Carrot-Zucchini Cake, 146
  Passover Carrot-Nut Cake, 40
  Rabbit Stew with Carrot
    Dumplings, 61
Casseroles
  Beef and Potato Bake, 18
  Cottage-Cheese Rice Bake, 144
  Easy Lasagna, 142
  Pecan-Pork Chop Casserole, 17
  Spaghetti Pizza, 130
  Spinach Matzo Pie, 40
  Tortilla-Beef Casserole, 16
Celeriac Soup, 121
Cheese
  Cannoli, 44
  Cheese 'n Chocolate Mini-Cakes, 90
  Cheese 'n Onion Popovers, 131
  Cheesy Carrot-Zucchini Cake, 146
  Cheesy Chili Rolls, 54
  Chunky Peanut Butter Spread, 54
  Chutney Spread, 171
  Cottage Cheese-Rice Bake, 144

Cheese (continued)
  Creamed Vegetable-Cheese
    Soup, 146
  Fluffy Cranberry-Cheese Pie, 186
  Fromajadas, 41
  Fruit-Topped Cheese Tart, 104
  Orange Cream Cheese, 91
  Sherry-Cheese Log, 171
  Shrimp in Cheddar Sauce, 15
  Spinach Frittata, 122
  Spinach Pistou, 62
  Summer Fruit Tart, 90
  Sunflower Cheese Balls, 53
  Surprise Cake Roll, 130
  Tuna-and-Cheese-Stuffed Pasta, 73
  Vegetable Basket with Very
    Cheesy Dip, 53
Cherries
  Cherry Vinegar, 120
  Dried Cherries, 121
  Dried Cherry Bread, 121
  Honey-Cherry Butter Horns, 175
Cherry Tomato Roses, 143
Chicken
  Chicken Soup with Matzo Balls, 40
  Chicken-Stuffed Cream Puffs, 174
  Curried Chicken in a Pot, 60
  Germantown Stew, 145
  Honey-Glazed Chicken, 144
  Indonesian Sâté with Peanut
    Sauce, 93
  Lahaina Chicken Rolls, 103
  Orange-Glazed Chicken with
    Matzo-Nut Stuffing, 41
  Orange-Sauced Chicken, 132
  Rosemary Chicken, 32
  Spanish-Style Chicken Paella, 187
Chilled Spumoni Soufflé, 102
Chive Crème Fraîche, 157
Chocolate
  Cheese 'n Chocolate Mini-Cakes, 90
  Chocolate Dough, 183
  Chocolate Genoise Cake with
    Espresso Buttercream, 156
  Florentines, 182
  Fudge Mint Sundaes, 144
  Pot de Crème Ice Cream, 104
Christmas Wreath, 186
Chunky Peanut Butter Spread, 54
Chutney Spread, 171
Citrus Cider, 174
Cocoa Kisses, 182
Coconut Crust, 106
Coconut-Pear Crisp, 17
Coffee Walnut Sauce, 179
Coloring Book Cake, 76
Cookies
  Almond Pinecones, 182
  Cocoa Kisses, 182
  Edible Christmas Cards, 178
  Fig-Filled Cookies, 44

Cookies (continued)
  Florentines, 182
  4-Grain Cookies, 134
  Honey-Cherry Butterhorns, 175
  Honey-Wheat Fruitcake
    Cookies, 182
  Lollipop Cookies, 51
  Pizzelles, 94
  Sesame Cookies, 43
  Sweet Fried Pretzels, 182
  Teddy Bears, Funny Faces,
    Elves, and Angels, 183
  Thumbprint Cookies, 119
Cottage Cheese-Rice Bake, 144
Crab-Artichoke Appetizers, 70
Crafts
  Homemade Candy Box, 179
  Plastic Christmas Card
    Envelopes, 178
Cranberries
  Banana Berry Jam, 179
  Candied Cranberries, 166
  Cranberry-Pork Loaf, 15
  Fluffy Cranberry-Cheese Pie, 186
Creamed Vegetable-Cheese Soup, 146
Cream of Winter Vegetable Soup, 31
Creamy Oyster Broccoli Stew, 186
Crumb-Topped Beans, 144
Cucumber Relish, 118
Curried Cheese Spread, 134
Curried Chicken in a Pot, 60
Curried Cocktail Sauce, 102
Curried Lamb Chop Platter, 32
Curried Rice Dinner Platter, 17
Curried Shrimp and Cucumber
  Cocktail, 102

D-G

Desserts (see also Cakes, Cookies,
  Pies)
  Baklava Tarts, 94
  Broiled Orange-Grape Boats, 133
  Cannoli, 44
  Caramel Apple Crisp, 146
  Chilled Spumoni Soufflé, 102
  Coconut-Pear Crisp, 17
  Dessert Crepes, 116
  Dessert Omelet Flambé, 29
  Farfel Pudding, 40
  Fresh Fruit Cookie Tarts, 55
  Fresh Fruit Snow, 52
  Fruited Barley Pudding, 134
  Fruit Salad Dessert, 18
  Fruit-Topped Cheese Tart, 104
  Fruit Tzimmes, 41
  Fruit Whip, 145
  Fruity Poached Apples, 133
  Fudge Mint Sundaes, 144
  Hingham Pudding, 165

Desserts (continued)
  Meringue and Fruit Flambé, 29
  Pastel Ribbon Bavarian, 158
  Peach Custard Crunch, 120
  Peach Mousse with Raspberry
    Sauce, 31
  Pignolatti, 43
  Pineapple Tarte Tatin, 30
  Poached Pears and Apples, 166
  Pot de Crème Ice Cream, 104
  Raspberry-Almond Tart, 116
  Raspberry Meringue, 116
  Red Raspberry Crepes, 116
  Rum-Raisin-Peach Sundaes, 18
  Spicy Fruit Sundaes, 51
  Strawberry Bavarian Dressing, 41
  Strawberry Shortcake Alaska, 106
  Summer Fruit Puff, 187
  Summer Fruit Tart, 90
Dilled Relish Tray, 186
Divinity, Almond Pinwheel, 174
Dried Cherries, 121
Dried Cherry Bread, 121
Easter Punch, 41
Easy Broccoli Eggs, 17
Easy Guacamole, 91
Easy Lasagna, 142
Edible Christmas Cards, 178
Eggs
  Dessert Omelet Flambé, 29
  Easy Broccoli Eggs, 17
  Italian Puffy Omelet, 133
  Pastel Ribbon Bavarian, 158
  Sherried Custard Sauce, 166
  Spinach Frittata, 122
  Tomato Quiche, 119
Endive with Dijon Sauce, 167
Farfel Pudding, 40
Favorite Pepper Salad, 117
15-Minute Pasta Primavera, 105
Fig-Filled Cookies, 44
Fish and Seafood
  Antipasto Tuna Tray, 105
  Crab-Artichoke Appetizers, 70
  Creamy Oyster Broccoli Stew, 186
  Curried Shrimp and Cucumber
    Cocktail, 102
  Fish à la Diable, 71
  Fish in Sour Cream, 92
  Fried Cod with Tomato-Olive
    Sauce, 43
  Frisky Shrimp, 29
  Italian Fish Platter, 72
  Monkfish-Zucchini Chowder, 72
  Oriental-Style Stuffed Fish, 72
  Pasta con Sarde, 43
  Pasta with Fish Sauce, 32
  Romano Shrimp-Stuffed
    Mushrooms, 170
  Salmon Quenelles with Chive
    Crème Fraîche, 157

Index

Fish and Seafood *(continued)*
  Scallop-Pasta Salad, 70
  Scandinavian Appetizer Tray, 165
  Seafood-Rice Chowder, 17
  Seafood Thermidor, 70
  Seaside Bundles, 72
  Shrimp in Cheddar Sauce, 15
  Shrimp Mousse, 175
  Smoked Mussels Rockefeller, 72
  Sole Patties Paprikash, 71
  Szechwan Lamb Soup with
    Wontons, 61
  Tabouli-Seafood Salad, 73
  Tri-Level Salmon-Tomato
    Appetizer, 73
  Tuna-and-Cheese-Stuffed Pasta, 73
  Turban of Broccoli and Fish, 71
  Veracruz Steaks, 73
  Wine-Poached Halibut, 133
Flaming Tea Punch, 29
Florentines, 182
Fluffy Cranberry-Cheese Pie, 186
4-Grain Cookies, 134
Fresh Cauliflower Salad, 122
Fresh Fruit Cookie Tarts, 55
Fresh Fruit Snow, 52
Fried Cod with Tomato-Olive
  Sauce, 43
Fried Won Ton Strips with Soy-
  Lemon Sauce, 92
Frisky Shrimp, 29
Fromajadas, 41
Frostings
  Buttercream Frosting, 76
  Icing, 171
  Powdered Sugar Icing, 42
  Royal Icing, 78
Frozen Meat Base, 16
Fruit and Granola Parfaits, 51
Fruitcake, Whole Wheat-Sour
  Cream, 175
Fruited Barley Pudding, 134
Fruited Ice Cubes, 171
Fruit Salad Dessert, 18
Fruit-Topped Cheese Tart, 104
Fruit Tzimmes, 41
Fruit Whip, 145
Fruity Poached Apples, 133
Fudge-Mint Sundaes, 144
Fudge, No-Cook Peanut, 174
Gazpacho, 117
Germantown Stew, 145
Gingerbread Dough, 183
Gingered Poppy Seed Dressing, 131
Glacéed Sandwiches, 32
Glazed Nectarine Pie, 119
Glazed Papaya, 103
Great Caesar Burgers, 102
Guacamole Soup, 105
Gugelhupf, 94

H-O

Ham
  Cranberry-Pork Loaf, 15
  Glacéed Sandwiches, 32
  Ham and Vegetable Bundles, 42
  Ham-Mushroom Rotini, 18
  Ham with Onion Sauce, 31
  Quince-Glazed Ham, 171
Haroseth, 40
Harvest Fruit Salad, 143
Harvest Grape Loaf, 156
Hashed Browns Salad, 89
Hearty Vegetable Stew, 132
Herbed Bechamel Sauce, 31
Herbed Lentil-Vegetable Soup, 31
Hingham Pudding, 165
Holiday Fruit Diamonds, 171
Hollandaise Sauce, 71
Homemade Candy Box, 179
Honey Butter, 52
Honey-Cherry Butterhorns, 175
Honey-Glazed Chicken, 144
Honey-Wheat Fruitcake Cookies, 182
Horseradish-Beef Sandwiches, 18
Hot Red Cabbage, 120
Icing, 171
Indonesian Sâté with Peanut
  Sauce, 93
Irish Coffee, 167
Italian Fish Platter, 72
Italian Puffy Omelet, 133
Italian-Style Liqueur, 178
Jams
  Banana Berry Jam, 179
  Nectarine-Pear Jam, 120
  Strawberry-Pineapple Jam, 118
Java Barbecue Sauce, 105
Jellies
  Bouquet Garni Jelly, 30
  Rosé Jelly, 165
Kulich, 42
Lahaina Chicken Rolls, 103
Lamb
  Curried Lamb Chop Platter, 32
  Indonesian Sâté with Peanut
    Sauce, 93
  Szechwan Lamb Soup with
    Wontons, 61
Lasagna, Easy, 142
Light Wassail Bowl, 166
Live Wire Cake, 77
Lollipop Cookies, 51
Maltaise Sauce, 42
Marinated Green Beans, 122
Marinated Potato Salad, 134
Matzo Balls, 40

Meatball Soup with Spinach
  Pistou, 62
Melon Daiquiri Slush, 102
Meringue and Fruit Flambé, 29
Mexican Christmas Salad, 167
Mideastern Green Salad, 93
Mini-Bagels, 55
Mixed Summer Vegetables, 122
Mock Hollandaise, 106
Mock Mayonnaise, 131
Molded Hard Sauce, 166
Monkfish-Zucchini Chowder, 72
Moroccan Orange Salad, 93
Muffins
  Banana Surprise Muffins, 132
  Blueberry Corn Muffins, 118
  Peach and Brown Sugar
    Muffins, 117
Mushrooms
  Artichoke-Mushroom Salad
    Remoulade, 92
  Ham-Mushroom Rotini, 18
  Onion-Mushroom Rice Mix, 17
  Romano Shrimp-Stuffed
    Mushrooms, 170
Nectarine-Cherry Chicken Salad, 121
Nectarine-Pear Jam, 120
No-Cook Peanut Fudge, 174
Nut and Seed Cake, 77
Nut Butter, 119
Nutmeg Cheese Sauce, 158
Occidental Stir-Fry, 144
Omelets
  Dessert Omelet Flambé, 29
  Italian Puffy Omelet, 133
Onions
  Caramelized Onions in Squash, 30
  Cheese 'n Onion Popovers, 131
  Ham with Onion Sauce, 31
  Onion Mums, 143
  Onion-Mushroom Rice Mix, 17
Open-Faced Sandwich Buffet, 90
Oranges
  Berry-Orange Aspic Molds, 146
  Broiled Orange-Grape Boats, 133
  Easter Punch, 41
  Moroccan Orange Salad, 93
  Orange Cream Cheese, 91
  Orange Glazed Chicken with
    Matzo-Nut Stuffing, 41
  Orange Pilaf Peppers, 104
  Orange-Sauced Chicken, 132
Oriental-Style Stuffed Fish, 72
Oriental Vegetables Tart, 32

P-R

Papaya, Glazed, 103
Parsley Pesto, 92
Parsnip Slaw, 122
Passover Carrot-Nut Cake, 40
Pasta con Sarde, 43
Pasta with Broccoli and Sausage, 122
Pasta with Fish Sauce, 32
Pastel Ribbon Bavarian, 158
PDQ Pickles, 103
Peaches
  Peach and Brown Sugar
    Muffins, 117
  Peach Custard Crunch, 120
  Peach Daiquiris, 119
  Peaches and Cream Pie, 120
  Peach Jam Bread, 118
  Peach Kuchen, 120
  Peach Mousse and Raspberry
    Sauce, 31
  Peach-Walnut Torte, 143
  Rum-Raisin-Peach Sundaes, 18
  Spicy Fruit Sundaes, 51
Peanut Sauce, 93
Pears
  Coconut-Pear Crisp, 17
  Harvest Fruit Salad, 143
  Nectarine-Pear Jam, 120
  Pearadise Pie, 130
  Poached Pears and Apples, 166
Pecan-Pork Chop Casserole, 17
Pesto, Parsley, 92
Pickles
  PDQ Pickles, 103
  Zucchini Pickles, 118
Pies
  Blueberry Pie, 119
  Caramel-Filigree Hazelnut Pie, 157
  Fluffy Cranberry-Cheese Pie, 186
  Glazed Nectarine Pie, 119
  Peaches and Cream Pie, 120
  Pearadise Pie, 130
  Piña Colada Chiffon Pie, 106
  Raspberry-Apple Pie, 117
Pies, Main Dish
  Applesauce-Beef Pie, 16
Pignolatti, 43
Piña Colada Chiffon Pie, 106
Pineapple
  Fruit Whip, 145
  Piña Colada Chiffon Pie, 106
  Pineapple Tarte Tatin, 30
  Spicy Fruit Sundaes, 51
  Strawberry-Pineapple Jam, 118
Pizzelles, 94
Plastic Christmas Card
  Envelopes, 178
Plum Pudding Candy, 179

Poached Pears and Apples, 166
Pork
  Cranberry-Pork Loaf, 15
  Germantown Stew, 145
  Pecan-Pork Chop Casserole, 17
  Pork Pastries, 170
  Rice-Stuffed Rib Crown, 143
  Scandinavian Appetizer Tray, 165
  Sombrero Ribs with Tortillas, 60
  Swedish Meatballs, 165
Potatoes
  Beef and Potato Bake, 18
  Carrot Mousse Tart, 158
  Hashed Browns Salad, 89
  Whipped Potatoes with
    Turnips, 165
Pot de Crème Ice Cream, 104
Poultry with Rockefeller
  Dressing, Roast, 164
Powdered Sugar Icing, 42
Pumpkin Butter, 170
Quince-Glazed Ham, 171
Rabbit Stew with Carrot
  Dumplings, 61
Rainbow Cake, 78
Raspberry-Almond Tart, 116
Raspberry-Apple Cider, 117
Raspberry-Apple Pie, 117
Raspberry Meringue, 116
Raspberry Sauce, 31
Red Raspberry Crepes, 116
Relishes
  Candied Cranberries, 166
  Cucumber Relish, 118
  Haroseth, 40,
  Spiced Parsnip Relish, 164
Rhubarb Bread, 118
Rice
  Cottage Cheese-Rice Bake, 144
  Curried Rice Dinner Platter, 17
  Easy Broccoli Eggs, 17
  Onion-Mushroom Rice Mix, 17
  Orange Pilaf Peppers, 104
  Pecan-Pork Chop Casserole, 17
  Rice-Stuffed Rib Crown, 143
  Seafood-Rice Chowder, 17
  Turmeric Rice, 94
  Wild Rice Pilaf Mix, 179
Rich Sour Cream Gravy, 164
Roast Poultry with Rockefeller
  Dressing, 164
Romano Shrimp-Stuffed
  Mushrooms, 170
Rosé Jelly, 165
Rosemary Chicken, 32
Royal Icing, 78
Rum-Raisin-Peach Sundaes, 18

S

St. Joseph's Bread, 42
Salad Dressings
  Gingered Poppy Seed Dressing, 131
  Mock Mayonnaise, 131
  Tofu Dressing, 131
  Zesty Salad Dressing, 131
Salads
  Artichoke-Mushroom Salad
    Remoulade, 92
  Beet-Spinach Salad, 18
  Berry-Orange Aspic Molds, 146
  Carrot-Zucchini Salad, 145
  Favorite Pepper Salad, 117
  Fresh Cauliflower Salad, 122
  Harvest Fruit Salad, 143
  Hashed Browns Salad, 89
  Marinated Potato Salad, 134
  Mexican Christmas Salad, 167
  Mideastern Green Salad, 93
  Moroccan Orange Salad, 93
  Parsnip Slaw, 122
  Vegetable Salads Alfresco, 91
  Wilted Salad Benedict, 106
Salads, Main Dish
  Scallop Pasta Salad, 70
  Spaghetti Salad, 54
  Tabouli-Seafood Salad, 73
Salmon Quenelles with Chive Crème
  Fraîche, 157
Sandwiches
  Bratwurst 'n Rye, 103
  Bulgur Salad Pockets, 132
  Cheesy Chili Roll, 54
  Great Caesar Burgers, 102
  Horseradish-Beef Sandwiches, 18
  Open-Faced Sandwich Buffet, 90
  Seaside Bundles, 72
  Steak Pinwheel Pitas, 89
Sauces
  Coffee Walnut Sauce, 179
  Curried Cocktail Sauce, 102
  Herbed Bechamel Sauce, 31
  Hollandaise Sauce, 71
  Java Barbecue Sauce, 105
  Maltaise Sauce, 42
  Mock Hollandaise, 106
  Molded Hard Sauce, 166
  Nutmeg Cheese Sauce, 158
  Orange Cream Cheese, 91
  Peanut Sauce, 93
  Raspberry Sauce, 31
  Rich Sour Cream Gravy, 164
  Sherried Custard Sauce, 166
  Strawberry Bavarian Dressing, 41
Sausage
  Bratwurst 'n Rye, 103
  Curried Rice Dinner Platter, 17

Index

Sausage *(continued)*
    Pasta with Broccoli and
      Sausage, 122
    Rosemary Chicken, 32
    Sausage and Vegetable
      Paprikash, 62
    Sausage-Bulgur Soup, 15
    Scandinavian Appetizer Tray, 165
    Sombrero Ribs with Tortillas, 60
    Spanish-Style Chicken Paella, 187
Scallop Pasta Salad, 70
Scandinavian Appetizer Tray, 165
Seafood-Rice Chowder, 17
Seafood Thermidor, 70
Seaside Bundles, 72
Seasoned French Loaf, 134
Sesame Cookies, 43
Sfinghi, 44
Sherried Custard Sauce, 166
Sherry-Cheese Log, 171
Shortcut Smoked Turkey with
    Orange Pilaf Peppers, 104
Shrimp
    Curried Shrimp and Cucumber
      Cocktail, 102
    Frisky Shrimp, 29
    Romano Shrimp-Stuffed
      Mushrooms, 170
    Shrimp in Cheddar Sauce, 15
    Shrimp Mousse, 175
    Sole Patties Paprikash, 71
    Szechwan Lamb Soup with
      Wontons, 61
    Tabouli-Seafood Salad, 73
Skillet Enchiladas, 142
Smoked Mussels Rockefeller, 72
Snack in a Glass, 55
Sole Patties Paprikash, 71
Sombrero Ribs with Tortillas, 60
Sonoma Sangria, 117
Soups
    Cauliflower-Leek Soup, 121
    Celeriac Soup, 121
    Chicken Soup with Matzo Balls, 40
    Creamed Vegetable-Cheese
      Soup, 146
    Cream of Winter Vegetable
      Soup, 31
    Gazpacho, 117
    Guacamole Soup, 105
    Herbed Lentil-Vegetable Soup, 31
    Meatball Soup with Spinach
      Pistou, 62
    Monkfish-Zucchini Chowder, 72
    Sausage-Bulgur Soup, 15
    Seafood Rice Chowder, 17
    Szechwan Lamb Soup with
      Wontons, 61
    Vegetable Rutabaga Soup, 121
Spaghetti Pizza, 130
Spaghetti Salad, 54
Spanish-Style Chicken Paella, 187

Spiced Parsnip Relish, 164
Spiced Spritzers, 171
Spicy Fruit Nut Sundaes, 51
Spinach Frittata, 122
Spinach Matzo Pie, 40
Spinach Pistou, 62
Spinach Ravioli with Squash
    Filling, 158
Squab Calvados with Fried Rice
    Sticks, 156
Squash
    Caramelized Onions in Squash, 30
    Spinach Ravioli with Squash
      Filling, 158
    Squash-Stuffed Baked Apples, 166
Stained-Glass Window Cake, 78
Steak Pinwheel Pitas, 89
Stews
    Creamy Oyster Broccoli Stew, 186
    Germantown Stew, 145
    Hearty Vegetable Stew, 132
    Rabbit Stew with Carrot
      Dumplings, 61
Strawberry Bavarian Dressing, 41
Strawberry-Pineapple Jam, 118
Strawberry Shortcake Alaska, 106
Stuffed Artichokes, 44
Summer Fruit Puff, 187
Summer Fruit Tart, 90
Sunflower Cheese Balls, 53
Surprise Cake Roll, 130
Swedish Meatballs, 165
Sweet Fried Pretzels, 182
Sweet-Sour Vegetables, 90
Szechwan Lamb Soup with
    Wontons, 61

T-Z

Tabouleh Bread, 93
Tabouli-Seafood Salad, 73
Taco Cups, 105
Teddy Bears, Funny Faces, Elves,
    and Angels, 183
Teriyaki Marinated Steak with
    Sweet-Sour Vegetables, 131
Thumbprint Cookies, 119
Thumbprint Sweet Rolls, 53
Toasted Pita Chips, 144
Tofu Dressing, 131
Tomato-Bacon Spread, 91
Tomato-Olive Sauce, 43
Tomato Pesto Tart, 92
Tomato Quiche, 119
Tortilla Beef Casserole, 16
Tri-Level Salmon-Tomato
    Appetizer, 73
Tuna-and-Cheese-Stuffed Pasta, 73
Turban of Broccoli and Fish, 71

Turmeric Rice, 94
Vanilla Dough, 183
Vegetables
    Beet-Spinach Salad, 18
    Caramelized Onions in Squash, 30
    Carrot Mousse Tart, 158
    Creamed Vegetable-Cheese
      Soup, 146
    Cream of Winter Vegetable
      Soup, 31
    Crumb-Topped Beans, 144
    Dilled Relish Tray, 186
    Endive with Dijon Sauce, 167
    15-Minute Pasta Primavera, 105
    Fish à la Diable, 71
    Gazpacho, 117
    Ham and Vegetable Bundles, 42
    Hearty Vegetable Stew, 132
    Herbed Lentil-Vegetable Soup, 31
    Hot Red Cabbage, 120
    Italian Fish Platter, 72
    Marinated Green Beans, 122
    Mixed Summer Vegetables, 122
    Occidental Stir-Fry, 144
    Orange Pilaf Peppers, 104
    Oriental Vegetable Tart, 32
    PDQ Pickles, 103
    Sausage and Vegetable
      Paprikash, 62
    Spinach Matzo Pie, 40
    Squash-Stuffed Baked Apples, 166
    Stuffed Artichokes, 44
    Sweet-Sour Vegetables, 90
    Teriyaki Marinated Steak with
      Sweet-Sour Vegetables, 131
    Vegetable Basket with Very Cheesy
      Dip, 53
    Vegetable Rutabaga Soup, 121
    Vegetable Salads Alfresco, 91
    Whipped Potatoes with
      Turnips, 165
    Zesty Vegetable Dip, 133
    Zucchini-Bulgur Stir-Fry, 15
Veracruz Steaks, 73
Whipped Potatoes with Turnips, 165
Whole Wheat Caramel Rolls, 30
Whole Wheat Nut Bread, 170
Whole Wheat-Sour Cream
    Fruitcake, 175
Wild Rice Pilaf Mix, 179
Wilted Salad Benedict, 106
Wine Poached Halibut, 133
Zesty Salad Dressing, 131
Zesty Vegetable Dip, 133
Zucchini
    Carrot-Zucchini Salad, 145
    Cheesy Carrot-Zucchini Cake, 146
    Monkfish-Zucchini Chowder, 72
    Zucchini Bread, 117
    Zucchini-Bulgur Stir-Fry, 15
    Zucchini Pickles, 118
    Zucchini Sandwich Filling, 91